THE COMPLETE

Wilton®

BOOK OF

Candy

EDITED BY EUGENE T. AND MARILYNN C. SULLIVAN

WILTON ENTERPRISES, WOODRIDGE, ILLINOIS 60517

Please address mail to:
   Wilton Book Division
   2240 West 75th Street
   Woodridge, Illinois 60517

Photographs and other material submitted for publication must be accompanied by a stamped, self-addressed envelope, if return is requested.

The Complete Wilton Book of Candy
is published by Wilton Enterprises,
2240 West 75th Street, Woodridge, Illinois 60517

For product information, write Department C-10

Printed and bound in the United States of America

FIRST EDITION

Library of Congress Catalog Card Number: 81-11681
International Standard Book Number: 0-912696-18-4

Library of Congress Cataloging in Publication Data
Main entry under title:

The Complete Wilton Book of Candy.
      Includes index.
         1. Confectionery.   2. Wilton Enterprises.
I. Sullivan, Marilynn.   II. Sullivan, Eugene T.
TX791.C65   641.8'53   81-11681
ISBN 0-912696-18-4   AACR2

INTRODUCTION

I grew up making candy. My dad was a candy maker—a first class one—and my mother a chocolate dipper, so I learned early the techniques of working fondant, boiling sugar and putting together all kinds of delicious sweets.

Candy is fun to work on! Start out by making some of the easy confections in the first chapter, learn good candy making habits and you'll be on your way toward mastering one of the most enjoyable and rewarding of the culinary arts.

Fondant has been my favorite candy ingredient for many years. In Chapter 10, in step-by-step pictures, I'll show you how to make the kind of fondants that go into the world's most distinguished candies.

I've also been fascinated by jewel-like hard candies. In Chapter 14, I'll show you a shimmering candy dish that looks like Venetian glass—but it's made of a simple sugar mixture.

I've enjoyed recapturing the thrills of fine candy making, and am glad to have shared in producing the most complete, easy-to-follow candy book I have ever seen.

NORMAN WILTON

FOREWORD

With today's interest in the preparation of delicious homemade sweets, we realized there was a need for a truly *complete* book of fine candies.

We worked for almost two years to prepare this book for you. We improved and clarified the formulas for old-fashioned favorites. We developed entirely new recipes that produce fine candies every bit as good, and even better than, traditional confections. Every recipe was tested and re-tested to make it foolproof in your own kitchen.

As this work was going on, we developed the tools and products you need to turn candy making into a joy, not a job. The use of these products will make it easy to give your candies a finished, professional appearance.

I'm proud to present *The Complete Wilton Book of Candy* to you. Best wishes for enjoyment in your candy making adventures.

VINCENT A NACCARATO
PRESIDENT, WILTON ENTERPRISES

The Complete Wilton Book of Candy

CO-EDITORS:
Eugene T. Sullivan
and Marilynn C. Sullivan

ASSISTANT TO THE EDITORS:
Ethel LaRoche

RECIPE TESTING:
Judy McKee. Wilton Test Kitchen
Knechtel Laboratories
The staff of the Wilton Book Division

DECORATING:
Yvonne Disharoon
Marie Kason
Amy Rohr

READERS' EDITOR:
Diane Kish

PHOTOGRAPHY:
Edward Hois

CONTRIBUTORS TO THIS BOOK

The help of a number of individuals and firms is most sincerely acknowledged for contributing to the accuracy and authority of recipes in this book. This help took the various forms of developing, testing and retesting recipes. It also took the form of reducing to non-technical terms important information relating to many of the products used in candy making. Among contributors the publisher wishes to thank are:

The Blommer Chocolate Company, Chicago, Illinois.

George Brunslik, master of the old world art of fine candy making and owner-operator of Old Fashioned Candies, Berwyn, Illinois.

Herb Knechtel, founder of Knechtel Laboratories, president of Knechtel Research Sciences, Inc. and internationally recognized authority in candy technology, Skokie, Illinois.

The Nestlé Company, Inc., White Plains, New York.

Chef Lutz Olkiewicz, European-trained patissier and Gold Medal winner in International Culinary Olympics, Chicago, Illinois.

Barton Siebers, consultant to The Nestlé Company, Inc. and operating head of The Chocolate Plantation, Hilton Head Island, South Carolina.

Norman Wilton, master in the art of fondant, pulled sugar and hard candy making. Founder of Wilton Enterprises, Chicago, Illinois.

Dear Friends,

We were determined to make this the very best recipe book on candy ever printed. We brought back old techniques, discovered new ones, and even developed brand new recipes that produce fine candy in a modern time-saving way.

Making candy is really an art. It's the pinnacle of achievement for any good cook—and it's an art in which any serious cook can achieve mastery. To make certain of this we tested and retested every recipe in this book to make it foolproof in your kitchen.

This is a unique book which you can use many different ways. First, use it just for fun—to enjoy the accomplishment of creating perfect homemade candies, and to delight others with sweets more delicious than you could ever buy.

How do we suggest you use this book? Use it as a course in fine candy making. After you've tried making a few of your favorites, we know you'll want to go on to more adventures. Make at least several candies in each chapter, following the chapters in order as they progress. Soon you'll become very adept and confident. You'll begin to understand the nature of ingredients and how they react to various degrees of heat. Soon you'll be making lavish continental chocolates with the ease of an old world patissier.

But even if your ambitions are more modest, be sure to read Chapter 2 very carefully. This chapter tells you what you need to make fine candy—and why you need it. Turn back to it from time to time as you prepare to make a new recipe. It will answer many questions, and solve some problems before they occur.

Also study the foreword that appears at the beginning of each chapter. This will tell you the general characteristics of the type of candy contained in the chapter and give guidelines for success in individual recipes.

Finally, we strongly suggest you use this book to bring back some of the elegance and flair of former days—days when confections were made with love and care and the finest ingredients. You will find your series of successes in making truly distinguished candies very rewarding!

With best wishes,

THE EDITORS

The Complete Wilton Book of Candy

Chapter 1
ANYTIME, EASY-DO CANDIES

If you have half an hour—or even less—and an urge to serve your family or friends a special treat, browse through this chapter. Select the recipe that appeals to you most, whether your taste is for a fresh flavored fruit jell, a delicate pastel bonbon, a rich chocolate-y fudge or a melt-in-the-mouth truffle. Then step in the kitchen and whip it up in next-to-no-time.

Each candy will have a delicious homemade flavor that purchased candy just can't match.

None of these recipes requires any equipment that the average kitchen doesn't provide. Look through your shelves—you probably have the ingredients too. You don't need to be experienced in candy making either. These recipes can be successfully made by a novice.

Don't be concerned if the day is hot or humid. These recipes are truly foolproof and work out beautifully in any weather. Some of the candies have a built-in bonus, too. They may be formed into centers for dipping as Chapter Three describes.

So turn today into a party! Make a batch of homemade candy and surprise and delight everyone. This chapter makes it very easy.

HURRY-UP
BUTTERSCOTCH FUDGE

A nice creamy fudge with the contrast of crunchy nuts. Children love to make it, and teen-agers think it's super. Successful in any weather.

> 1⅔ cups (400ml or 375g) granulated sugar
> ⅔ cup (160ml) or one small can evaporated milk
> Pinch of salt
> 1 six-ounce package (170g) butterscotch morsels
> 1½ cups (360ml or 85g) miniature marshmallows
> 1 cup (240ml or 112g) coarsely chopped walnuts, crisped
> 1 teaspoon (5ml) butterscotch flavoring (optional)

Before you begin, line a 5" x 9" (12.7 x 22.9cm) loaf pan smoothly with foil, then lightly but thoroughly butter the foil. Preheat oven to 300°F (149°C), spread chopped nuts on a cookie sheet and place in oven. Turn off oven and leave nuts in oven 15 minutes to crisp.

1. Put sugar, milk and salt in a heavy three-quart (three-liter) saucepan and turn heat to medium. Stir constantly with a wooden spoon to dissolve sugar. When mixture comes to a boil, set timer (or watch clock) and allow to boil for five minutes as you continue to stir.

2. Remove from heat, add butterscotch morsels and marshmallows. Stir until blended. Add flavoring and nuts and stir until thick, about five or more minutes. Pour into prepared pan and cool until firm at room temperature, about one hour. Or cool in the refrigerator about a half hour.

3. Turn out on board, peel off foil, cut into 1" (2.5cm) squares. Yield: 45 pieces.

4. *Store, well wrapped,* before cutting, in refrigerator for up to two weeks.

TO VARY THIS RECIPE

This is really a very creative candy—you may make changes to suit your own taste.

For chocolate fudge, substitute chocolate morsels for the butterscotch morsels and substitute vanilla for butterscotch flavoring.

For mint chocolate fudge, omit vanilla and add a few drops of oil of peppermint.

For coconut fudge, in either the chocolate or butterscotch versions, substitute one cup (240ml) lightly toasted coconut for the nuts.

At right: an elegant choice of delectable sweets. Clockwise from top center: Quick Two-tone Fudge, Four-Star Nut Fudge, Hurry-up Butterscotch Fudge, Chocolate Corn Flake Clusters, Classic Chocolate Truffles, Stuffed Dates, Sparkle Jells, Lemon Drop Bonbons and Rosy Fruit Balls.

CLASSIC CHOCOLATE TRUFFLES*

Make this utterly luxurious, silky-textured candy with just two main ingredients and very little time! Serve a guest a truffle or two with black coffee for a most sophisticated dessert.

  9 ounces (252g) milk chocolate (purchase in 8-ounce packages in grocery store)

  ⅜ cup (90ml) whipping cream

  3 tablespoons (45ml or 45g) cocoa

Before you begin, line two cookie sheets with wax paper.

1. Chop the chocolate coarsely on a board and set aside.

2. Place cream in a small saucepan over medium heat. Bring to a boil, stirring constantly with wooden spoon. As soon as cream reaches boiling point, remove from heat, add the chopped chocolate and cover the pan. Leave covered for three minutes to allow chocolate to melt.

3. Stir the mixture until perfectly blended and smooth. Place pan in refrigerator for 30 minutes to cool and stiffen mixture.

4. Remove from refrigerator and drop by dessert spoon into mounds on prepared cookie sheet. Place cookie sheet in refrigerator for one hour.

5. Spread cocoa in a small flat dish. (A small pie tin is ideal.) Remove cookie sheet from refrigerator and form each truffle mound into a ball by rolling between your palms. Drop balls into cocoa and roll to coat. You may form three or four balls, roll in cocoa then place on second cookie sheet. If mixture becomes too soft, place in freezer a few minutes. Continue until all truffles are formed and coated.

6. Store in refrigerator for several weeks, or, if the weather is not warm or humid, for three days at room temperature. Yield: about 36 candies.

TO VARY THIS RECIPE:

Roll the truffle balls in sifted confectioners' sugar instead of cocoa.

For nut truffles, roll the truffles in finely chopped nuts. (First crisp nuts by preheating oven to 300°F (149°C). Spread nuts on cookie sheet, place in oven, turn off heat and leave for 15 minutes.)

RUM RAISIN TRUFFLES

Here is an elegant variation on the classic truffle. To prepare the candies, you will need a decorating bag, tube 12, about 40 small paper candy cups and just basic decorating skill.

  ½ cup (120ml or 56g) raisins

  1½ cups (360ml) water

  1½ tablespoons (22.5ml) rum

  1 recipe Classic Chocolate Truffles

Before you begin. Do this a day or two before making the truffles. Place raisins in a small heatproof bowl, bring water to a boil and pour over raisins. Allow raisins to soak and plump 15 minutes, then drain well. Put raisins back in bowl, add rum and cover. Allow to stand at room temperature for one or two days.

1. Prepare Classic Chocolate Truffles through step 3 in recipe above. Have ready a plastic decorating bag fitted with tube 12. Set about 40 paper candy cups on a tray.

2. Remove truffle mixture from refrigerator. Beat with electric hand mixer about three minutes at high speed. Put truffle mixture into decorating bag and pipe into mounds in the paper cups. Hold bag straight up, apply pressure, stop, then lift. Drain the raisins on a paper towel and press several into each candy. Harden in refrigerator about an hour before serving or cover closely with plastic wrap and freeze for months. Store up to several weeks in refrigerator. If weather is not warm or humid, truffles may be kept covered, at room temperature, for up to three days. Yield: about 40 candies.

Would you like to make other versions of delectable truffles? Turn to Chapter 9.

BIG-BATCH FUDGE*

This is the recipe to use when you want to make a lot of fudge! It's good to take on a picnic, send to school or whip up for a tree-trimming party. Or you can cut the finished pan of fudge in half, freeze some for future treats and serve the rest as soon as it's cool. This fudge makes an ideal candy center for dipping (see Chapter Three) with a rich, almost truffle-like flavor.

13 ounces (390ml) evaporated milk

4½ cups (1.125 liters or 1kg) granulated sugar

⅛ teaspoon or pinch of salt

¼ pound (120ml or 112g) butter

12 ounces (336g) semi-sweet chocolate morsels

16 ounces (two 8-ounce bars, 448g) milk chocolate (purchase in grocery store)

16 large marshmallows, quartered

5 teaspoons (25ml) vanilla extract

1½ cups (360ml or 168g) chopped walnuts, crisped

Before you begin, crisp the nuts. Heat oven to 300°F (149°C), spread nuts on cookie sheet and place in oven. Turn off heat and leave in oven 15 minutes. Chop the milk chocolate bars on a cutting board. Cut each marshmallow into four pieces with a scissors (dip scissors in cold water). Line a 9" x 13" (23cm x 33cm) pan with foil and lightly butter the foil.

1. Put milk, sugar and salt into a heavy four-quart (four-liter) saucepan. Add the butter, cut in thin slices. Set pan on medium-high heat and bring to a rolling boil, stirring constantly. This will take about ten minutes. Reduce heat to medium and cook for five minutes, stirring to prevent sticking.

2. Remove from heat, add the chocolate morsels, chopped milk chocolate, marshmallows and vanilla. Stir with a wooden spoon until mixture is thoroughly blended and beginning to thicken. Stir in the nuts.

3. Pour into prepared pan and cool completely. For faster cooling, place in refrigerator about one hour. Turn out of pan, remove foil and cut in 1" (2.5cm) squares. To store in the refrigerator for several weeks, wrap uncut candy in plastic wrap or foil. To freeze for up to six months, wrap uncut candy closely in plastic wrap or foil. Yield: about 115 pieces.

TO VARY THIS RECIPE

Substitute chopped candied fruit for the nuts. Use cherries, pineapple or any candied fruit you like.

For coconut fudge, substitute toasted shredded coconut for the nuts. Toast the coconut on a cookie sheet in a 350°F (177°C) oven just until delicately browned, ten minutes or less. Stir frequently.

CREAMY CREAM CHEESE FUDGE*

Here's a nice chocolate-y fudge that stays moist and creamy for up to two weeks. You may freeze it for months for future treats or to have on hand for dipping.

3 ounces (84g) cream cheese, room temperature

½ teaspoon (2.5ml) vanilla

⅛ teaspoon or pinch of salt

2 cups (480ml or 200g) sifted confectioners' sugar

2 ounces (56g) unsweetened chocolate

Before you begin, remove cheese from refrigerator and set out to bring to room temperature. Chop chocolate on a cutting board. Put water in lower pan of small double boiler to depth of 1" (2.5cm), bring to simmer. Remove from heat, place upper pan in position and add chopped chocolate. Cover pan to melt chocolate. Line a 9" x 5" (22.9cm x 12.7cm) loaf pan with foil, and butter foil lightly.

1. Whip cheese, vanilla and salt until fluffy with hand mixer set on medium speed.

2. Set mixer on low speed and blend in sugar, one-third at a time. For last addition of sugar, use a wooden spoon to blend.

3. Thoroughly blend in melted chocolate with wooden spoon and put mixture into prepared pan. Refrigerate about two hours, or until firm. Turn out onto board, remove foil, and cut into 1" (2.5cm) squares. You may store this candy for several weeks in the refrigerator, closely wrapped in foil or plastic wrap and uncut. Or freeze it for up to six months. Bring to room temperature to cut. Yield: about 45 pieces.

TO VARY THIS RECIPE

For nut fudge, blend in ½ cup (120ml or 56g) of crisped chopped nuts of your choice along with the chocolate. (To crisp the nuts, heat oven to 300°F (149°C). Spread on cookie sheet, place in oven and turn off heat. Leave nuts in oven 15 minutes.)

*May be used as centers for dipping

DATES STUFFED WITH ORANGE CREAM*

This creamy, refreshing filling sets off the rich tropical sweetness of the dates to perfection. In Chapter Three you'll see how to use Orange Cream as a marvelous center for dipped candies.

    1 tablespoon (15ml or 15g) butter

    2 cups (480ml or 200g) sifted confectioners' sugar (approximate)

    2 tablespoons (30ml) fresh orange juice

    2 drops of orange liquid food color

    1 teaspoon (5ml) grated orange rind

    8 ounces (225g) pitted dates

Before you begin, grate the orange rind on a small hand grater, measure and set aside on wax paper. Squeeze the orange and measure. Line a cookie sheet with wax paper.

1. Cream butter with a wooden spoon until fluffy. Gradually stir in the confectioners' sugar, alternating with a few drops of orange juice. When mixture becomes too stiff to stir, knead with your hands to incorporate the sugar. Place the food color on the mixture, knead until evenly spread, then knead in the grated orange rind. The completed filling should be perfectly smooth and easy to form into a ball, like pie dough.

2. Open the dates and place on the prepared cookie sheet. Pinch off a little of the orange cream and roll between your palms into a rounded oval, about the size of a date. Insert the oval into a date and press lightly to secure. The filling should protrude attractively from the cut edges of the date. Continue until all dates are filled.

Serve immediately, or store in refrigerator, well wrapped in foil or plastic wrap for several weeks. The flavor will ripen and become even better. Yield: about 32 dates.

TO VARY THIS RECIPE

Substitute 2 tablespoons (30ml) frozen, undiluted orange juice for the fresh orange juice. Omit the grated orange rind and use only one drop of orange food color. The flavor will be more assertive and very tangy.

LEMON DROP BONBONS*

This delicately tangy candy looks so attractive in its coconut coating that guests will think you're a professional candy maker!

    5 drops yellow liquid food coloring

    ½ teaspoon (2.5ml) milk

    1½ cups (360ml or 112g) shredded coconut (approximate)

    3½ cups (840ml or 396g) sifted confectioners' sugar (approximate)

    ⅓ cup (80ml or 74g) instant, nonfat dry milk

    ¼ cup (60ml or 56g) butter

    ½ cup (120ml) light corn syrup

    1 tablespoon (15ml) water

    2 teaspoons (10ml) vanilla extract

    1 teaspoon (5ml) grated lemon rind

Before you begin, mix food color and ½ teaspoon milk in a small container. Place coconut in a plastic bag and add diluted food color. Close the bag tightly, then knead it with your fingers until the coconut is evenly tinted. Empty onto a small pie tin or plate. Grate the rind of a lemon with a small hand grater, measure and set on wax paper. Line an 8" (20.3cm) square pan with foil, lightly butter the foil.

1. Sift the sugar and dry milk together into a mixing bowl. Set aside.

2. Cut butter into thin slices, place in top pan of small double boiler. Bring water in lower pan to a simmer, put top pan in position and allow butter to melt.

3. Bring water in lower pan to boiling and stir in corn syrup, water and vanilla. Blend in half of dry ingredients, stirring constantly with a wooden spoon until smooth. Add second half of dry ingredients, stirring again until smooth. Remove from heat, blend in lemon rind and turn into prepared pan.

4. Cool at room temperature until firm, or in the refrigerator for about 1½ hours. Turn out on board, remove foil and cut into 48 squares. Roll the squares in your palms into balls and place on prepared tray. If mixture seems too soft, put in freezer for a few minutes to harden.

5. Drop balls into tinted coconut and roll to coat. If coconut does not cling to balls, roll over a damp towel, then in coconut. Store closely covered in plastic wrap in refrigerator for up to a week, or in freezer for up to six months. Yield: 48 candies.

*May be used as centers for dipping

OLD-FASHIONED
MASHED POTATO FUDGE*

Use prepared instant or regular mashed potato. If this is left-over from a previous meal, whip up to original consistency, adding milk as necessary.

- 3 ounces (84g) unsweetened chocolate
- 1 tablespoon (15ml or 15g) butter
- ¼ cup (60ml or 56g) prepared mashed potato
- ½ teaspoon (2.5ml) vanilla
- 2 cups (480ml or 200g) sifted confectioners' sugar (approximate)

Before you begin, line a 9" x 5" (22.9cm x 12.7cm) loaf pan with foil and lightly butter the foil. Coarsely chop the chocolate.

1. Heat water to a low simmer in bottom pan of a one-quart (one-liter) double boiler. Put chopped chocolate and butter in top pan of boiler, place over lower pan and melt, stirring constantly. Remove top pan.

2. Stir in potato and vanilla. Add confectioners' sugar gradually. When mixture becomes difficult to stir, turn out on surface and knead in more sugar with your hands. Use enough sugar to form a pliable mass. Press into prepared pan, cool until stiff, peel off foil and cut in 1" (2.5cm) squares. Fudge may be refrigerated, uncut and closely wrapped in foil or plastic wrap for up to two weeks — or freeze for up to six months. Yield: about 45 pieces.

PEANUT BUTTER
MASHED POTATO FUDGE*

- ⅔ cup (160ml or 154g) prepared mashed potato
- ½ cup (120ml or 112g) creamy peanut butter
- 4 cups (960ml or 400g) sifted confectioners' sugar (approximate)
- ½ cup (120ml or 112g) chopped peanuts, crisped

Before you begin, crisp the nuts. Preheat oven to 300°F (149°C), spread nuts on cookie sheet, put in oven and turn off heat. Leave for 15 minutes. Line an 8" (20.3cm) square pan with foil—lightly butter the foil. If you are using leftover mashed potato, whip up to original consistency, adding milk as necessary.

1. Mix potato and peanut butter in a large bowl. Gradually knead in sugar and nuts to form a pliable but stiff mass.

2. Press into prepared pan. Let stand for an hour before cutting into 1" (2.5cm) squares. Refrigerate, uncut and closely wrapped in foil or plastic wrap for up to two weeks. Yield: 64 pieces.

QUICK TWO-TONE FUDGE

Easy to do, delicious, and very professional looking!

Make a recipe of Old-Fashioned Mashed Potato Fudge and press into a 10" (25.5cm) square pan, lined with foil, then buttered. Cover it with a recipe of Peanut Butter Mashed Potato Fudge, and press the two together. Allow the candy to harden for an hour before cutting into 1" (2.5cm) square pieces. Yield: 100 pieces.

FOUR-STAR NUT FUDGE*

Old-fashioned taste! Chocolate-y! Marvelous texture! These are some of the comments you'll hear when you offer a plate of this delectable fudge to your family.

- 1 pound (454g) confectioners' sugar
- ½ cup (120ml or 56g) cocoa
- ¼ teaspoon (1.25ml) salt
- 3 ounces (90ml or 84g) butter
- ¼ cup (60ml) milk
- 1 tablespoon (15ml) vanilla extract
- 1 cup (240ml or 112g) chopped pecans or walnuts, crisped

Before you begin, line a 9" x 5" (23cm x 12.7cm) loaf pan with foil and butter the foil. Crisp the nuts. First heat oven to 300°F (149°C). Spread nuts on cookie sheet, place in oven and turn off heat. Leave nuts in oven for 15 minutes.

1. Heat water in lower pan of small double boiler until simmering. Place all ingredients except nuts in upper pan of boiler, place top pan over lower pan and stir with wooden spoon until smooth.

2. Work quickly at this point. Remove from heat, stir in nuts and spread in prepared pan. Cool completely for about two hours at room temperature, or for about one hour in the refrigerator. Turn out of pan onto cutting board, remove foil and cut into 1" (2.5cm) squares. Store, uncut and closely wrapped in refrigerator for several weeks. Yield: 45 pieces.

RUM BALLS

One of the best known and most loved of all confections, Rum Balls are surprisingly easy to make. They're traditionally, served at holidays, but they make an elegant dessert at any time of year.

   1 cup or 3½ ounces (98g) vanilla wafers, crushed (about 24)

   1 cup (240ml or 100g) sifted confectioners' sugar

   1 cup or 3½ ounces (98g) ground almonds

   2 tablespoons (30ml or 15g) cocoa

   1½ tablespoons (23ml) light corn syrup

   ¼ cup (60ml) rum

   3 tablespoons (45ml or 42g) confectioner's sugar for coating

Before you begin, place wafers in a tightly sealed plastic bag and crush with a rolling pin. Measure. Line a cookie sheet with wax paper.

1. Combine crushed wafers, one cup of sugar, almonds, and cocoa in a mixing bowl. Stir with a wooden spoon until well blended. Add syrup and rum and stir until thoroughly mixed into a compact mass.

2. Take off dessert spoon-sized portions and roll between buttered palms into 1" (2.5cm) balls. Place on prepared cookie sheet. Put two tablespoons sugar into a small bowl and drop in balls, rolling to coat. Set completed balls on a small tray and cover tightly with foil or plastic wrap. Refrigerate two or three days to mellow the flavor. Bring to room temperature to serve. Refrigerate in a sealed container for several weeks, or freeze for up to six months. Yield: about 30 balls.

TO VARY THIS RECIPE

Make Bourbon Balls by substituting bourbon for the rum. If you and your friends are real chocolate lovers, roll the balls in cocoa instead of confectioners' sugar.

RAISIN DROPS

You'll need only a few minutes to stir this candy together! Raisin drops have a luscious truffle-like texture and flavor.

   8 ounces (224g) dark or milk chocolate

   ⅔ cup (160ml) sweetened condensed milk

   1 cup (240ml or 130g) raisins

Before you begin, line a 12" x 18" (30.5cm x 45.7cm) cookie sheet with wax paper.

1. Chop the chocolate. Put it in the top of a double boiler and place it over the lower pan with water just at a low simmer. Stir until melted.

2. Remove the top pan with the melted chocolate, add the milk and stir until smooth. Stir in the raisins. Drop by teaspoonfuls onto prepared cookie sheet. Let stand at room temperature for about two hours or until firm. Refrigerate, closely covered, for up to three weeks. Or wrap tightly in foil or plastic wrap and freeze for up to six months. Yield: 36 clusters.

CHOCOLATE CORN FLAKE CLUSTERS

Make this chewy, not-too-sweet and very satisfying candy very easily—or let the children make it themselves with just a little supervision from you. It's a recipe you'll make again and again because the family enjoys it so.

   ½ cup (120ml or 112g) butter

   30 large marshmallows, quartered

   1 teaspoon (5ml) vanilla

   ½ cup (120ml or 112g) semi-sweet chocolate morsels

   4½ cups (1.2 liters or 126g) cornflakes

Before you begin, cut marshmallows in quarters with a kitchen scissors dipped in cold water. Place cornflakes in a large mixing bowl and warm in lowest temperature oven until ready to mix. Line a cookie sheet with wax paper.

1. Melt butter in small saucepan over low heat. Add cut-up marshmallows and stir constantly with a wooden spoon until marshmallows are completely melted.

2. Remove from heat, stir in vanilla. Sprinkle chocolate morsels over cornflakes. Pour syrup over cornflakes and morsels and stir just until evenly coated. Drop by heaping teaspoonfuls onto prepared cookie sheet and let dry about one hour at room temperature. Refrigerate for several weeks in a tightly closed plastic bag. Yield: about 36.

ROSY FRUIT BALLS*

Everyone enjoys the tangy fresh flavor of this pink and pretty candy. Use your favorite flavor of gelatin—the red-tinted varieties give the nicest color.

½ cup (120ml) light corn syrup

⅓ cup (80ml or 84g) butter

1 package (3 ounces or 84g) fruit-flavored gelatin

1 pound (450g) sifted confectioners' sugar

1½ cups (360ml or 112g) flaked coconut

Before you begin, line an 8" (20.3cm) square pan with foil and butter the foil. Line a cookie sheet with wax paper.

1. Combine corn syrup, butter and gelatin in a three-quart (three-liter) saucepan. Stir constantly over low heat until gelatin is completely dissolved, about three minutes. Add the sugar, one-third at a time, stirring until well blended after each addition. Remove from heat and turn into prepared pan.

2. When candy is cool enough to handle, form into a ball. Empty coconut into a small pie tin. Take off teaspoon-sized portions from the mixture and roll between your palms into balls, about ¾" (2cm) in diameter. Drop balls into coconut and roll until coated. You may form four or five balls before rolling them in coconut. Place coated balls on cookie sheet to harden. Store in a tightly closed plastic bag in the refrigerator for several weeks. Yield: about 50 candies.

COCONUT WON'T STICK?

If the formed balls of candy harden a little and the coconut tends to fall off, don't despair. Mix equal quantities of water and light corn syrup in a small bowl, drop in a formed candy and immediately take out and roll in coconut.

SPARKLE JELLS

Just two ingredients and a very few minutes will turn out candy that shimmers like jewels and tastes fresh-picked. This is an ideal candy for summer when you'd like a light, fruity treat, but it's so pretty you'll make it year-round. Children love it, and they can make it themselves, too. Use your favorite flavor of gelatin.

1 cup (240ml) water

2 three-ounce packages (84g each) fruit-flavored gelatin

Before you begin, oil a 6" (15.2cm) square pan with vegetable oil.

1. Bring water to a full boil in saucepan, remove from heat and add gelatin. Stir constantly with a wooden spoon until gelatin is completely dissolved. If necessary, place pan over very low heat and continue stirring until dissolved, but do not allow to boil.

2. Pour into prepared pan and refrigerate until firm, about two hours. Turn out on wax paper and cut in 1" (2.5cm) squares. To store for several weeks in the refrigerator, wrap closely, uncut, in plastic wrap. Yield: 36 squares.

TO VARY THIS RECIPE

Sparkle Jells mold easily into many pretty shapes—hearts, flowers, fluted cups or squares. Brush plastic molds thoroughly with vegetable oil, fill cavities with a spoon and refrigerate until firm. Pop candies out onto wax paper by pressing back of mold. Use the shapes to add shimmer to a candy tray, to decorate holiday cakes or trim simple desserts.

*May be used as centers for dipping

Chapter 2

WHAT YOU NEED TO MAKE CANDY

Making delectable homemade candy is just like putting together any fine recipe—follow the steps carefully, use the best quality ingredients and suitable equipment. You'll have perfect results, even the first time. As you make the candy again and again, the process will become very easy because you're used to it.

The only difference between creating a fine candy and making a delicious entrée is the absolute necessity of following the recipe accurately. Size and type of cooking pan, degree of heat, timing, even the size of the pan you used for cooling and firming—all are extremely important.

So follow the recipes in this book *carefully* and be assured of success. And read the guidelines that follow to gain an understanding of what is needed, and why it is needed. For information on where to purchase needed materials, see the last page in this book.

ORDERLY WORK HABITS

Work in an orderly, methodical fashion. This is advisable for any task, but for making candy it's a must. Follow the simple recommendations below and turn candy-making into a joy, not a job.

1. *Read the foreword* that is printed at beginning of the chapter in which the recipe appears. This will tell you general characteristics of the type of candy you are making, and the reason for certain procedures. The pictures of the finished candy help, too.

2. *Read the recipe through completely* before starting. Then you'll know just what to expect as you make the candy.

3. *Get out everything you need*—tools, pans, measured ingredients, and place them within easy reach. Then there's no chance of a forgotten ingredient or a frantic search for a necessary piece of equipment.

4. *Follow the printed procedure* in order, step by step. And don't forget the very first step of all, *"Before you begin"*. The importance of starting out right with everything "at the ready" cannot be over-emphasized.

SUITABLE WEATHER

You can make fine candy almost anytime, *except* when the weather is hot and humid. The ideal candy-making weather is a temperature in your work area of about 68°F (20°C) and humidity of 50% or less. If your kitchen is air conditioned, you can duplicate this atmosphere easily. But most candy is quite forgiving—it can be made at a temperature as much as ten or more degrees higher. Just try to have the room free of steam.

What do you do in really warm, steamy weather when the temperature and the humidity are both sky-high? Use any of the recipes in Chapter 1. They're proven successful anytime.

At left, some of the tools and ingredients you'll need to make fine candy: the indispensable thermometer, measuring cups and spoons, dipping forks for bonbons and chocolates, a marble slab and metal candy bars. Heavy saucepans, double boilers and wooden spoons you probably already own. A timer is a great convenience.

USE TOP QUALITY INGREDIENTS

You'll put a lot of love and care into making a batch of fine candy. Don't risk a mediocre result by using less than the finest and freshest ingredients.

Sugar is the basic ingredient in most candies. Be sure to use *granulated cane sugar*, not beet sugar. Beet sugar tends to foam when heated.

Confectioners' sugar (also called powdered sugar or 10X sugar) is used mainly for uncooked candies. Always sift confectioners' sugar before measuring.

Brown sugar, usually the light variety, should be free of lumps and lightly packed in the measuring cup.

Syrups lend sweetness, smoothness and flavor to many candies. Usually light corn syrup is called for, but in some recipes dark corn syrup is used for its distinctive butterscotch flavor. Light molasses and honey are also used in candies. Both tend to scorch easily—so watch carefully.

Dairy products give richness to your homemade candies. Unless otherwise stated, use lightly salted butter. And use butter for greasing your pans too, unless the recipe states otherwise. Milk should be whole milk, not skim, and cream should be rich whipping cream. Evaporated and condensed milks offer a special smoothness.

Be sure to use *Grade A Large* eggs when a recipe calls for eggs. This will assure correct proportions.

Chocolate is almost synonymous with candy! Experiment with different brands to find the one you like the best —each maker produces a chocolate of a somewhat different flavor. Never confuse *chocolate* with *confectionery coating*.

Chocolate comes in many forms. *Unsweetened*, or bitter, chocolate is usually used when chocolate is one of the ingredients in a recipe. *Semi-sweet* and *milk chocolate* come in small morsels as well as the familiar bars. They are a blend of chocolate, sugar, flavoring and dried milk. *Cocoa* is unsweetened chocolate from which most of the cocoa butter has been removed.

For dipping or molding, chocolate must be tempered. Read about this fascinating process in Chapter 11.

Nuts give a lot of crunch and flavor to many deluxe candies. To bring out their full delicious taste and texture, *always crisp chopped nuts before using them.*

This takes next-to-no time. Preheat your oven to 300°F (149°C), spread the nuts on a cookie sheet, place in oven and turn off heat. Remove in ten minutes.

Roast whole nuts before using. Spread on a cookie sheet and place in a preheated 350°F (177°C) oven for about eight to ten minutes. Stir frequently for even browning. Use no butter or oil.

Nuts to be coated in chocolate should never be buttered or oiled. Oil or butter may break down the chocolate.

To toast coconut to a delicate brown, spread on a cookie sheet and place in a preheated 350°F (177°C) oven for eight to ten minutes. Stir very frequently so coconut does not scorch.

Almond paste consists principally of finely ground almonds. Purchase it in eight-ounce or larger cans.

Confectionery coating is a convenient product used for dipping bonbons, molding all types of figures and as an ingredient in fudges, nougats and truffles. It is available in pastels, as well as two chocolate-flavored varieties.

Never confuse confectionery coating with chocolate. Every candy expert strongly urges that you remember this fact. The two substances are completely different and require totally different techniques when handling.

Flavoring and food colors add charm and appeal to your fine candies.

Pure extracts are the flavorings you'll use the most. Purchase clear vanilla— in some candies the dark variety will destroy their delicate tint.

Flavoring oils are needed for hard candies and may also be used for lower-temperature candies. Measure drop by drop—flavoring oils are very strong.

Liquid food colorings may be used in all types of candies.

MOST EQUIPMENT NEEDED IS ALREADY IN YOUR KITCHEN

For cooking, *any good household range,* either gas or electric, will give satisfactory results. For high-temperature candies, preheat the heat unit on an electric range for quicker, more professional results.

Use heavy saucepans, whether aluminum, steel or copper. Many candies scorch easily in lightweight pans. If you have them, pans with non-stick interiors are most convenient for pouring out candies to cool and firm, but they are not essential. One and a half-quart, three-quart and four-quart (one and a half, three and four-liter) sizes will handle any of the recipes. Be sure to use the correct size of pan to prevent messy boil-overs.

Pastry brushes are little tools you'll use a lot. Whenever a recipe calls for a hot, cooked sugar mixture, you'll need to wash down the sides of the pan with a brush dipped in hot water. This prevents crystallization which would ruin the batch. Before you start to cook the candy, set a two-cup measuring cup filled with hot water with the pastry brush in it near the heat unit. This is the best insurance for perfect results.

Double boilers in one and a half-quart and two-quart (one and a half and two-liter) sizes are needed for many recipes.

For measuring, accuracy is essential. Here are the tools you'll need.

A *thermometer* is your most essential measuring tool. Except for the candies in Chapter 1, a thermometer is a must for perfect results. It should measure from 100°F to 400°F (40°C to 200°C). Very experienced candy makers may use cold water tests, but even these tests should be done in combination with thermometer readings.

Buy one with a clip that attaches to the side of your pan. When you start to cook your candy, have the thermometer nearby, resting in a container of hot water. Then it will be preheated when you lower it into the hot mixture. When you remove the thermometer, put it back into the hot water. This will make it much easier to clean.

Wash the thermometer separately in warm sudsy water, and hold it under the tap to rinse. When storing, it's best to hang it on a hook, rather than putting it in a drawer where it may be jostled.

Always test the thermometer for accuracy before starting on a batch of candy. Place it in a pan of cold water and bring to a full boil. It should register 212°F (100°C) at or near sea level. This test will do two things. First, it will tell you if your thermometer is slightly inaccurate. Secondly, it will indicate the boiling temperature of water at the altitude in your area. (Consult the Appendix for more information.) If the thermometer registers higher or lower, adjust cooking temperature accordingly. For example, if the thermometer registers 214°F (101°C) at boiling and the recipe calls for cooking to 240°F (116°C) cook to 242°F (117°C). If it registers 210°F (98°C), cook to 238°F (114°C).

A *low-temperature thermometer* is needed for chocolate molding and for dipping and molding *confectionery* coating. Buy one that measures from 60°F to 120°F (15°C to 49°C).

Measuring cups and spoons are needed in multiples. For liquids, heat-proof glass cups are ideal. For dry ingredients, always use metal cups that can be filled to overflowing, then leveled off with a spatula. Either metal or plastic measuring spoons are satisfactory. *All measurements for recipes in this book are level.*

A *timer is a great convenience.* In making candy, time should be measured too! It's very helpful to hear the reassuring ring that tells you the nuts have crisped, or that you're nearing the end of the cooking period.

Please turn the page

For mixing and beating, *use wooden spoons* to blend and stir candies. They have many advantages over metal spoons. With a wooden spoon you can tell by feel and sound if all the sugar crystals in a mixture are dissolved. It will feel cool and comfortable to your hand and will not scratch the suface of your pans, or destroy the non-stick coating. And there's no unpleasant clatter!

An electric mixer is a great labor-saver for finishing some candies. Either a good hand-held mixer or a table model is satisfactory. A table model is more convenient when pouring a hot syrup into the mixing bowl as you beat—but if you have a helper, a hand-held mixer will do the job. Use heat-proof bowls.

For cooling and firming cooked candies you'll need several shallow metal pans, no more than 2" (5cm) high. Baking pans are fine.

Use square pans in 6", 8" and 10" (15.2cm, 20.3cm and 25.4cm) sizes as directed in the recipe. Size is important so that the finished pieces of candy will be of the proper height—usually about 3/4" (1.9cm). Occasionally you will need a 9" x 13" (23cm x 33cm) sheet cake pan, or 12" x 18" (30.5cm x 45.7cm) cookie sheets.

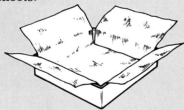

Always line pans with foil as the diagram shows.* Cut or fold a length of foil to the width of the pan and press it smoothly into the pan. Crisscross it with a second length. Lightly butter the foil-lined pan. When your candy is firm, simply lift it out of the pan by the edges of the foil. Turn out on a cutting board, peel off the foil and cut the candy. There's never a chance of sticking, or of crumbling the first few pieces. Pans stay free of knife scratches, too.

Some candies require a different treatment as recipes note.

SPECIAL EQUIPMENT, JUST FOR CANDY

As you gain experience, you'll want to invest in a few tools to make your work easier and more professional.

A marble slab. Once you have one, you'll wonder how you ever did without it! Buy one about 15" x 25" (38cm x 63.5cm) and at least 1" (2.5cm) thick. Any larger would be too heavy, unless it is mounted in its own table or counter. Old marble is just as good as new, maybe better—and any color is fine. Perhaps you can claim a piece of marble when a building is being demolished. Or look under "marble" in your telephone directory. A high polish is unnecessary, as long as the surface is smooth.

What do you use the marble for? Lots of things! The dense texture of marble makes it ideal for even cooling of fondant, hard candy, brittles and caramels. The smooth surface of marble is best for working fondant and tempering chocolate. You'll pour lollipops and form candy logs on it. You can set a hot pan on it without concern.

A marble slab is a big help in everyday cooking projects, too. You'll knead bread dough, roll pastry and cut cookies on its smooth surface—all with ease.

Marble is easy to maintain. When you've finished your candy, just wash it off with diswashing suds, rinse and dry with a clean towel. Never apply polish or preservative.

Place a clean towel, folded in thirds, on the counter under your marble slab. Then it's easy to slide it out of the way.

Metal candy bars. These are companions to your marble slab, and like the slab, you'll wonder how you ever did without them. Sometimes called fondant bars, or caramel bars, these heavy steel bars come in sets of four—two 18" (45.7cm) long and two 12" (30.5cm) long. They are square-cut—each side 3/4" (1.9cm). Their weight makes them rest securely on the slab with never a shift. Their height gives a convenient guide to the depth of the finished candy.

How do you use the bars? For cooling fondant, arrange them on the slab to form the largest rectangle possible—then pour in the cooked fondant. The bars will contain the hot mixture as it cools. No chance of any dribbling off.

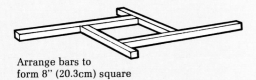

Arrange bars to
form 8" (20.3cm) square

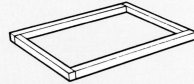

Bars form 12" x 18" (30.5cm x 45.7cm) area

For cooling and firming caramels and many other candies, arrange the bars to form the exact area you want. When the candy has firmed, simply remove the bars. You'll have a block of candy with neat, trim edges and perfectly square corners, ready to cut.

It's easy to maintain the metal bars. Just wash, rinse and dry them as you would any cooking utensil. They're a lifetime investment in fine candy making.

Scrapers. These are just paint scrapers with a sturdy wooden handle and a somewhat flexible metal blade. Get the widest blade possible, about 5" (12.7cm).

You'll need these for working fondant and tempering chocolate. Scrapers are handy for breaking up brittles and barks too. Buy them at the hardware store.

Professional candy scrapers make the work even easier. These have a 5" (12.7cm) rectangular blade topped by a 5" (12.7cm) wood handle.

A household scale. This is most convenient for measuring chocolate or *confectionery* coating to be used for dipping or molding. It's essential for the fine Continental Chocolates in Chapter 15.

Dipping forks for dipping centers in *confectionery* coating, chocolate and fondant. These specially designed forks make dipping easy. Purchase the best quality—they'll last for many years.

Molds. Some candies seem cuter and more appealing when they're molded in fancy shapes. With molds you can form chocolate and *confectionery* coating into stand-up three dimensional figures, shape lollipops and elegant bonbons.

Molds fall into two groups—those for high-temperature hard candies, and those used for low-temperature candies.

High-temperature molds are made of metal or a special synthetic material. They will accept mixtures as hot as 320°F (160°C).

Low-temperature molds are usually made of a clear plastic with a very smooth, shiny finish. Use them for chocolate, *confectionery* coating, fondant, marshmallow or other low-temperature mixtures. Many high-temperature molds may be used for molding low-temperature candies.

Some baking pans such as heart-shaped cupcake pans or egg-shaped cupcake pans may serve as molds for either high or low temperature candies.

Care of molds. The smoother the cavity of the mold, the shinier the finished molded candy. So be very careful not to scratch the inner surface of the mold. Store flat so they do not warp. If they need washing, use *warm* (not hot) sudsy water, rinse and dry with a soft cloth.

Cotton gloves (cosmetic gloves) made of a thin knit material are used for handling chocolate and *confectionery* coating molded items. Wear them and you'll never leave a fingerprint!

Cotton work gloves take the heat out of making brittles. Before using, soak the palm side liberally with any clear vegetable oil. Wear them for thinning and stretching the hot poured candy.

A mint patty funnel. This simple device makes it easy to form dainty colorful mints. It consists of a metal funnel with a handle, and a wooden stick that closes the opening.

Packaging materials to show off your gift candies—boxes, dainty paper doilies and fluted paper bonbon cups. The Appendix will give you many ideas for pretty packaging.

Chapter 3

CANDY MAGIC WITH

CONFECTIONERY COATING

Everyone who makes candy has an ambition to create luxurious dipped bonbons and cute molded candies in holiday shapes—Christmas trees, Santas, hearts, bunnies, eggs, flowers and many more. The substance that makes it easy to create such candy masterpieces is confectionery coating. This product is often called summer coating or compound coating. It is produced by the leading chocolate manufacturers and is offered under the trade names of these firms. *Confectionery coating is easy and fun to use.* Just read this chapter carefully—then go on to create colorful, professional-looking candies everyone will admire.

Confectionery coating is composed of sugar, various fats and oils, milk solids, flavoring and food colors. Cocoa is added to the light and dark chocolate-flavored coatings. This product has a relatively high melting point—about 99°F (36°C)—therefore it is suitable to use even in warm weather. It is available in pretty pastels as well as dark and light brown.

Never confuse confectionery coating with chocolate. The two substances are completely different and require totally different methods of handling. Of the two, confectionery coating is less delicate and much more suited for dipping and molding by a novice in candy making.

Purchase confectionery coating in two forms. "Wafers" are button-shaped discs, quick and easy to melt for dipping or molding. Ten-pound blocks must be chopped before melting, but you'll want to have them on hand if you plan to dip or mold a number of candies for gifts or special occasions. Of course, blocks are more economical than the wafers. If you haven't used confectionery coating before, we recommend you buy a few pounds of the wafers and enjoy the thrill of turning out bonbons, candy bars and dimensional molds. Then you will want to invest in the ten-pound blocks.

Confectionery coating is easy to store. Keep either wafers or blocks in tightly sealed plastic bags at a temperature of 72°F (22°C) or less, with a humidity of 50% to 60%. A cool dry cupboard, basement or hallway is ideal. Make sure the plastic bag is tightly sealed to prevent foreign odors from affecting the coating. The coating will keep for many months, ready for your candy making adventures.

There is no waste in confectionery coating. In the directions that follow, the approximate amount needed is given. There will always be melted coating left over. Just take it out of the pan with a rubber scraper onto a sheet of foil. When hardened, store in a tightly sealed plastic bag to use for the next project. When preparing to dip or mold candies, we recommend you use no more than half previously melted coating combined with half new, or never melted, coating.

Confectionery coating may be flavored as you wish. To flavor, use *oil-based flavors only.* Two drops per pound of coating is sufficient, added when the coating is almost melted. Never use flavoring extracts.

A word of caution. Never allow any moisture, water or steam, to enter the coating as you melt it. Moisture will stiffen and ruin the coating for dipping or molding. This is the reason you use oil-based flavorings.

Watch temperature carefully. Never let the temperature of the melted coating exceed 115°F (46°C). Higher temperature will cause an unattractive gray "bloom" on the finished candy. Invest in a handy low-temperature thermometer. Soon you will be familiar with the coating's proper temperature by appearance and feel—but the thermometer is needed insurance.

Above: just see the magic you can make with confectionery coating! Dipped and molded bonbons, some set off with cut-outs, a stand-up bunny and a molded basket of Easter eggs

HOW TO MAKE DIPPED BONBONS WITH CONFECTIONERY COATING

Coating chopped and ready to melt

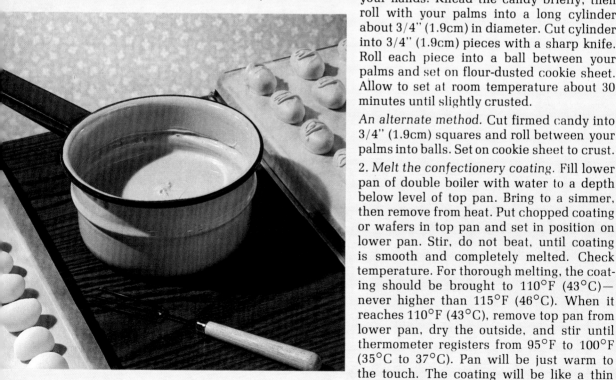

Set up your work area conveniently

It's easy and fun to produce a tray of delicious bonbons you'll be proud to serve to your friends. Choose any tint of coating you desire, or make a variety with centers of different flavors. Here's what you'll need.

  About 50 formed centers

  A double boiler, two-quart capacity

  Low-temperature thermometer

  One pound (454g) confectionery coating, chopped, or one pound of wafers

  Dipping fork

  Two cookie sheets, backs covered with wax paper. Dust one lightly with flour.

Before you begin, arrange your work area. Flour-dusted cookie sheet containing centers will be at your left side, cookie sheet to receive dipped bonbons at your right. Leave space for pan of melted coating in center.

1. *Form the centers.* Use any of the recipes in Chapter 1 starred with an asterisk—or any of the starred recipes in this book.

Work with a third or a half of the recipe at a time. Lightly flour a smooth surface and your hands. Knead the candy briefly, then roll with your palms into a long cylinder about 3/4" (1.9cm) in diameter. Cut cylinder into 3/4" (1.9cm) pieces with a sharp knife. Roll each piece into a ball between your palms and set on flour-dusted cookie sheet. Allow to set at room temperature about 30 minutes until slightly crusted.

An alternate method. Cut firmed candy into 3/4" (1.9cm) squares and roll between your palms into balls. Set on cookie sheet to crust.

2. *Melt the confectionery coating.* Fill lower pan of double boiler with water to a depth below level of top pan. Bring to a simmer, then remove from heat. Put chopped coating or wafers in top pan and set in position on lower pan. Stir, do not beat, until coating is smooth and completely melted. Check temperature. For thorough melting, the coating should be brought to 110°F (43°C)—never higher than 115°F (46°C). When it reaches 110°F (43°C), remove top pan from lower pan, dry the outside, and stir until thermometer registers from 95°F to 100°F (35°C to 37°C). Pan will be just warm to the touch. The coating will be like a thin mayonnaise or a warm pudding.

3. *Dip centers.* Drop a center into the coating with your left hand. Tumble with the dipping fork to coat, then lift out on fork with your right hand. Tap fork on side of pan to remove excess coating, then deposit coated center on prepared cookie sheet upside down. With the coating that clings to the fork, try to make a little swirl on top of the bonbon. As you dip the centers, stir the coating occasionally with the dipping fork.

4. Allow dipped bonbons to firm at room temperature, about 15 minutes. Use a rubber scraper to scrape remaining coating from pan onto a length of foil. Let harden, then store in tightly sealed plastic bag to use for a future project.

TIPS ON DIPPING CONFECTIONERY COATING

A temperature of about 68°F (20°C) in your work area is ideal for dipping—but you can have satisfactory results at a temperature as high as 78°F (26°C). Open the window—the flow of air is helpful in drying the bonbons to a gloss.

The cooler the temperature of the melted coating, the thicker the covering of the bonbons. Those dipped at 95°F (35°C) will have a heavier coating than those dipped at 100°F (37°C).

Form a rhythm as you dip. While right hand is tapping the fork to remove excess coating, left hand is tossing center into pan.

If coating becomes too thick as you dip, set top pan over lower pan filled with very warm water. Stir until coating is proper consistency—or check with thermometer.

Bonbons keep very well—the coating keeps the center fresh and moist. Place finished bonbons in paper candy cups and arrange snugly in a box. Cover with plastic wrap, then put cover on box. Store in a cool place for one to two months.

MOLDING CONFECTIONERY COATING

Molded candies have a special appeal—their clear-cut shapes have a very professional look that is easy to achieve with coating. Confectionery coating offers the added appeal of dainty pastel colors, too.

Molds to use. The most satisfactory molds for confectionery coating are made of a special clear plastic. These clear molds have several advantages. After the mold is filled you can hold it above eye level and see if any air bubbles remain. You can tell if the molded coating has been sufficiently cooled and is ready to be unmolded by the frosted appearance of the filled mold. Best of all, the clear plastic molds give the finished candies a very shiny surface.

Other molds may also be used for confectionery coating. Any mold made for high-temperature candies will work equally well for confectionery coating—but you will sacrifice the advantages of the clear molds.

Care of molds. The smoother the inner surface of the mold, the glossier the finished candy. Therefore, take care not to scratch or mar the cavity of the mold. To wash molds, just swish through *warm* (not hot) suds, rinse in warm water and dry with a soft cloth. Heat may cause molds to warp.

Store molds flat in a dust-free cupboard so they do not bend or warp. If you stack the molds, place soft tissue or paper toweling between them.

Molds come in one or two pieces. *One-piece* molds are the easiest to use. With them you can mold a whole alphabet, fancy shaped bonbons, flowers, hearts, candy bars, Easter eggs and many more shapes. Your finished candies can be hollow or solid. All will have a flat back and a molded upper surface.

Two-piece molds make upright three-dimensional figures that delight everyone. One piece shapes the front of the figure, the second piece shapes the back. Projections on one piece of the mold fit neatly into hollows on the other piece, so you can easily align the mold, then clip it together. The three-dimensional figures you mold may be hollow or solid. If the mold is hollow, it may be filled with a variety of fillings.

TIPS ON MOLDING CONFECTIONERY COATING

White spots or streaks. This is usually caused by molding at too high a temperature. Streaks are also caused by not stirring the coating frequently enough as it melts. Stir the melted coating occasionally, too, as you fill the molds. This keeps all the melted coating at the same temperature.

A grainy texture is caused by over-heating the coating when melting. It is still edible and need not be wasted.

Thickening is usually caused by moisture getting into the coating. It may also be caused by over-heating when melting the coating. You may salvage the melted coating by stirring in a very small amount of solid white vegetable shortening—no more than one half teaspoon at a time. This will lower the melting point of the coating so be very careful to add the shortening *sparingly.*

Chopping a lot of coating? If you plan to mold large items, or a quantity of small ones, use a six-pronged ice pick to chop the coating. Then go back and chop the pieces with a large chopping knife. This is easier and quicker than chopping with the knife alone.

Wear light cotton gloves (cosmetic gloves) when handling the completed molded candies. The candies have a fine glossy finish that shows up fingerprints.

Put small candies in paper candy cups after unmolding. When you need to handle them, touch only the paper cups.

Wrap larger molded candies in soft tissue for storage. For gift-giving, wrap in clear plastic or thin foil.

Confectionery coating picks up odors readily. To avoid an off-flavor, store small candies in a box slipped into a plastic bag and tightly sealed. Place tissue-wrapped larger candies in tightly sealed plastic bags.

HOW TO MOLD SOLID CANDIES IN ONE-PIECE MOLDS

This quick, easy procedure is summed up in three words—*melt, fill, chill.* As confectionery coating cools and hardens within molds, it contracts. This allows the candies to drop easily out of the molds. Choose any molds you like, those that include a number of bonbon-shaped cavities are ideal. Have the molds at room temperature.

1. *Melt* the confectionery coating as described on page 22. Use about 3/4 pound (340g) of chopped coating or wafers. This will make about 40 to 50 candies, about 1" (2.5cm) in diameter. Check temperature with a thermometer. It should not exceed 115°F (46°C). Stir to cool to 103°F (38°C), the ideal temperature for molding.

2. *Fill* the cavities of the molds with a spoon or a small ladle. Or use cone method, page 26. Do not over-fill so that coating mounds up. From a height of two or three inches, drop filled mold on surface several times to eliminate air bubbles. Check clear molds by viewing when held above eye level. If any bubbles are visible, drop or tap again.

3. *Chill* the filled molds in the freezer until hardened. For small bonbon molds, this will take only eight to ten minutes. Candy will be hardened if outside of cavity appears frosty. If a dark area appears on mold, return to freezer until entire mold appears frosty. Then it is ready to unmold.

4. *Unmold* the candies by inverting the mold and holding about an inch above a towel-covered table top. Very gently flex mold, or tap mold, and candies will fall out. Remove remaining coating from pan with a rubber scraper onto foil. When hardened, store in tightly sealed plastic bag for months.

At right: lollipops molded in confectionery coating, pretty as a flower garden. Place sticks in position on molds and pour in melted coating. Rotate sticks. This will assure that they remain firmly in the candy. Chill for ten to 20 minutes in freezer, then unmold. Decorate with confectionery coating and buttercream flowers.

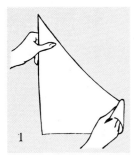 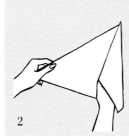  

THE PARCHMENT CONE METHOD FOR FILLING SMALL MOLDS

This is a quick, very professional method for filling molds. It's especially suitable for filling molds with multiple cavities.

Make cone from purchased parchment paper triangles, or use wax paper cut in triangles two short sides about 12" (30.5cm) long. Follow the diagram above.

1. Lay triangle with longest side away from you. Grasp right hand corner with thumb and forefinger of your right hand and turn inward.

2. Roll your right hand toward the center, holding left hand corner firmly with your left hand. A cone shape will start to form.

3. Twirl left hand corner all the way around cone, sliding it back and forth until point of cone is needle sharp.

4. Staple or tape cone to secure. With just a little practice you'll be able to make a cone in seconds.

Fill cone with melted confectionery coating. Use a small metal measuring cup with handle, and fill no more than a third to a half full. Fold the top of the cone securely in a "diaper" fold. Cut a tiny opening in point of cone with a scissors.

Fill mold by holding cone in your right hand, upright, a little above mold. A very light squeeze will release the coating into the mold cavity. As you move from one cavity to the next, keep your left forefinger over the point of the cone. Squeeze unused coating back into the pan. Or let coating harden in the cone. Open cone, take out hardened coating and put in plastic bag to use again.

HOW TO MOLD HOLLOW CANDIES IN ONE-PIECE MOLDS

This procedure is similar to that of molding solid candies.

To mold nut-filled candies. Spoon just enough of the melted confectionery coating into the mold cavity to cover the bottom. Drop in a small nut, or broken piece of a larger nut. (Nuts should be roasted *without* fat or oil—fat or oil might break down the coating.) Add enough melted coating to bring it to the top of the mold cavity. Tap to eliminate air bubbles, chill and unmold.

For candies with soft fillings, fill mold cavities with melted coating. Place in freezer just two or three moments until candies have hardened on the outside, then invert mold over foil to empty excess coating. Return to freezer a moment or two until hardened. Remove from freezer, but do not remove from mold. Spoon or pour in filling to about 1/8" (.3cm) from top of mold. Or use cone method, above. Seal molds with melted coating. Chill again to harden, then unmold.

Use this procedure when you want a hollow item, like a liqueur glass or dessert shell, too. Omit filling, just empty excess coating and chill to harden before unmolding.

Fondant is used most often for filling. See recipes in Chapter 10. Heat the fondant until it is just barely pourable, adding a few teaspoons of liquid if necessary.

HOW TO USE TWO-PIECE MOLDS WITH CONFECTIONERY COATING

Two piece molds make enchanting three-dimensional figures in confectionery coating.

For Solid Molded Candies

1. Line up the two pieces of the mold by fitting projections on one piece into hollows on second. Clip securely.

2. Improvise a stand for holding mold upright. An easy way to do this is to crumple a little foil in the bottom of a tumbler or container large enough to receive the mold.

3. Melt coating as directed on page 22. Stir until temperature lowers to about 103°F (38°C). Set clipped mold into prepared stand, upside down. Make a paper cone (page 26), cut point to make an opening ¾" to 1" (1.9cm to 2.5cm) in diameter and insert in opening of mold. Pour melted coating into mold through cone, using a metal measuring cup with handle. Drop stand holding mold on table several times to eliminate air bubbles — then add more coating if necessary to fill mold. Remove cone. Put mold, in stand, in freezer to harden. This method is neat, quick and professional.

An alternate method. Hold clipped mold in your left hand as you spoon in melted coating with your right hand. Tap to eliminate air bubbles and place in stand. Put in freezer to harden.

4. Remove clips from mold, lay mold on its side and lift off upper piece. Use a dull knife, if necessary, slipped between the two pieces of the mold. Invert second piece over surface and very gently flex mold. It will drop out. Wearing light cotton gloves, trim off any rough edges at the seam of the molded candy with a small sharp knife.

For Hollow Molded Candies

1. Follow the steps for Solid Molded Candies, filling the mold completely and tapping to remove air bubbles. Put in freezer for just two or three minutes, just until the outside of the mold is hardened. Remove from freezer and pour out the still-liquid coating from the interior of the mold onto foil. Return mold to freezer to harden completely.

2. Unmold and trim seam, just as for Solid Molded Candies. Seal the opening at the bottom of the candy with melted coating applied with a small spatula. Allow seal to harden at room temperature.

Below: molding a dimensional Santa. Mold is in improvised stand, paper cone inserted in opening. Completed Santa has piped trim.

ADD COLOR CONTRAST
WITH THE FLOW-IN METHOD

This is the easiest, quickest and neatest way to give the magic of color to your confectionery coating molds. When making several molds, do them in assembly-line fashion, color by color. Here is the way we did the Christmas wreath pictured below. Use the same method for two-piece molds.

1. Start with red berries. Since these areas are so small, we melted just a few red wafers in a small glass jar set in hot water. Stir until coating is smooth and completely melted. Put into parchment cone (see page 26). Fill just the areas of the berries, giving the cone a very light squeeze. Drop mold to level. Let set a few minutes until firm.

2. Fill a second cone with melted yellow confectionery coating. Fill in the letters, then the bow, working from outer edges in. Do not over-fill areas. Drop mold on table to level and remove air bubbles and let set a few minutes until firm. Now fill in the green area of the wreath, going right over the top of the berries. Drop mold to level and let set.

3. Now fill entire mold with chocolate-flavored confectionery coating. Drop mold sharply several times to remove air bubbles. Place filled mold in freezer about 20 minutes to harden, then unmold.

THE CROCK POT METHOD
FOR MELTING COATING

If you plan to mold a number of rather large pieces in confectionery coating, your crock pot is a handy tool for melting the coating.

1. Chop all the coating you need at one time. A crock pot holds up to five pounds (2.3kg) of confectionery coating—plan to melt at least 3½ pounds (1.6kg).

2. Place about one pound (454g) of the chopped coating in the crock pot and *set at low.* (Never use higher setting.) As the coating melts, stir occasionally. When it is almost completely melted (about 20 minutes) add another pound of chopped coating.

3. Stir occasionally until coating is almost melted, then add a third pound of chopped coating. Continue until all the coating is melted. Five pounds of coating will melt in about 45 minutes.

4. When temperature reaches 105°F (40°C), turn off crock pot. Temperature will rise to 110°F (43°C). Stir to lower to 103°F (38°C). Or add a little chopped coating to reduce temperature. Check the temperature from time to time. It may be necessary to turn heat on and off at intervals. Don't forget to stir occasionally.

QUICK TREATS WITH CONFECTIONERY COATING

You'll always have melted confectionery coating left over after you've dipped bonbons or made molded pieces. If you'd rather not store it for a later use, here are some quick and delicious ways to use up the last of the melted coating.

Raisin clusters. Stir raisins into enough confectionery coating to cover well. Add chopped homemade orange or lemon peel if you have it on hand. Drop with a small spoon into clusters on wax paper. Harden for eight or ten minutes in the freezer.

Nut clusters. Stir crisped broken nuts into the remaining coating. Drop by spoonfuls onto wax paper. Harden in freezer eight or ten minutes.

Dipped pretzels. Miniature pretzels are surprisingly good when dipped in confectionery coating. Use a two-tined dipping fork to dip. See directions on page 23.

Dipped animal crackers. Children love these! Just dip in confectionery coating as you would a bonbon. See directions on page 23.

Peanut butter squares. Best with butterscotch or chocolate flavored confectionery coating. Stir about one tablespoon of peanut butter, creamy or chunky, into remaining coating. Spread into small metal baking pan, lined with foil. Let set up at room temperature, then score into 1" (2.5cm) squares with a knife. Chill to harden, then break into squares.

Easter egg nests. Green or yellow confectionery coating is best for these. Stir in flaked coconut, drop by tablespoon into mounds and make a depression in each. After hardening, fill with candy.

Above: Lemon Marble Bark, dipped miniature pretzels. Candy Mushrooms and Jack-o-lanterns trimmed with piping gel.

DECORATING FINISHED MOLDS

Decorating adds the final touch of charm and color to make your finished confectionery coating molds special. There are several methods of decorating—with just a little practice all will become quick and easy.

COATING CUT-OUTS MAKE CHARMING TRIMS

This is the quickest and easiest method of all, and gives a very pretty finish to molded bonbons. See picture above. To cut the trims from confectionery coating, use tiny truffle cutters or large round decorating tubes, 9 through 12, for circles. To cut small squares or diamonds, a small sharp knife is all you need.

1. Cover the back of a cookie sheet with foil, shiny side up. Tape edges to secure. Melt about a half-pound of confectionery coating according to directions on page 22.

2. Spread the melted coating smoothly over the foil with a large spatula, keeping surface as smooth as possible and the coating about 1/16" thick.

3. Wait until the confectionery coating has just set up but not completely hardened. If your work area is 72°F (22°C), this will take about 5 minutes. Cut the shapes just as you would cut out cookies, pressing the cutter or tube firmly through the coating. For squares or diamonds, use knife to cut long straight lines, then cross with a second series of lines.

4. Allow coating to harden completely, about ten minutes at room temperature. Remove tape from foil and slide your hand gently beneath foil. Cut-out shapes will pop up. Attach cut-outs to candies with dots of melted coating. Save scraps to melt again.

DECORATING WITH CONFECTIONERY COATING

This is the best way to write names, or pipe colorful trims or features on any finished confectionery coating mold.

1. Make a paper decorating cone (page 26) for each color of coating you plan to use. Using the large Easter eggs on page 21 as an example, you will need three cones—one for white coating, one for yellow and one for pink.

2. Melt confectionery coating as directed on page 22. If you are melting just a small quantity of coating, use this method. Fill a small square pan with hot water from the tap to a depth of about 1" (2.5cm). Place chopped coating or wafers in colors desired in small glass jars and set in water. Stir with a small spoon or popsicle stick to proper consistency, like thinned mayonnaise or warm pudding. Make sure no water gets into coating. Meanwhile, set a cookie sheet over a sheet cake pan of warm water.

3. Fill cones with melted coating, no more than half full, fold to seal securely and place

filled cones on cookie sheet over warm water. Do not cut points of cones. The gentle heat of the cookie sheet will keep the coating at the proper consistency.

4. To pipe names, cut about ¼" (.6cm) from point of cone, then tape tube 1 *to the outside* of the cone. This will keep coating from oozing out. With very light pressure, squeeze the cone as you pipe the name. Use your whole arm, not just your fingers to pipe the letters. For dots and lines, use tube 1. For tiny leaves, use tube 65. For a shell border, use tube 13.

If you are decorating a large number of molds, do them in assembly-line fashion, completing all trim in one color on all molds before starting with a second color.

DECORATING MOLDS WITH BUTTERCREAM

This is a very satisfactory method for decorating confectionery coating molds. Use your favorite buttercream for decorating recipe or the one below. It's ideal for any decorating purpose.

WILTON SNOW-WHITE BUTTERCREAM

⅓ cup (80ml) water

2 tablespoons (30ml or 28g) Wilton meringue powder

⅝ cup (150ml or 140g) solid white vegetable shortening, room temperature

5 ¾ cups (1.4 liters or 575g) sifted confectioners' sugar

¼ teaspoon (1.2ml) salt

⅛ teaspoon (.6ml) butter flavoring

¼ teaspoon (1.2ml) almond flavoring

¼ teaspoon (1.2ml) clear vanilla

liquid food coloring, as desired

1. Combine water and meringue powder and whip with electric mixer at high speed until peaks form. Add two cups (480ml) sugar, one cup (240ml) at a time, beating after each addition at low speed.

2. Alternately add shortening and remainder of sugar. Add salt, flavorings and food coloring and beat at low speed until smooth and fluffy. For line work, thin with one teaspoon of light corn syrup. May be stored, well covered, in refrigerator for several weeks, then brought to room temperature and rebeaten. Yield: four cups (960ml).

3. Make a paper decorating cone (page 26), cut about ¼" (.6cm) from the point and drop in the proper decorating tube. Use tube 1 for lines and dots, tube 3 or 4 for larger dots, tube 13 for shells, tube 65 for leaves. Fill the cone about half full with buttercream, fold top to seal securely, then squeeze cone with your right hand and guide it with your left forefinger to decorate molded pieces. Allow decorations to dry about 30 minutes at room temperature. Leftover buttercream may be used to ice or decorate cakes or cookies.

DECORATING MOLDS WITH PIPING GEL

Piping gel makes glistening, showy trims on confectionery coating molds. See the Jack-o-lanterns on page 29.

1. Stir enough liquid food coloring into clear piping gel to attain the tint you want. Work with just a small quantity of gel—a third-cup (80ml) will trim at least a dozen molds.

2. Make a paper cone (page 26) and fill no more than half full with tinted gel. Fold to seal securely and cut just a tiny opening from point of cone. Squeeze cone gently to fill in areas on finished mold. Dry at room temperature about 30 minutes. Leftover gel may be refrigerated, well covered, to use for decorating again.

FLOWER TRIMS

This is the sweetest way to trim a confectionery coating mold. See picture at left.

1. Make a paper decorating cone (page 26), cut about ¼" (.6cm) from the point, and drop in the proper decorating tube. Tubes 107, 224, or 17 all pipe quick pretty blossoms. Fill cone about half full with Wilton Snow-White Buttercream.

2. Cover the back of a cookie sheet with wax paper. Hold cone straight up above cookie sheet, touch lightly to surface, squeeze cone, stop pressure and move away. Result is an instant star-like flower. You can pipe dozens of them in minutes. To finish the flowers, pipe a dot in center with tube 1.

3. Allow flowers to dry thoroughly at room temperature—about an hour. To release, run a spatula under the wax paper. Attach flowers to molded pieces with a dot of melted confectionery coating. If you wish, add leaves piped through tube 65.

DECORATIVE PETITS FOURS

These little confections add a fashionable accent to a gift box of candy—and they're so delicious they'll be the first to be eaten! Use your imagination in dreaming up color schemes. The dainty tints of confectionery coating make it easy to provide a pretty variety of miniature cakes

    1 purchased pound cake about 7" x 3½" (17.8cm x 8.9cm)

    ½ cup (120ml) jelly for filling

    1½ cups (360ml) apricot preserves

    2 pounds (908g) confectionery coating, chopped, or 2 pounds wafers

Before you begin, freeze the cake.

1. Using a serrated knife, trim off all crusty edges. Slice the frozen cake horizontally into even layers ½" (1.2cm) high. Start at the base of the cake, measure ½" (1.2cm) up at intervals around the sides and mark with toothpicks as guides for even layers. Continue for additional layers. Spread a layer with jelly, top with second layer. Continue until all layers are filled. Press tops of cakes with a baking pan to firm, then refrigerate for 30 minutes.

2. Cut cakes in 1" (2.5cm) squares with a serrated knife. Heat apricot jam to boiling and strain. Using a pastry brush, coat top and sides of cake cubes with hot strained jam. Set on wax paper to dry, about 30 minutes.

3. Melt confectionery coating (page 22). Place the little cakes on a baking rack set on a cookie sheet, and spoon the melted coating over them to cover.

When coating has hardened, dip the bottoms of the cakes in melted coating to seal them on all sides. Wear light cotton gloves to hold while dipping. This will avoid fingerprints. Decorate, if desired, with trims piped with contrasting melted confectionery coating. Place in paper candy cups, then in a covered box to store for up to six weeks. Yield: about 42 petits fours.

TO VARY THIS RECIPE

Cut fruitcake into 1" (2.5cm) cubes and cover with melted confectionery coating, chocolate flavor. Garnish with roasted nuts or bits of candied fruit.

MOLD A MONOGRAM IN CONFECTIONERY COATING

Your friend will be delighted to receive this thoughtful little gift on the occasion of a birthday, graduation or any day you'd like to make special. Monograms make spectacular cake decorations, too.

You will need about six ounces (168g) of confectionery coating to mold three letters. Melt the coating as described on page 22. Stir to cool to a temperature between 100°F (37°C) and 107°F (42°C)—103°F (39°C) is ideal. Fill the letter molds with a spoon or with the parchment cone method, page 26. Drop filled mold sharply on table several times to eliminate air bubbles. Place in freezer about 15 minutes, or until entire area of mold appears frosty. Unmold.

Dress up the completed molds with scrolls and dots piped with tube 1 and confectionery coating. See page 30 for method.

CANDY MUSHROOMS

Exactly like real mushrooms! These cute confections delight everyone. Confectionery coating sets off the crisp, crunchy meringue.

    4 egg whites, room temperature

    pinch of salt

    ¼ teaspoon (1.2ml) cream of tartar

    1 cup (240ml or 200g) granulated sugar

    1 teaspoon (5ml) vanilla

    2 tablespoons (30ml or 14g) cocoa

    1 pound (454g) confectionery coating, dark chocolate flavor, chopped, or 1 pound wafers

Before you begin, chop the confectionery coating. Line two cookie sheets with foil. Make two paper cones (page 26) and pre-

heat the oven to 225°F (108°C). Adjust two racks in oven to divide height into thirds.

1. Place egg whites in small bowl of electric mixer and beat at low speed until foamy. Add salt and cream of tartar and continue beating until the mixture holds its shape when beaters are lifted. Add the sugar, one tablespoon (15ml) at a time, beating after each addition until thoroughly blended. Add vanilla, turn speed to high and continue beating for about eight minutes, until meringue is very stiff.

2. Drop a tube 10 into each paper cone and fill cones with the meringue mixture. Fold tops securely to seal. Pipe mushroom tops first on one prepared cookie sheet. Hold cone straight up, tube just touching surface of cookie sheet. Squeeze cone gently with your right hand, lifting cone as a rounded dome shape builds up. Stop pressure and lift cone away. Shapes should be about 1½" (3.8cm) in diameter. If a point forms on top of mushroom, touch with a damp finger.

3. Pipe stems with second cone on second prepared cookie sheet. Hold cone straight up, resting lightly on cookie sheet. Squeeze very gently with right hand, lifting cone as form builds up to a height of 1" to 1½" (2.5cm to 3.8cm). Stop squeezing, then move cone away. Place cocoa in a fine sieve and gently sift over mushroom tops and stems. Place cookie sheet with mushroom tops on lower shelf of oven, stems on upper shelf. Bake for one hour, turn off oven, open door slightly, and allow mushrooms to remain in oven until oven is cool.

4. Put stems and tops together with confectionery coating. You may do this several days after baking the mushrooms. Keep loosely covered at room temperature. Melt coating as directed on page 22. Spread bottom of mushroom top with coating using a small spatula. Coating should be 1/8" (.3cm) in thickness or less. Press a mushroom stem into coating and lay upside down on a towel to harden, about ten minutes. Store completed mushrooms at room temperature, lightly covered, for up to two months. Yield: about 45 mushrooms.

LEMON MARBLE BARK

A very pretty candy that you can vary by using a different oil flavoring and different tints of confectionery coating.

- 1 pound (454g) white confectionery coating, chopped, or 1 pound wafers
- ½ pound (227g) yellow confectionery coating, chopped, or ½ pound wafers
- 2 drops oil of lemon

Before you begin, line a 10" (25.4cm) square pan with foil. Chop the coatings.

1. Melt the white and yellow coating separately in two double boilers. Follow directions on page 22.

2. Remove top pan containing melted white coating and dry outside with a towel. Stir in oil of lemon and pour into prepared pan.

Pour melted yellow coating over white coating in swirls. Use a spatula to cut through both colors, making a marble pattern. Allow to set at room temperature until set but still soft. Run the tines of a fork over the surface for a bark-like texture. Score into 1½" (3.8cm) squares with a sharp knife. Continue cooling at room temperature until candy has hardened, about an hour, or in the refrigerator for about 30 minutes. To store for several months in a cool place, wrap, uncut, in a tightly sealed plastic bag. To store for several days at room temperature place on tray or in box and cover with plastic wrap. Break into squares to serve. Yield: about 36 generous pieces.

MINT SANDWICHES

Decorative, delicious and very easy to make with confectionery coating.

   1 pound (454g) confectionery coating,
      light chocolate flavored, chopped, or
      1 pound wafers
   ½ pound (227g) green confectionery
      coating, chopped, or ½ pound wafers
   3 drops oil of peppermint

Before you begin, line a 8" (20.3cm) square pan smoothly with foil (see page 18). Chop the coating.

1. Melt the two coatings separately as directed on page 22. Stir the oil of peppermint into the green coating. Spread half of the chocolate flavored coating in the prepared pan. Cover with green coating, then the remainder of the chocolate flavored coating.

2. Let the candy set up at room temperature, just until firm. Cut into 1" (2.5cm) squares, then cut each square in two, diagonally. Place in refrigerator about 30 minutes to harden. Store in tightly sealed box for months in a cool place. Yield: 128 pieces.

Opposite page: Mint sandwiches and molded flowers and leaves, all flavored with oil-based flavorings.

AMOUNT OF COATING AND FREEZER TIMES FOR VARIOUS MOLDS

Consult this chart for amount of confectionery coating to melt for various molds. Remember, always melt a little more coating than listed. Surplus can be saved and used again. Time needed for molds to harden in freezer is also approximate. Never allow the molds to remain in freezer longer than necessary. Over-cooling may cause cracking or moisture condensation.

Mold	Coating Needed (Approx.)	Freezer Time (Approx.)
Greeting cards	8 oz. (227g) or less	20 minutes
Bonbon shapes	2 to 3 oz. (56g to 85g) for 6	8 minutes
Liqueur glasses	8 oz. (227g) for 4	3 minutes
Pumpkins, 1-piece	10 oz. (284g) for 4	5 minutes
Lollipops, large	4 oz. (114g) each	20 minutes
Lollipops, medium	2 oz. (56g) each	15 minutes
Lollipops, small	1 oz. (28g) each	10 minutes
3-D figures 4¼" high (10.8cm)	5 oz. (140g)	35 minutes
House	Sides & chimney, 1½ pounds (681g)	20 minutes each piece
	Roof, ½ pound (227g)	
	Base, 1½ pounds (681g)	

Chapter 4

CEREAL AND POPCORN CANDIES

Crunchy, chewy, easy to do and just plain fun! All of these candies are especially suitable for children—caramel corn makes a nice lunchtime treat, and a cereal candy bar is just the thing for an after-school snack. And just see the colorful creations you can make with popcorn!

Many of these candies are made by coating dry cereal or popped corn with a cooked hot syrup. Always warm the cereal or popcorn in an oven set at lowest temperature before pouring on the syrup, so it does not cool down too quickly. This gives you time to combine the ingredients thoroughly and completely.

If popcorn balls become difficult to form, place the syrup-popcorn mixture in a low oven for a few minutes. It will soften enough to become pliable again.

Cereal bars dry out rapidly. Wrap them closely in plastic wrap and serve within a few days. Even better, dip in summer coating or chocolate. They'll stay fresh and crisp for weeks.

HOW TO POP CORN

If you own a corn popper, follow the instructions that come with it. Or pop the corn this easy way.

Pour one-quarter cup (60ml) of vegetable oil into a heavy four-quart (four-liter) saucepan, equipped with a close fitting cover. Put pan over medium-high heat. When oil starts to smoke slightly, add one-half cup (120ml or 113g) of corn and cover the pan. As soon as you hear the corn begin to pop, lift the pan about 1" (2.5cm) away from the heat and shake constantly until popping stops. Remove from heat and sprinkle lightly with salt, stirring to distribute evenly. Discard any unpopped kernels. Use in any of the recipes that follow. Store in a large plastic bag, tightly sealed. Yield: about eight cups of popped corn.

ONE-STEP POPCORN BALLS

This is a quick way to make crunchy chewy popcorn balls—so easy the children can do it with a little supervision.

½ cup (120ml) dark corn syrup

½ cup (120ml or 100g) granulated sugar

½ teaspoon (2.5ml) salt

¼ cup (60ml) vegetable oil

½ cup (120ml) or 112g) unpopped corn

Before you begin, mix syrup, sugar and salt in a two cup (480ml) glass measuring cup or small bowl. Butter a 9"x13" (22.9cm x 33cm) sheet cake pan.

1. Heat oil over medium high heat in a heavy four-quart (four-liter) saucepan until it just begins to smoke. Add popcorn and cover the pan. As soon as you hear corn begin to pop, raise pan about 1" (2.5cm) from heat and shake constantly until popping stops.

Add syrup-sugar-salt mixture to pan, turn heat to medium and stir constantly for about five minutes until corn is evenly coated with mixture. Remove from heat.

2. Spread into prepared pan and mark into eight portions. Butter your hands and form each portion into a ball about 2½" (6.3cm) in diameter. Use light pressure. Wrap each ball in a square of plastic wrap, securing with twist tie. Store at room temperature for months. Yield: eight popcorn balls.

At right, starting clockwise at top right: a Popcorn Christmas Tree, dipped Peanut Crunch Squares, dipped Cereal Bars, Holiday Popcorn Balls, Deluxe Caramel Corn, Molasses Date Puffs and a jolly Popcorn Snowman.

HOLIDAY POPCORN BALLS

The syrup used to coat the popcorn for these balls takes food color well, so you can tint it any color you like—dainty pink, Christmas red or green or Halloween orange. Recipe may be cut in half.

    12 cups (336g) popped corn
    1 cup (240 ml or 200g) granulated sugar
    1 cup (240 ml) light corn syrup
    ½ cup (120ml) water
    2 tablespoons (30ml or 56g) butter
    2 teaspoons (10ml) vanilla
    15 drops (2.5ml) liquid food color
       (approximate)

Before you begin, butter the inside of a large heat-proof bowl, place the popped corn in it and put in oven set at lowest temperature to warm. Remove bowl when ready to mix with cooked syrup. Line a cookie sheet with wax paper.

1. Combine sugar, syrup and water in a three-quart (three-liter) heavy saucepan. Add butter, cut in thin slices. Place over medium heat and stir with a wooden spoon until all sugar crystals are dissolved. Wash down sides of pan with a pastry brush dipped in hot water.

Clip on thermometer and continue cooking until temperature reaches 240°F (118°C). Remove from heat and stir in vanilla and food coloring, drop by drop, until desired color is reached.

2. Pour syrup over the warmed popcorn and toss with two forks until corn is evenly coated. When mixture is cool enough to handle, butter your hands and form into balls about 2½" (6.3cm) in diameter. Place on prepared cookie sheet to harden at room temperature. Wrap each ball in a square of plastic wrap, twisting at top, then securing with a twist tie. These will keep for months at room temperature. Yield 13 to 15 balls.

3. For balls to hang on the Christmas tree, tie with a narrow ribbon after wrapping in plastic. Form a loop for hanging with the ends of the ribbon.

POPCORN SNOWMEN

Use your artistic talents to create a pair of jaunty snowmen. They'll make a jolly center-piece for a holiday party or cute gifts for your visitors.

    1 recipe Holiday Popcorn Balls, untinted
    ¼ recipe Basic Marzipan (Chapter 12)
    1 recipe Corn Syrup Glaze using 1 table-spoon water (Chapter 12)
    A few currants, candied cherries, marsh-mallows and cinnamon candies

1. Follow the recipe for Holiday Popcorn Balls, omitting food coloring. Form two balls about 4" (10cm) in diameter for bases, two about 2¾" (6.9cm) for upper bodies and two more about 2" (5cm) in diameter for heads. Stack balls to form snowmen, inserting toothpicks to secure. Form rough cone shapes and toothpicks to bodies for arms. (if coated popcorn becomes difficult to work with, warm in lowest temperature oven a few minutes.) With remaining popcorn, make a few popcorn balls.

2. Make the snowmen's hats and scarves from rolled marzipan (Chapter 12). Tint one-third of the marzipan green, the rest red. For scarf, roll out green marzipan and cut ½" (1.3cm) wide strips. Wrap 6" (15cm) lengths around necks, securing ends at side with a little egg white. For scarf ends, cut 2" (5cm) strips and fringe ends with a sharp knife. Attach at sides of necks.

For hat brims, roll out red marzipan and cut out with a 2" (5cm) round cookie cutter. Lay on wax paper, propping with two skewers to curve the sides. For crowns of hats, cut 1" x 3½" (2.5cm x 9cm) strips of marzipan. Insert toothpicks into bottoms of two marshmallows, paint sides with egg white and wrap strips around sides. Trim seams and secure with egg white. Cut 1" (2.5cm) circles with a cookie cutter, paint tops of marshmallows with egg white and cover with circles. Attach crown to brim with egg white. Dry hats overnight.

3. Attach hats to snowmen's heads with toothpicks. Prepare Corn Syrup Glaze and use as glue to secure currants for eyes and buttons, cinnamon candies for nose and slivers of cherry for smiles. Brush completed snowmen, hats and all, with glaze. Set this merry pair in the center of the party table.

A POPCORN CHRISTMAS TREE

Form popcorn balls into a shining cone, trim with candied cherries and you've created a Christmas decoration the children will love! After the big day, they'll take the tree down and enjoy it even more as they eat it!

    Paper cone (see below)
    1½ recipes Holiday Popcorn Balls tinted with liquid green food color
    1 recipe Corn Syrup Glaze using 1 table-spoon water (Chapter 12)
    20 candied cherries

1. First make the paper cone that serves as foundation for the tree. Cut a half circle, 18" (45.7cm) in diameter, from stiff paper or light cardboard. Twirl it into a cone, 9" (22.9cm) high and 3¼" (8.3cm) in diameter at base. Tape securely, then cover smoothly with wax paper and tape again.

2. Make the syrup for the popcorn balls. As this cooks, make the Corn Syrup Glaze and keep warm in the top of a double boiler over hot water.

Mark a circle on a piece of wax paper by tracing an 8" (20.3cm) round pan. Dip the bottom of the paper cone in the glaze and set in the middle of the circle.

3. Build the tree. For the base layer, form seven popcorn balls, each about 2½" (6.3cm) in diameter. Flatten the side of each and press flat side against the cone, continuing until cone is circled at the base. Circle on wax paper will serve as guide. For next layer, form five balls and surround cone just as before. Secure with toothpicks as needed. For third layer, use three popcorn balls. The top of the tree is one ball, pushed over point of cone. If balls become difficult to form, place syrup-coated corn in a warm oven for a few minutes.

4. Trim the tree. Carefully cut off excess wax paper with a sharp knife. Attach a paper doily to a dinner plate with a few dabs of Corn Syrup Glaze. Set tree on doily. Cut all but two of the cherries in half and press half-cherries to crevices in tree, using glaze to secure if necessary. Thread two whole cherries on a toothpick and insert in tree top. Brush finished tree with glaze. Dry thoroughly and display with pride!

Form leftover popcorn mixture into balls as extra treats.

MOLASSES-NUT CARAMEL CORN

This version of caramel corn has a nice deep color and an assertive flavor similar to the confection that comes in a box with a tiny toy. If you like molasses you'll love this treat.

　　5 cups (1.2 liters or 140g) freshly popped corn

　　1 cup (240ml or 112g) salted peanuts

　　1 cup (240ml or 200g) granulated sugar

　　¼ cup (60ml) light corn syrup

　　½ cup (120ml) water

　　2 tablespoons (30ml or 28g) butter

　　¾ teaspoon (3.75ml) salt

　　2½ tablespoons (33ml) molasses

Before you begin, butter two 12" x 18" (30.5cm x 45.7cm) cookie sheets. Butter a large heat-proof mixing bowl, combine popcorn and nuts in it and place in oven set at lowest temperature to warm. Remove when ready to mix with cooked syrup.

1. Combine sugar, corn syrup and water in a heavy three-quart (three-liter) saucepan. Set over high heat and stir with a wooden spoon until all sugar crystals are dissolved. Wash down sides of pan with a pastry brush dipped in hot water. Clip on thermometer and continue cooking until temperature reaches 260°F (127°C). Lower heat to medium, add butter, salt and molasses and cook to 290°F (143°C) and syrup is golden brown. Stir occasionally to prevent scorching. Remove from heat and pour over warmed popcorn-nut mixture. Mix quickly with two forks until nuts and popcorn are well coated. Spread out on prepared cookie sheets. Butter your hands and press into a thin layer. Cool about 30 minutes, then break into clusters. Store at room temperature in tightly closed containers or a tightly sealed plastic bag. Keeps for months. Yield: seven cups.

TO VARY THIS RECIPE

Make popcorn balls instead of clusters. After popcorn and nuts have been well coated with the syrup, allow to stand only until cool enough to handle. Butter your hands and press lightly between your palms to form balls about 2½" (6.3cm) in diameter. If mixture becomes too cool to form, place bowl in oven for a few minutes to soften. Cool balls to room temperature, then wrap each in plastic wrap, securing with twist tie. Yield: about ten popcorn balls.

CHOCOLATE POPCORN CLUSTERS

These clusters have a nice sheen and color and an unusual flavor to please chocolate lovers. Dates add richness and flavor.

　　5 cups (1.2 liters or 112g) popped corn

　　1 cup (240ml or 224g) pitted chopped dates

　　2 ounces (56g) unsweetened chocolate

　　1 cup (240ml) light corn syrup

　　1 cup (240ml or 200g) granulated sugar

　　½ cup (120ml) water

　　2 tablespoons (30ml or 56g) butter

　　1 teaspoon (5ml) vanilla

Before you begin, butter two cookie sheets. Put popcorn and dates in a large buttered heat-proof mixing bowl. Place in oven set at lowest temperature to warm. Remove when ready to mix with cooked syrup. Chop the chocolate finely.

1. Bring about 1" (2.5cm) of water in lower pan of one-quart (one-liter) double boiler to simmer, then remove from heat. Put chopped chocolate in upper pan, place over lower pan and cover to melt. Stir occasionally until melted.

2. Combine syrup, sugar and water in a heavy three-quart (three-liter) saucepan. Add butter, cut in thin slices. Cook over medium heat, stirring constantly until mixture almost comes to a boil. Wash down sides of pan with a pastry brush dipped in hot water. Clip on thermometer and cook, still stirring to 290°F (143°C), about 20 minutes. Wash sides of pan twice more as mixture cooks. Remove from heat and blend in melted chocolate and vanilla.

3. Pour the hot syrup over the warmed popcorn-date mixture. Toss quickly with two forks until popcorn and dates are well coated. Spread on prepared cookie sheets. When cool enough to handle, break into clusters. Cool completely. Store at room temperature in tightly covered containers or tightly sealed plastic bags. Keeps for months. Yield: seven cups.

MOLASSES DATE PUFFS

These puff balls are just the thing when you want something mildly sweet and crunchy. Children love to find one or two tucked in their lunch box.

 1 cup (240ml or 224g) pitted chopped dates
 4 cups (960ml or 56g) puffed cereal, wheat or rice
 1 cup (240ml or 200g) granulated sugar
 ¾ cup (180ml) water
 ¼ cup (60ml) molasses
 Pinch of salt
 1 teaspoon (5ml) white vinegar
 1 teaspoon (5ml) vanilla extract
 1 tablespoon (15ml or 15g) butter

Before you begin, butter a large heat-proof bowl, combine the dates and cereal in it and place in oven set at lowest temperature to warm. Remove when ready to mix with cooked syrup.

1. Combine sugar, water, molasses and salt in a heavy three-quart (three-liter) saucepan. Set over medium heat and stir with a wooden spoon until sugar is completely dissolved. When mixture is almost boiling, wash down sides of pan with a pastry brush dipped in hot water. Clip on thermometer and continue to cook to 256°F (123°C), about 30 minutes. Add vinegar and cook for a half-minute more.

2. Remove from heat and stir in vanilla and thinly sliced butter. Pour syrup over warmed date-cereal mixture. Working quickly, toss with two forks until cereal and dates are well coated. Cool about ten minutes. Butter your hands and form mixture into balls about 1¼" (3cm) in diameter. Wrap each in plastic wrap and seal with a twist tie. Store for a few days at room temperature. Yield: about 45 puffs.

TO VARY THIS RECIPE

Substitute raisins or any combination of dried or candied fruits for the dates.

DELUXE CARAMEL CORN

The very best you've ever tasted! Deluxe Caramel Corn has a good crisp texture, plenty of crunchy nuts and a rich caramel flavor. This candy keeps and travels well so it's a much-appreciated gift.

 5 cups (1.2 liters or 140g) freshly popped corn
 1 cup (240ml or 112g) dry roasted salted cashews
 1 cup (240ml) dark corn syrup
 1 cup (240ml or 2ᶜ Jg) granulated sugar
 ¼ cup (60ml) water
 ¼ cup (60ml or 56g) butter

Before you begin, butter two 12" x 18" (30.5cm x 45.7cm) cookie sheets. Combine popped corn and cashews in a large buttered heat-proof mixing bowl and place in oven set on lowest temperature. Remove when ready to mix with cooked syrup.

1. Combine corn syrup, sugar and water in a heavy three-quart (three-liter) saucepan. Add butter, cut in thin slices. Place pan on medium heat and stir constantly with a wooden spoon until mixture comes to a boil. Wash down sides of pan with a pastry brush dipped in hot water. Clip on thermometer. Continue cooking, stirring occasionally until temperature reaches 280°F (136°C). Remove from heat.

2. Pour over warmed popcorn mixture in bowl. Toss quickly with two forks until nuts and popcorn are well coated. Spread out on prepared cookie sheets. Butter your hands and press into thin layers. Cool about 30 minutes, then break into clusters. Store at room temperature for up to several months in tightly covered containers, or in tightly sealed plastic bag. Yield: seven cups.

CHOCOLATE CEREAL BARS*

A nice chewy, crunchy bar with an intriguing caramel-chocolate flavor.

   ¾ cup (180ml) dark corn syrup

   ¼ cup (60ml or 50g) granulated sugar

   2 tablespoons (30ml or 30g) butter

   1 teaspoon (5ml) vanilla

   2 cups (480ml or 56g) corn flakes

   1 cup (240ml or 28g) crisp rice cereal

   1 cup (240ml or 112g) coarsely chopped nuts (crisped)

   1 cup (240ml or 225g) semi-sweet chocolate morsels

   2 pounds (908g) confectionery coating, light or dark chocolate flavor (optional)

Before you begin, crisp the nuts (Chapter 2). Line a 9" x 5" (22.9cm x 12.7cm) loaf pan with foil and butter the foil. Put nuts and cereal in a large, buttered, heat-proof bowl and place in oven set at lowest temperature to warm. Remove when ready to mix.

1. Combine syrup, sugar and butter in a heavy three-quart (three-liter) pan. Set over medium heat and stir constantly with a wooden spoon until mixture almost comes to a boil. Wash down sides of pan with a pastry brush dipped in hot water. Clip on thermometer and continue boiling until temperature reaches 230°F (110°C), about three minutes. Remove pan from heat and take off thermometer. Cool for five minutes.

2. Add vanilla to cooked mixture and beat about two minutes with wooden spoon until mixture thickens and becomes lighter in color. Add chocolate morsels to bowl of warmed cereal and nuts and pour in cooked mixture. Working quickly, toss with two forks to coat evenly. Pack into prepared pan and cool at room temperature until set, about an hour. Turn out of pan, peel off foil, and cut into ½" (1.3cm) slices to form bars about 1" x 4½" x ½" (2.5cm x 11.4cm x 1.3cm). Use a sharp, serrated knife. To store for a few days, wrap each bar tightly in plastic wrap. Needs no refrigeration. Yield: about 18 bars.

3. For a delicious extra touch, dip each bar in confectionery coating according to directions in Chapter 3. The coating will keep the bars fresh and crisp for weeks.

PEANUT SUPREMES*

Everybody loves this candy with a rich mellow taste and pleasantly crisp texture enhanced by a dip in chocolate or confectionery coating. This uncooked confection is a deluxe treat that takes only about 15 minutes to put together, ready for dipping.

   2 cups (480ml or 450g) peanut butter, chunky style

   ¾ cup (180ml or 168g) butter

   3½ cups (840ml or 350g) sifted confectioners' sugar (approximate)

   3 cups (720ml or 85g) crisp rice cereal

   2 pounds (908g) chocolate or confectionery coating (approximate)

Before you begin, line a 9" x 13" (22.9cm x 33cm) pan or two 8" (20.3cm) square pans with foil. Butter the foil.

1. Cut butter in thin slices and put in a three-quart (three-liter) heavy saucepan over low heat. Add peanut butter and stir constantly with a wooden spoon until butter is melted and mixture is smooth. Remove from heat.

2. Stir in confectioners' sugar, a third at a time, blending well after each addition. Gently knead in cereal. Add more confectioners' sugar as necessary to form a stiff but pliable mass. Pack into prepared pan and refrigerate about an hour until very firm. Remove pan, peel off foil and cut into 1¼" (3.2cm) squares with a sharp knive. Dip in confectionery coating (Chapter 3) or chocolate (Chapter 11). Allow to harden, then pack in a wax paper-lined box. Store for several weeks in a cool place. Yield about 70 candies.

TO VARY THIS RECIPE

Make balls instead of squares. Cut the candy into squares as above, then form each square into a ball by rolling firmly between your palms. Dip immediately.

For a special treat, dip either Chocolate Cereal Bars or Peanut Crunch Squares in Wilton Caramel for Dipping (Chapter 6). After dipping, place in pan of crisped chopped nuts and tumble to cover. Wrap in wax paper or plastic wrap. These candy bars will stay fresh for a month or more.

PEANUT CRUNCH SQUARES*

One of the most delectable of cereal candies! These squares make a sweet surprise in the lunch box, taste good with a glass of milk and pack well for a gift box.

    3 cups (720ml or 85g) crisp rice cereal
    1 cup (240ml or 150g) salted peanuts
    ½ cup (120ml or 100g) granulated sugar
    ½ cup (120ml) light corn syrup
    ½ cup (120ml or 140g) creamy peanut
        butter
    1 teaspoon (5ml) vanilla extract

Before you begin, combine cereal and nuts in a large buttered heat-proof bowl and place in oven set at lowest temperature to warm. Remove when ready to mix. Line two 6" (15.2cm) square pans with foil, then butter the foil (Chapter 2). Or use your marble slab and metal bars. Butter the marble, then arrange the bars to form an area about 6" x 12" (15.2cm x 30.5cm). Butter inner sides of the bars.

1. Combine sugar and syrup in a heavy three-quart (three-liter) saucepan. Set over medium heat and stir constantly until mixture comes to a full rolling boil. This will take about five minutes.

2. Remove from heat and add peanut butter and vanilla. Stir until well blended. Working quickly, pour over the warmed cereal-nut mixture and toss with two forks to coat. Turn into the two prepared pans and pat to level. Or pack into the prepared marble slab. Cool to room temperature, then cut into 1½" (3.8cm) squares. Wrap each in a square of wax paper or plastic wrap. Put wrapped squares in a tightly sealed plastic bag to keep for months. Yield: 32 squares.

TO VARY THIS RECIPE

Dip the squares in confectionery coating to make a good thing even better. Consult Chapter 3 and melt about two pounds of either butterscotch or milk chocolate flavored coating. Store in a wax paper-lined box.

MARDI GRAS

Make this surprisingly luxurious candy for holiday parties or for special gifts. It's crunchy and creamy at the same time — and so easy to make the children can do it.

    ¼ cup (60ml or 56g) chopped candied
        cherries
    1 cup (240ml or 112g) dry roasted
        cashews, broken
    ¼ cup (60ml or 56g) toasted coconut
    1 pound (454g) white confectionery
        coating
    1 cup (240ml or 28g) doughnut-shaped
        cereal
    1 cup (240ml or 28g) crisp rice cereal
    1 cup (240ml or 56g) miniature marsh-
        mallows

Before you begin, chop the cherries, break cashews into large pieces and toast the coconut (Chapter 2). Line two cookie sheets with wax paper.

1. Chop confectionery coating and melt in a two-quart (two-liter) double boiler as directed in Chapter 3. Leave top pan over hot water in lower pan.

2. Stir in coconut, nuts, cereals, cherries and marshmallows and blend well.

3. Drop by teaspoonfuls on prepared cookie sheets. Allow to harden at room temperature, about twenty minutes. Store at room temperature in a tightly closed plastic bag for up to two months. If weather is warm and humid, store in refrigerator. Yield: about 60 clusters.

*May be used as centers for dipping

Chapter 5

FABULOUS FUDGES...BEST LOVED OF ALL HOMEMADE CANDIES

The best fudge is made at home—and the very best homemade fudges are here in this chapter! All contain lavish amounts of fresh, wholesome ingredients—butter, rich milk or cream, syrup and chocolate that give off a heavenly aroma as you cook and stir. There's a wonderful variety of fudges, too—try delicate Orange Coconut Fudge, Coffee Cinnamon Fudge, Maple Syrup Fudge or Wilton Penuche. We've included a number of authentic Praline recipes too—straight from New Orleans.

Fudge can be formed in other ways than the conventional neat squares. See the last page of this chapter for directions for forming luscious fudge logs, or centers to be dipped in chocolate or coating. You can create a fudge candy bar, too!

Perfect fudge is easy to make—rich and creamy with a delicate toothsome grain as you bite into a piece. Just follow these guidelines—you'll never have a sugary, over-grained candy.

Cook fudges carefully. Use a heavy saucepan and medium heat, stir just enough to avoid scorching. Wash down sides of pan as recipes direct to eliminate sugar crystals. And be sure to follow noted temperatures. *A thermometer is your best friend* in cooking fudges.

Cool fudges, undisturbed, after cooking as recipe directs. This cooling-off period is another secret to avoid graininess.

Want a glossy surface on your fudge? Brush lightly with milk or cream after fudge has been put into pan for firming.

Good news! New no-beat fudges have been developed just for this book. These new fudges are especially formulated to eliminate the time and energy needed to make fudge the traditional way— and the results are just as rich and creamy as the good old-fashioned fudges. Read the pages that follow for details and brand new recipes.

First aid for failed fudges. Yes, you can restore a *traditional fudge* that has turned grainy and sugary. Scrape it out of the pan into a heavy saucepan and add two or more tablespoons of water. Place over medium heat, break up the fudge with a wooden spoon, and stir constantly until the mixture is smooth and temperature reaches the degree stated in the recipe. This will take just a few minutes. Remove from heat, cool, undisturbed, to 110°F (43°C), then beat as recipe directs. Firm in foil-lined buttered pan. The fudge will be smooth and delicious, but a little firmer than most fudges.

Another way to rescue a grainy fudge. Scrape into a saucepan, add 1/3 cup or more of cream, milk or water and stir over medium heat until smooth. You'll have a delicious fudge sauce. Store in a tightly sealed container in the refrigerator. Serve warm over ice cream.

At right, clockwise from top: Honey Walnut Fudge, No-beat Penuche, Wilton Basic Fudge, Layered Fudge, Snow White Fruited Fudge, Orange Coconut and Cinnamon Coffee Logs, Chocolate Dipped Fudge and a selection of Pralines.

NO-BEAT FUDGES WITH CONFECTIONERY COATING

A minor miracle occurs when you stir confectionery coating into fudge after a brief cooling period. As soon as the confectionery coating is incorporated, the fudge will thicken to almost a pudding-like consistency. You can turn it into a pan for cooling and be assured of a delicate grain and creamy texture. Don't be afraid to scrape out the cooking pan—we recommend using a rubber scraper.

The confectionery coating serves a second purpose, too. The specialized fats in the coating lubricate the candy, and make it very easy to cut for serving. Try the brand new Wilton recipes that follow—we know you'll agree that these no-beat fudges are among the very best you've ever tasted—with the bonus of saving the time and energy needed for beating.

Please note: in a few of the no-beat recipes, chopped chocolate is added after a short cooling period, instead of confectionery coating. The chocolate serves the same purpose as the coating but may take just a bit more stirring to thicken.

Caution: Do not attempt to knead or work coating or chocolate no-beat fudges. It will break them down.

MILK CHOCOLATE FUDGE

A new, no-beat chocolate fudge.

If you like a fudge with a delicate flavor that's not too sweet, here's the one for you. Sour cream gives a distinctive but very subtle tang.

  3½ cups (840ml or 650g) granulated sugar

  2 tablespoons (30ml) light corn syrup

  2 cups (480ml) sour cream

  6 tablespoons (90ml or 85g) butter

  6 ounces (168g) milk chocolate, chopped

  1 teaspoon (5ml) vanilla extract

Before you begin, line an 8" (20.3cm) square pan with foil and butter the foil. Chop the chocolate finely.

1. Combine sugar, corn syrup and sour cream in a three-quart (three-liter) heavy pan. Add butter, cut in thin slices. Place over medium heat and stir constantly with a wooden spoon until all sugar crystals are dissolved. Wash down sides of pan with a pastry brush dipped in hot water, then clip on thermometer.

2. Continue cooking, stirring occasionally, until thermometer registers 234°F (112°C), about 30 minutes. During this time, wash down sides of pan twice more. Remove from heat. Take off thermometer.

3. Let stand, undisturbed, for ten minutes. Do not stir. Add chocolate and vanilla and stir until thoroughly blended. Mixture will thicken quickly to almost a pudding-like consistency. Turn into prepared pan, using a rubber scraper. Cool in refrigerator until firm, about an hour. To serve, cut in 1" (2.5cm) squares. To store for up to a month, wrap uncut candy closely in foil or plastic wrap and refrigerate. Yield: 64 pieces.

TASTERS' CHOICE DOUBLE CHOCOLATE FUDGE

A new, no-beat chocolate fudge.

A panel of discriminating chocolate fudge lovers gave this candy an A plus. Cocoa and chocolate, cream and butter combine for a deep delicious flavor.

  3 cups (720ml or 600g) granulated sugar

  3 tablespoons (45ml or 15g) cocoa

  2 tablespoons (30ml) light corn syrup

  2 cups (480ml) whipping cream

  6 tablespoons (90ml or 85g) butter

  3 ounces (85g) semi-sweet chocolate, chopped, or semi-sweet morsels

  ½ teaspoon (2.5ml) vanilla

  1 cup (240ml or 112g) chopped nuts, crisped

Before you begin, line an 8" (20.3cm) square pan with foil and lightly butter the foil. Chop the chocolate and crisp the nuts.

1. Combine sugar and cocoa in a heavy four-quart (four-liter) saucepan and mix thoroughly. Add corn syrup and cream and place pan on medium heat. Stir constantly until all sugar crystals are dissolved, then wash down sides of pan with a pastry brush dipped in hot water. Clip on thermometer.

2. Continue cooking, stirring occasionally and washing down sides of pan twice more. When thermometer registers 234°F (112°C),

remove from heat. This will take about 25 minutes. Take off thermometer. Allow candy to cool, undisturbed, for ten minutes. As it cools, cut butter in thin slices and lay on surface of candy. Do not stir.

3. After ten minutes, add chopped chocolate. Stir until chocolate is melted and butter is thoroughly incorporated. Mixture will thicken quickly. Fold in vanilla and nuts and turn into prepared pan, using a rubber scraper. Cool at room temperature for ten minutes, then refrigerate for about 40 minutes to firm. Cut in 1" (2.5cm) square pieces to serve, or wrap tightly, uncut, in foil or plastic wrap and refrigerate for up to a month. Yield: 64 pieces.

SOUR CREAM FUDGE

New, no-beat confectionery coating fudge

Make this new and distinctive fudge the easy, no-beat, Wilton way. It has a nice little tang, a lovely ivory color and a rich creamy texture set off by crunchy nuts.

  3 cups (720ml or 600g) granulated sugar

  1 tablespoon (15ml) light corn syrup

  2 cups (480ml) sour cream

  6 tablespoons (90ml or 85g) butter

  3 ounces (85g) white confectionery coating, chopped, or 3 ounces wafers

  1 cup (240ml or 112g) chopped nuts, crisped

  ½ teaspoon (2.5ml) vanilla

Before you begin, line an 8" (20.3cm) square pan with foil and lightly butter the foil. Crisp the nuts and chop the coating.

1. Combine sugar, corn syrup and sour cream in a heavy three-quart (three-liter) saucepan. Place over medium heat and stir constantly with a wooden spoon until all sugar crystals are dissolved. Clip on thermometer. Continue cooking, stirring frequently, until thermometer registers 237°F (114°C), about 40 minutes. During cooking process, wash down sides of pan twice more. Remove from heat. Take off thermometer.

2. Allow to stand, undisturbed for ten minutes. Place butter, cut in thin slices, on surface of mixture to melt, but do not stir. Add chopped coating, then stir until coating has melted and mixture is smooth and slightly thickened. Stir in nuts and vanilla. Turn into prepared pan, using a rubber scraper.

3. Firm in refrigerator about an hour. Cut into 1" (2.5cm) squares to serve. To store for up to a month, wrap, uncut, in foil or plastic wrap and refrigerate. Bring to room temperature to cut. Yield: 64 pieces.

SNOW WHITE FRUITED FUDGE

New, no-beat confectionery coating fudge

We're including this recipe in the fudge chapter because it gives such a pretty contrast to the darker fudges on a candy tray — but it's really more of a firm truffle. You'll like its creamy texture and festive jewelled appearance.

  2 pounds (900g) white confectionery coating, chopped, or 2 pounds wafers

  1 cup (240ml) whipping cream

  ¼ teaspoon (1.2ml) salt

  ½ cup (120ml or 112g) chopped candied cherries

  ⅓ cup (80ml or 70g) chopped candied pineapple

Before you begin, chop the confectionery coating. Chop and measure the candied fruits. Line an 8" (20.3cm) square pan with foil and lightly butter the foil.

1. Place chopped confectionery coating in top pan of double boiler. Bring about 1" (2.5cm) of water in lower pan to simmer and place top pan in position. Stir coating constantly until melted. Remove from heat, leaving top pan in position on lower pan.

2. Heat cream and salt in a small pan over low heat, stirring constantly with wooden spoon. When thermometer registers 160°F (70°C), remove from heat. Remove top pan of double boiler containing melted coating from lower pan and pour in heated cream. Stir the mixture until completely smooth, then blend in fruit. Pour into prepared pan and refrigerate an hour or more until firm. Let stand at room temperature a few minutes before cutting into 3/4" (1.9cm) squares. Store uncut, closely wrapped in foil or plastic wrap, for up to a month in the refrigerator. Yield: about 100 pieces.

More no-beat fudges on the next page

WILTON NO-BEAT PENUCHE

New, no-beat confectionery coating fudge

This fudge has everything a penuche fudge should have—a rich caramel flavor, a delicate grain and the crispness of pecans

  2 cups (480ml or 400g) granulated sugar

  1 cup (240ml or 170g) light brown sugar, lightly packed

  1 tablespoon (15ml) light corn syrup

  2 cups (480ml) whipping cream

  6 tablespoons (90ml or 85g) butter

  3 ounces (85g) white confectionery coating, chopped, or 3 ounces wafers

  1 cup (240ml or 115g) chopped pecans, crisped

Before you begin, line an 8" (20.3cm) square pan with foil and lightly butter the foil. Chop the coating and crisp the nuts.

1. Combine sugars, syrup and cream in a heavy four-quart (four-liter) saucepan. (This candy foams up as it heats.) Place over medium heat and stir constantly with a wooden spoon until all sugar crystals are dissolved. Clip on thermometer. Continue cooking, stirring occasionally, and washing down sides of pan twice more. When thermometer registers 237°F (114°C), remove from heat. Take off thermometer. Total cooking time is about 30 minutes.

2. Allow to stand, undisturbed, about ten minutes. While mixture is standing, cut butter in thin slices and lay on surface to melt—do not stir in.

3. Add chopped coating and stir thoroughly until coating is melted, butter is incorporated and mixture thickens. Stir in nuts and turn into prepared pan, using a rubber scraper. Refrigerate about 40 minutes until firm. Cut into 1" (2.5cm) squares for serving. To store for up to a month, wrap closely, uncut, in foil or plastic wrap, and refrigerate. Yield: 64 pieces.

FAMOUS FUDGE

A no-beat chocolate fudge

Hundreds of thousands of pounds of this enticing fudge have been sold to eager customers the country over. Now make it yourself, following this authentic recipe. It will taste even better because you'll enjoy it at its freshest. Very rich, very creamy and as a bonus, very easy to put together.

  4 cups (960ml or 800g) granulated sugar

  1 cup (240ml) milk

  1 cup (240ml or 224g) butter

  25 large marshmallows, cut in quarters

  1 teaspoon (5ml) vanilla

  11½ ounces (322g) milk chocolate morsels

  12 ounces (336g) semi-sweet chocolate morsels

  1 cup (240ml or 112g) chopped nuts, crisped

Before you begin, crisp the nuts. Cut each marshmallow in quarters using a scissors dipped in cold water. Line a 9" x 13" (22.9cm x 33cm) sheet pan with foil and butter the foil.

1. Combine sugar, milk and butter, cut in thin slices, in a four-quart (four-liter) heavy saucepan. Place over medium heat. Stir constantly with a wooden spoon until mixture comes to a full boil. Allow to boil for two minutes, then remove from heat.

2. Add marshmallows and stir until marshmallows have dissolved and mixture is smooth. Add vanilla, milk chocolate and semi-sweet chocolate morsels and stir again until mixture is smooth. Blend in nuts. Pour into prepared pan and refrigerate until firm, about 40 minutes. Cut into 1" (2.5cm) squares, or store, uncut, and closely wrapped in foil or plastic wrap for up to a month in refrigerator. Yield: about 120 pieces.

YOGURT WALNUT FUDGE

New, no-beat confectionery coating fudge

Make this new fudge to delight and intrigue your friends. The flavor has an almost lemon-y tang, and the texture is smooth.

  3 cups (720ml or 600g) granulated sugar

  1 tablespoon (15ml) light corn syrup

  2 cups (480ml) plain yogurt

  6 tablespoons (90ml or 85g) butter

  3 ounces (85g) white confectionery coating, chopped, or 3 ounces wafers

  1 cup (240ml or 115g) walnut pieces, crisped

  ½ teaspoon (2.5ml) vanilla

Before you begin, line an 8" (20.3cm) square pan with foil and lightly butter the foil. Chop the confectionery coating.

1. Combine sugar, syrup and yogurt in a four-quart (four-liter) heavy saucepan. (This

candy foams up as it heats.) Place over medium heat and stir constantly with a wooden spoon until all sugar crystals are dissolved. Wash down sides of pan with a pastry brush dipped in hot water, then clip on thermometer. Stir very frequently as mixture continues to cook, and wash down sides of pan twice more during cooking process.

2. Continue cooking until thermometer registers 236°F (113°C), about 35 minutes. Remove from heat and lay butter, cut in thin slices, on surface. *Do not stir.* Allow to stand undisturbed for ten minutes.

3. Now add chopped coating and stir vigorously until coating is melted and mixture is smooth. Stir in nuts and vanilla and pour into prepared pan. Refrigerate until firm, about an hour. Cut into 1" (2.5cm) pieces. Store, uncut and closely wrapped in foil or plastic wrap in the refrigerator for up to a month. Yield: 64 pieces.

MAPLE SYRUP FUDGE

New, no-beat confectionery coating fudge

Make this fudge for dear friends whose expensive tastes include a passion for maple syrup. It's very rich, with a robust maple flavor and a lovely peachy beige color.

3 cups (720ml or 600g) granulated sugar

1½ cups (360ml) pure maple syrup

1 tablespoon (15ml) corn syrup

2 cups (480ml) whipping cream

6 tablespoons (90ml or 85g) butter

3 ounces (85g) white confectionery coating, chopped, or 3 ounces wafers

Before you begin, line an 8" (20.3cm) square pan with foil and lightly butter the foil. Chop the confectionery coating.

1. Combine sugar, syrups and cream in a six-quart (six-liter) heavy saucepan. (This candy foams up as it heats—be sure to use a six-quart (six-liter) pan.) Place over medium heat and stir constantly with a wooden spoon until all sugar crystals are dissolved. Wash down sides of pan with a pastry brush dipped in hot water, then clip on thermometer. Continue cooking, stirring very frequently until thermometer registers 238°F (114°C). Wash down sides of pan twice more during cooking process—about 30 minutes. Remove from heat and let stand undisturbed ten minutes. *Do not stir.*

2. Cut butter in thin slices and lay on surface of mixture to melt. Do not stir in. When

butter is melted, add chopped coating. Stir until coating is melted and mixture is smooth and slightly thickened. Pour into prepared pan and firm in refrigerator about an hour. Cut into 1" (2.5cm) squares. To store, wrap, uncut, in foil or plastic wrap and refrigerate for up to a month. Yield: 64 pieces.

CARAMEL FUDGE

New, no-beat confectionery coating fudge

A generous amount of milk and butter gives this fudge a rich caramel flavor. Butterscotch flavored confectionery coating adds to flavor and russet color.

1½ cups (300ml or 250g) granulated sugar

1 tablespoon (15ml) dark corn syrup

2 cups (480ml) milk

3 tablespoons (45ml or 43g) butter

1½ ounces (43g) butterscotch flavored confectionery coating, chopped, or 1½ ounces wafers

1 teaspoon (5ml) vanilla

½ cup (120ml or 56g) pecans, coarsely chopped and crisped

Before you begin, line a 6" (15.2cm) square pan with foil and lightly butter the foil. Chop coating and crisp pecans.

1. Combine sugar, corn syrup and milk in a three-quart (three-liter) heavy saucepan. Place over medium heat and stir constantly with a wooden spoon until all sugar crystals are dissolved. Wash down sides of pan with a pastry brush dipped in hot water. Clip on thermometer. As candy cooks, stir occasionally and wash down sides of pan twice more. When temperature reaches 235°F (113°C), about 35 minutes, remove from heat. Take off thermometer.

2. Allow mixture to stand, undisturbed for ten minutes. During this time, lay butter, cut in thin slices, on surface. *Do not stir.*

3. Add chopped coating and vanilla and stir thoroughly until all butter is incorporated, coating is melted and mixture is smooth. Mixture will rapidly thicken to a pudding-like consistency. Turn into prepared pan, using a rubber scraper. Sprinkle nuts evenly over surface and pat to secure. Refrigerate until firm, about 30 minutes. Cut into 1" (2.5cm) squares to serve. Store, uncut and tightly wrapped in foil or plastic wrap, for up to a month in the refrigerator. Yield: 36 pieces.

NEW NO-BEAT FONDANT FUDGES

Would you like to make fudge in a hurry and skip the rather lengthy cooling off and vigorous beating required to make traditional fudges? Just add fondant. (Fondant recipes are in Chapter 10.) It will set the fudge up to a creamy, delicately grained consistency so quickly you won't believe it! No beating and very little waiting for candy to cool and firm.

Even if you don't plan on using fondant for centers or mints, it's well worth making it just to have on hand for fudge. Try one of the new no-beat fondant recipes that follow—each is a proven winner.

You may knead no-beat fondant fudges very easily to form centers or logs for dipping. Just stir briefly until stiff, turn out on a lightly buttered smooth surface and knead very lightly—then form centers or logs. Or store the kneaded fudge in a tightly sealed container or plastic bag in the refrigerator for up to three weeks. Bring to room temperature, then form the centers or logs for dipping.

TRIPLE-RICH NUT FUDGE*

A new, no-beat fondant fudge

Cream, evaporated milk and butter combine to give this fudge its rich, not-too-sweet flavor. The texture is smooth and creamy, almost like a caramel.

- 2 cups (480ml or 400g) granulated sugar
- ½ cup (120ml) whipping cream
- ⅔ cup (160ml) evaporated milk
- ½ cup (120ml) corn syrup
- 1 teaspoon (5ml) salt
- 2 tablespoons (30ml or 28g) butter
- 1 cup (240ml or 400g) Wilton Fondant either Cream of Tartar or Corn Syrup, Chapter 10

- 4½ ounces (125g) unsweetened chocolate, finely chopped
- 1 cup (240ml or 112g) chopped nuts
- ½ teaspoon (2.5ml) vanilla

Before you begin, finely chop the chocolate. Crisp the nuts. Line an 8" (20.3cm) square pan with foil and butter the foil. Bring fondant to room temperature and measure.

1. Place sugar, cream, evaporated milk, corn syrup and salt in a three-quart (three-liter) heavy pan. Set on medium heat and stir constantly with a wooden spoon until sugar crystals are dissolved. Wash down sides of pan with a pastry brush dipped in hot water. Clip on thermometer.

2. Continue cooking, stirring occasionally until thermometer registers 234°F (112°C), about 15 minutes. Wash down sides of pan again during this period. Add butter, cut in thin slices.

3. Continue cooking, stirring occasionally until thermometer registers 237°F (114°C). This will take about five minutes. Wash down sides of pan once more during this period. Remove from heat.

4. Allow mixture to stand, undisturbed, for five minutes. Scatter fondant, cut in small pieces, and chocolate over surface of mixture, but do not stir or agitate in any way. The fondant and chocolate will help to cool the mixture.

Let stand undisturbed another five minutes. then stir to incorporate thoroughly the fondant and chocolate. Mixture will thicken quickly. Blend in nuts and vanilla. Spread in prepared pan, using a rubber scraper, then refrigerate until firm, about one hour. Cut into 1" (2.5cm) pieces. This fudge may be stored in the refrigerator for a month, uncut and closely wrapped in foil or plastic wrap. Bring to room temperature before cutting. Yield: 64 pieces.

MAPLE PECAN PENUCHE*

A new, no beat fondant fudge

Everybody loves this delicious brown sugar version of fudge. It's smooth, rich and creamy, yet has the delicate grain characteristic of penuche.

1 cup (240ml or 170g) light brown sugar, lightly packed

1 cup (240ml or 200g) granulated sugar

½ cup (120ml) whipping cream

½ cup (120ml) light corn syrup

⅔ cup (160ml) evaporated milk

1 teaspoon (5ml) salt

3 tablespoons (45ml or 42g) butter

1 cup (240ml or 400g) prepared Wilton fondant, either Cream of Tartar or Corn Syrup, Chapter 10

1 cup (240ml or 112g) chopped pecans, crisped

½ teaspoon (2.5ml) maple flavoring

Before you begin, crisp the nuts. Line an 8" (20.3cm) square pan with foil and butter the foil. If fondant is refrigerated, bring to room temperature and measure.

1. Combine brown and white sugars, cream, syrup, evaporated milk and salt in a heavy three-quart (three-liter) saucepan. Place over low heat and stir constantly with wooden spoon until all sugar crystals are dissolved. Increase heat to medium and wash down sides of pan with a pastry brush dipped in hot water. Clip on thermometer.

2. As candy continues to cook, wash down sides of pan twice more. When thermometer registers 238°F (114°C), remove from heat. Cooking time is about 25 minutes. Allow to stand five minutes, undisturbed.

Lay butter, cut in thin slices, and fondant, broken in small bits, on surface of mixture. Allow to stand undisturbed, an additional five minutes.

3. Stir mixture thoroughly to incorporate butter and fondant. Blend in nuts and flavoring. Turn into prepared pan, using a rubber scraper. Allow to cool until firm at room temperature, about an hour or more. Cut into 1" squares. Store uncut, closely wrapped in foil or plastic wrap, in the refrigerator for up to a month. Bring to room temperature before cutting and serving. Yield: 64 pieces.

COCOA WALNUT FUDGE*

A new, no-beat fondant fudge

A treat for confirmed chocolate lovers! Cocoa adds an especially rich chocolate flavor and a deep delicious color.

2 cups (480ml or 400g) granulated sugar

½ cup (120ml or 56g) cocoa

½ cup (120ml) whipping cream

⅔ cup (160ml) evaporated milk

½ cup (120ml) light corn syrup

1 teaspoon (5ml) salt

3 tablespoons (45ml or 42g) butter

1 cup (240ml or 400g) Wilton fondant, either Cream of Tartar or Corn Syrup, Chapter 10

1 cup (240ml or 112g) chopped walnuts, crisped

½ teaspoon (2.5ml) vanilla

Before you begin, crisp the walnuts. Line an 8" (20.3cm) square pan with foil and butter the foil. Bring fondant to room temperature and measure.

1. Mix sugar and cocoa thoroughly in a four-quart (four-liter) heavy saucepan with a wooden spoon. Add cream, evaporated milk, corn syrup and salt. Place over medium heat and stir constantly until all sugar crystals are dissolved. Wash down sides of pan with a pastry brush dipped in hot water, then clip on thermometer.

2. Continue cooking until thermometer registers 234°F (112°C), about 20 minutes, then add butter, cut in thin slices. During this time, wash down sides of pan twice more, and stir occasionally to prevent scorching. Continue cooking and stirring until thermometer registers 237°F (114°C), just a few more minutes.

3. Remove from heat and allow mixture to stand, undisturbed, for five minutes. Scatter fondant, cut in small chunks, over surface and let stand, undisturbed, for five minutes more. Add nuts and vanilla, then stir thoroughly until fondant is incorporated and mixture is smooth. Work quickly, the candy will stiffen fast. Turn into prepared pan, using a rubber scraper and allow to firm about 30 minutes at room temperature. Cut into 1" (2.5cm) squares. Store, uncut and closely wrapped in foil or plastic wrap, in refrigerator up to a month. Yield 64 pieces.

*May be formed into centers or logs

TRADITIONAL BEATEN FUDGES

These are the delicious old-fashioned fudges — carefully cooked, cooled to 110°F (43°C) without stirring—then beaten vigorously for about ten minutes and put into a pan for final cooling and firming. The beating stiffens the fudge and creates its delicate grain.

Traditional fudges are fun to make — the whole family can take turns at beating while anticipation rises for sampling the finished candy. As the fudge is beaten, it will become lighter, lose some of its gloss and finally thicken. Watch carefully—the candy will stiffen rapidly at this point and may become too stiff to press into the pan. (Kneading will restore its texture.)

Do not disturb or stir the fudge while it is cooling. If butter or flavoring is to be added, simply place them on the surface of the mixture, don't stir them in. *And never stop beating*, once you start, until the candy is almost too thick to stir.

WILTON BASIC FUDGE*

A traditional, beaten fudge

This is the fudge you remember from your childhood—rich, very chocolate-y, smooth and creamy. You can dream up many variations—add crisped chopped nuts, chopped candied fruit or coconut. It's a winner!

- ⅔ cup (160ml) light cream (half & half)
- 2 cups (480ml or 400g) granulated sugar
- 2 ounces (2 squares or 60g) unsweetened chocolate
- 2 tablespoons (30ml) light corn syrup
- 2 tablespoons (30ml or 30g) butter, cut in thin slices
- pinch of salt
- 1 teaspoon (5ml) vanilla

Before you begin, chop chocolate coarsely. Line a 6" (15.2cm) square pan with foil and lightly butter the foil.

1. Combine all ingredients except vanilla in a three-quart (three-liter) heavy saucepan. Place pan over medium heat and stir constantly with a wooden spoon until all sugar crystals are dissolved. Wash down sides of pan with a pastry brush dipped in hot water, then clip on thermometer. Stir occasionally. When temperature reaches 236°F (113°C), immediately remove pan from heat. Leave thermometer in position. Total cooking time is about 18 minutes.

2. Place vanilla on surface of mixture. Do not stir or move pan until thermometer registers 110°F (43°C), about 30 minutes.

3. Beat the mixture vigorously with a wooden spoon until it loses some of its gloss, turns a lighter color and thickens, about ten minutes. Turn into prepared pan and press lightly with spoon to level surface. *Do not scrape pan.* Cool at room temperature about 40 minutes, then cut in 1" (2.5cm) squares. Or wrap uncut candy closely in foil or plastic wrap and refrigerate for up to a month. Yield: 36 pieces.

LAYERED FUDGE

Make a recipe of Wilton Basic Fudge and press into an 8" (20.3cm) square pan that has been lined with foil, then buttered.

Now prepare another complete recipe, following the same procedures, but omitting the chocolate. Use clear vanilla. While beating, add two drops of red liquid food color and 3/4 cup (180ml or 150g) chopped candied cherries. Spread onto chocolate fudge in the pan. Press with spoon to flatten a little. Yield: 64 pieces, 1" (2.5cm) square.

ORANGE COCONUT FUDGE*

A traditional, beaten fudge

A sophisticated member of the fudge family!

- 2 cups (480ml or 400g) granulated sugar
- ⅔ cup (160ml) milk
- 2 tablespoons (30ml) light corn syrup
- pinch of salt
- 2 tablespoons (30ml or 30g) butter
- 1 teaspoon (5ml) dried grated orange peel
- 2 drops orange food color
- 1 cup (240ml or 84g) flaked coconut

Before you begin, line a 6" (15.2cm) square pan with foil and butter the foil.

1. Combine sugar, milk, corn syrup and salt in a three-quart (three-liter) heavy saucepan. Set on medium heat and stir constantly with wooden spoon until all sugar crystals are dissolved. Wash down sides of pan with a pastry brush dipped in hot water and clip on thermometer. As candy cooks, wash sides of pan twice more. When thermometer registers 238°F (114°C), remove from heat. Entire cooking time is about 25 minutes.

2. Place butter, cut in thin slices, and orange peel on surface of candy. Do not stir. When mixture has cooled to 110°F (43°C), about 30 minutes, add food color and beat with wooden spoon. When candy lightens in color, add coconut and beat until mixture thickens and begins to lose gloss, about ten minutes. Pack into prepared pan, without scraping, and cool at room temperature until firm, about an hour. Cut in 1" (2.5cm) squares, or wrap, uncut, closely in plastic wrap and refrigerate for a month. Yield: 36 pieces.

CINNAMON COFFEE FUDGE*

A traditional beaten fudge

A pronounced coffee flavor enhanced by a spicy whiff of cinnamon makes this amber fudge distinguished enough to serve as the finale for an elegant dinner.

    1 cup (240ml) water

    1 tablespoon (15ml) dry instant coffee

    2 cups (480ml or 400g) granulated sugar

    1 tablespoon (15ml) cream

    1 tablespoon (15ml or 15g) butter

    pinch of salt

    ¼ teaspoon (1.2ml) cream of tartar

    ¼ teaspoon (1.2ml) cinnamon

Before you begin, line a 6" (15.2cm) square pan with foil and butter the foil.

1. Combine water and coffee in a three-quart (three-liter) heavy saucepan, place on high heat and bring to a boil, stirring constantly with a wooden spoon. Reduce heat to medium and add remaining ingredients. Stir until all sugar crystals are dissolved. Wash down sides of pan with a pastry brush dipped in hot water. Clip on thermometer and continue cooking, stirring occasionally. Wash down sides of pan twice more as mix-

ture cooks. When thermometer reaches 236°F (113°C), remove from heat. Cooking time is about 15 minutes.

2. Allow to cool, undisturbed, to 110°F (43°C). Beat with a wooden spoon about ten minutes, or until candy begins to lose its gloss and thickens. Spread into prepared pan without scraping, and firm at room temperature about an hour. Cut into 1" (2.5cm) squares, or wrap uncut candy tightly in plastic wrap and refrigerate for a month. Yield: 36 pieces.

HONEY WALNUT FUDGE*

A traditional, beaten fudge

For a real treat, form fudge into logs, dip in chocolate, then cover with nuts.

    2 tablespoons (30ml or 30g) butter

    2 ounces (60g) unsweetened chocolate, chopped

    1 cup (240ml) milk

    3 cups (720ml or 600g) granulated sugar

    ¼ cup (60ml) honey

    pinch of salt

    1 teaspoon (5ml) white vinegar

    1 teaspoon (5ml) vanilla

    1¼ cups (300ml or 170g) finely chopped walnuts, crisped.

Before you begin, crisp the nuts. Line an 8" (20.3cm) square pan with foil and butter foil.

1. Place butter (cut in thin slices) and chocolate in a four-quart (four-liter) heavy saucepan, set on low heat and stir with wooden spoon until melted and blended. Add sugar, milk, honey and salt, turn heat to medium and stir constantly until all sugar crystals are dissolved. Clip on thermometer, and cook to 240°F (116°C). Stir occasionally, washing down sides of pan twice more as candy cooks. Remove from heat and add vinegar. Do not stir. Entire cooking process takes about 30 minutes.

2. Cool to 110°F (43°C), about 35 minutes. Add vanilla and beat until mixture begins to lighten. Add nuts and continue to beat until mixture thickens—about ten minutes. Spread in prepared pan without scraping. Cool at room temperature until firm, about an hour. Cut into 1" (2.5cm) squares. Or wrap, uncut, in plastic wrap and refrigerate for a month. Yield: 64 pieces.

May be formed into logs or centers

NEW ORLEANS BUTTERMILK PRALINES

Countless thousands of these pralines have been enjoyed by New Orleans natives and eagerly devoured by visitors. Now you can create the very best pralines ever in your own kitchen with this authentic recipe.

- 2 cups (480ml or 400g) granulated sugar
- 1 teaspoon (5ml) baking soda
- 1 cup (240ml) buttermilk
- Pinch of salt
- 2 tablespoons (30ml or 28g) butter
- 1 tablespoon (15ml) light corn syrup
- 2 cups (480ml or 216g) pecan halves, roasted

Before you begin, butter a cookie sheet or marble slab. Or butter cupcake pans—recipe will yield about 20 candies, 2½" in diameter. Roast pecans.

1. Combine sugar, soda, buttermilk and salt in a heavy four-quart (four-liter) saucepan. (Be sure to use a four-quart (four-liter) pan —candy foams up as it heats.) Place over medium heat and stir constantly with a wooden spoon until all sugar crystals are dissolved. Wash down sides of pan with a pastry brush dipped in hot water, then clip on thermometer. When temperature reaches 210°F (99°C), about five minutes, stir in butter, cut in thin slices, syrup and pecans.

2. Continue cooking, stirring very frequently, until temperature reaches 236°F (113°C), about 17 minutes. Wash down sides of pan twice more during cooking process. Remove from heat.

3. Beat with a wooden spoon just two or three minutes until mixture begins to thicken. Working quickly, drop by tablespoon into 2½" (6.3cm) patties on prepared cookie sheet or slab—or spoon into cupcake pans. If candy thickens too much before you have formed patties, stir in two or three teaspoons of hot water. Cool until firm, about 20 minutes. Loosen patties from cookie sheet or slab with a spatula, or remove from cupcake pans with tip of knife. Wrap individually in plastic wrap. To store for a month at room temperature, place wrapped patties in a tightly sealed plastic bag. Yield: about 20 pralines.

QUICK AND EASY PRALINES

Pralines are really traditional fudges with a pronounced grain. This grain is achieved by beating or stirring the candy as soon as it is removed from the heat—rather than allowing the mixture to cool before beating.

Pralines were first made in France and were simply sugar-coated almonds. In early New Orleans, Creole cooks elaborated on the recipe and substituted their native pecans, thus creating the famous candy sold in shops and on street corners to natives and visitors. The candy is formed by dropping the mixture from a spoon into patties—but you may also form pralines in cupcake pans for neat circular shapes. Always wrap pralines as soon as they are cool. This candy dries out rapidly.

Pralines are an easy and very quick candy. You can be enjoying a praline about 30 minutes after you put the pan on the stove to cook.

BUTTERSCOTCH ALMOND PRALINES

Here is the enticing blonde of the praline family. Roasted almonds give a delicate crunch, sour cream a fascinating tang.

- 1 cup (240ml or 170g) light brown sugar, lightly packed
- 1 cup (240ml or 200g) granulated sugar
- ½ cup (120ml or 112g) dairy sour cream
- 2 tablespoons (30ml or 30g) butter
- pinch of salt
- 1 cup (240ml or 120g) roasted almonds
- ½ teaspoon (2.5ml) butterscotch flavoring

Before you begin, roast the almonds. Lightly butter two cookie sheets or butter your marble slab.

1. Combine sugars, cream, butter (cut in thin slices) and salt in a three-quart (three-liter) heavy saucepan. Put on medium-low heat, stirring constantly until mixture comes to a boil. Wash down sides of pan with a

pastry brush dipped in hot water and clip on thermometer. Stirring occasionally, cook until thermometer registers 236°F (113°C). Remove from heat. Entire cooking time will be about 25 to 30 minutes.

2. Immediately add nuts and flavoring. Stir briefly, just until mixture begins to thicken —then drop by tablespoon on prepared cookie sheets or slab, working quickly. If mixture becomes too thick, stir in one or two teaspoons of hot water. These pralines will form more of a cluster than a flat patty. Cool at room temperature about 30 minutes. Wrap each patty in plastic wrap. Place wrapped patties in a tightly sealed plastic bag to store for a month at room temperature. Yield: 24 pralines.

NEW ORLEANS DELUXE PRALINES

A popular New Orleans recipe—this candy is crowded with crisp pecan halves, has a creamy delicate grain and a rich caramel flavor. Like all pralines, they're very quick and easy to make.

 1 cup (240ml or 170g) dark brown sugar, lightly packed
 1 cup (240ml or 200g) granulated sugar
 2/3 cup (160ml) evaporated milk, undiluted
 1/2 teaspoon (2.5ml) vanilla extract
 2 cups (480ml or 216g) pecan halves, roasted

Before you begin, roast the pecans (Chapter 2). Lightly butter two cookie sheets, or butter your marble slab.

1. Combine sugars and milk in a heavy three-quart (three-liter) saucepan. Place over medium heat and stir constantly with a wooden spoon until all sugar crystals are dissolved. Wash down sides of pan with a pastry brush dipped in hot water, then clip on thermometer. Turn heat to medium-low and continue cooking to 236°F (113°C). Entire cooking time is about 25 to 30 minutes. Remove from heat.

2. Add vanilla and nuts and stir briefly, just until nuts are well coated and mixture becomes a little lighter. Immediately drop from a tablespoon onto prepared cookie sheets into patties about 2½" (6.3cm) in diameter. If mixture becomes too stiff to drop, stir in one (5ml) or two (10ml) teaspoons of hot

water. Cool at room temperature until firm, about 30 minutes. Wrap individually in plastic wrap. To store for a month, place wrapped patties in a tightly sealed plastic bag. Yield: about 27 pralines.

FULL CREAM PRALINES

Rich creamy pralines with a delicate "tooth". You'll be interested in the time-honored way the praline grain is achieved.

 2 cups (480ml or 400g) granulated sugar
 1 cup (240ml or 170g) light brown sugar, lightly packed
 1 cup (240ml) whipping cream
 6 ounces (170g) pecan halves, roasted
 ½ teaspoon (2.5ml) salt
 ¼ cup (60ml or 56g) butter

Before you begin, butter a cookie sheet or marble slab. Roast the nuts.

1. Combine sugars and cream in a three-quart (three-liter) heavy saucepan. Place over medium heat and stir constantly with a wooden spoon until all sugar crystals are dissolved. Wash down sides of pan with a pastry brush dipped in hot water, then clip on thermometer. Continue cooking to 230°F (110°C), about ten minutes, then stir in pecans, salt and butter, cut in thin slices. Wash down sides of pan twice more during cooking process.

2. Stir occasionally as mixture cooks to 236°F (113°C), about five more minutes. Remove from heat. Use a 1/3 cup (80ml) metal measuring cup to ladle a portion from the batch. Stir portion with a dessert spoon until the candy lightens and begins to grain, then deposit in a patty on prepared cookie sheet. Continue until all patties are formed. After the first portion is ladled out, the succeeding portions will grain almost immediately as you stir the candy in the cup.

3. Allow to firm at room temperature about 15 minutes. Wrap each patty in plastic wrap. To store for a month at room temperature, place wrapped patties in a tightly sealed plastic bag. Yield: about 27 pralines, 2½" (6.3cm) in diameter.

More pralines on next page

CRUNCHY CREOLE PRALINES

Make this very simple candy to delight everyone. One or two pralines make a nice take-home gift for visitors. An authentic New Orleans recipe.

2 cups (480ml or 400g) granulated sugar

1 cup (240ml or (170g) light brown sugar, lightly packed

pinch of cream of tartar

1½ cups (360ml) water

1½ cups (360ml or 180g) chopped pecans, crisped

Before you begin, crisp the nuts. Butter two cookie sheets or your marble slab. Or, if you wish neatly circular pralines, butter cupcake pans to use as molds. You will need two or three pans for a total of 24 molds.

1. Combine all ingredients except nuts in a heavy three-quart (three-liter) saucepan. Set on high heat and bring to a boil, stirring constantly with a wooden spoon. Wash down sides of pan with a pastry brush dipped in hot water, then clip on thermometer.

2. Reduce heat to medium and continue cooking, without stirring, until thermometer registers 236°F (113°C). Entire cooking process takes about 20 minutes. Remove pan from heat. Add nuts, then immediately stir mixture with a wooden spoon for about five minutes, or until mixture lightens in color and becomes thicker.

3. Working quickly, spoon onto prepared cookie sheets or slab in patties, or spoon into cupcake pans. Cool at room temperature about 30 minutes, or until firm. Remove from sheets or slab with a spatula, or insert point of a paring knife at sides of cupcake pans to loosen. Wrap each praline in plastic wrap. To store at room temperature for a month, put wrapped patties into a tightly sealed plastic bag. Yield: about two dozen pralines, 2½'' (6.3cm) in diameter.

HOW TO FORM FUDGE BY WORKING OR KNEADING

Kneading the fudge gives an even creamier texture than beating alone and can even rescue a batch beaten too long that refuses to leave the pan. Any fudge, *except no-beat confectionery coating or chocolate fudges*, can be kneaded. Beat the fudge (or stir a no-beat fondant fudge) until it is very stiff. Turn it out of the pan onto a lightly buttered surface and knead like bread dough a very few minutes, just until pliable. Work in nuts, coconut or dried fruit as you knead. Press it into a foil-lined buttered pan, or form it into logs or centers.

Caution: don't knead fudge any longer than necessary. If you knead too long, it may break down and become soupy.

Working the fudge like fondant is a time saver, because the fudge cools very rapidly with this method. It will be especially smooth and creamy, too. *Only traditional fudges* may be worked.

Before starting to cook the fudge, arrange metal candy bars on a marble slab to form a 12" x 18" (30.5cm x 45.7cm) area. (Or use the alternate cookie sheet method, Chapter 10.) As soon as the fudge has cooked to the proper temperature, pour it out on the slab to cool. If butter or flavoring is to be added, just lay them on the surface, do not disturb the mixture.

After just a few minutes, test for coolness by touching an edge. If the mixture is about body temperature and holds the imprint of your finger, it is ready to work. Do this with a scraper, exactly as the picture lesson on fondant in Chapter 10 describes. It will take about ten minutes. As soon as the fudge is stiff, press into a foil-lined buttered pan. Or knead briefly and form the candy into logs or centers.

You may store worked fudge for a month in the refrigerator in a tightly sealed container. Bring to room temperature, knead briefly and form into logs or centers.

HOW TO FORM FUDGE LOGS AND CENTERS

Fudge logs are luxurious and especially good for gifts, as the coating they are dipped in keeps the candy fresh and creamy. To form the logs, roll lightly kneaded fondant or traditional fudge into cylinders about 1" (2.5cm) in diameter and about 6" (15.2cm) long. Work with a portion at a time on a lightly buttered work surface. Wrap closely in wax paper and refrigerate for an hour or several days.

Bring to room temperature, still wrapped, and pat with your hands to re-form. For dipping, use a double boiler whose top pan is at least 7" (17.8cm) in diameter. Dip in confectionery coating or chocolate — Chapters 3 and 11 give methods. Wrap dipped logs closely in plastic wrap and store for a month or more in a cool place. Refrigeration is not necessary. To serve, cut in ¼" (.6cm) slices.

Yield depends on size of recipe. A recipe containing two cups of sugar will make four logs, about 6" (15.2cm) long. One that contains three cups of sugar will yield six logs. Cut the kneaded fudge into corresponding portions before rolling into logs.

To make fudge centers, start with kneaded traditional or fondant fudge. Work with one-fourth of the recipe at a time on lightly buttered surface. Roll the fudge into cylinders about 3/4" (1.9cm) in diameter. Cut off 3/4" (1.9cm) pieces and roll between buttered palms into balls. Dip in confectionery coating or chocolate — see Chapters 3 and 11. A fudge recipe that contains two cups of sugar will yield about 50 centers. Fudge centers are firm and are especially easy to dip.

Another method, especially suited to no-beat *confectionery* coating or chocolate fudges. Cool and firm the fudge in a pan a size larger than noted in the recipe. (For example, use 10" (25.4cm) pan instead of a recommended 8" (20.3cm) pan.) Cut into ½" (1.3cm) squares and dip.

Chapter 6

PERFECT CARAMELS...
THE EASY WAY

Caramels might just be the most delicious candies you can make! A perfect caramel is luxuriously rich, delicately chewy—never tough or sticky—and has a silky, grainless texture. There's a unique flavor in caramels made at home, too—buttery, creamy, with a tantalizing undertone of butterscotch.

Caramels are also versatile. Accents of coffee, orange or chocolate give new dimensions to their flavors. They add richness to dipped marshmallows, nougat, fudge logs and cereal bars. You can even gild the lily by folding crisp nuts into caramels or dipping them in chocolate.

Caramels are easy to make. Follow the guidelines below for perfect caramels every time.

1. *All caramels are rich* in butter, cream or milk, so they scorch easily. Cook them at medium or lower heat and stir very frequently. Do not clip the thermometer to the side of the pan — the candy might scorch under it. Instead, just lay the thermometer in the pan and move it as necessary as you stir.

2. *The cold water test* is essential to achieve the consistency you like. As the temperature of the cooking mixture nears the degree indicated in the recipe, drop a little into a small container of ice water. Test the cooled ball of candy between your thumb and forefinger. The consistency will be the same as that of the entire finished batch. Repeat the test every few minutes—when consistency is satisfactory, immediately remove pan from heat. The temperature recommended in each recipe gives a good average consistency—but you may like your caramels softer or firmer.

3. *For a grainless texture,* stir the caramels as little as possible after removing from heat. Just fold in flavoring or nuts, then pour out immediately. *Never scrape the pan.* (After pouring, you may scrape out the remaining mixture onto a saucer or small pan for a family treat.)

4. *A marble slab,* buttered and fitted with buttered metal candy bars is ideal for the even cooling and firming of caramels. But a square pan lined with buttered foil is satisfactory, too.

5. *Let caramels firm overnight.* It takes hours for the candy to cool evenly and firm to its finished consistency.

6. *Cut finished caramels* with a long sharp, buttered knife. Use back-and-forth repeated movements. First cut into long strips, then cut strips into squares.

7. *Always wrap caramels individually*—they have a tendency to spread. Use small squares of foil, cellophane, wax paper or plastic wrap.

First aid for caramels. If you're interrupted by the phone or the doorbell and your caramels turn out less than perfect, here are two good remedies.

If your caramels grain, just cut them and serve them as fudge or pralines. They'll still taste delicious and delight the family.

If your caramels don't firm, and remain a little runny, just scoop the batch into a pan and refrigerate. Later, turn it into the best caramel sauce you've ever tasted. Warm over hot water, thinning with milk or cream as needed.

WILTON LIGHT CARAMELS*

Caramels at their simplest and most distinctive—so rich in butter, milk and cream that they need no other flavoring.

  1½ cups (360ml) light corn syrup

  1 cup (240ml or 200g) granulated sugar

  1⅓ cups (320ml) sweetened, condensed milk

  2 cups (480ml) whipping cream

  ½ cup (120ml or 112g) butter, cut in thin slices

Before you begin, line an 8" (20.3cm) square pan with foil and lightly butter the foil. Or lightly butter an area on your marble slab, arrange metal candy bars on it to form an 8" (20.3cm) square and lightly butter the inside surfaces of the bars.

1. Blend all ingredients in a four-quart (four-liter) heavy saucepan and place on medium heat. Stir constantly with a wooden spoon until all sugar crystals are dissolved. Wash down sides of pan with a pastry brush

*May be used as centers for dipping

dipped in hot water. *Lay* thermometer in pan (do not clip on).

2. Stir *frequently*, moving thermometer as necessary, until mixture cooks to about 238°F (114°C). At this point, start testing a small amount of mixture in ice water. When candy reaches 245°F (118°C), or is at the consistency you like, remove from heat. As mixture cooks, wash down sides of pan at least twice more. Cooking process will take about 45 minutes.

3. Pour into prepared pan or on slab—do not scrape pan. Allow to firm overnight. Lift out of pan onto cutting board and peel off foil—or remove metal candy bars. Butter the blade of a long sharp knife and cut into 3/4" (1.9cm) squares, using a sawing motion. Wrap each square individually. These may be left at room temperature for several days. Refrigerate to store for three weeks. Yield: about 100 caramels.

Above, clockwise from lower left: on table, Rum Caramel Kisses. In dish, Wilton Chocolate Caramels, Butterscotch Caramels, Wilton Light Caramels

COFFEE AND CREAM CARAMELS*

These candies are even better than a cup of full-bodied coffee laced with rich cream—there's a hint of butterscotch and the characteristic rich caramel texture.

> 1 cup (240ml or 200g) granulated sugar
>
> ½ cup (120ml or 100g) light brown sugar, lightly packed
>
> ½ cup (120ml) light corn syrup
>
> 2 tablespoons (30ml or 28g) dry, instant coffee
>
> ½ cup (120ml) whipping cream
>
> ¼ cup (60ml or 56g) butter
>
> pinch of salt
>
> 1 teaspoon (5ml) vanilla extract

Before you begin, line a 6" (15.2cm) square pan with foil and lightly butter the foil. Or, butter a marble slab and arrange buttered candy bars to form a 6" (15.2cm) square.

1. Cut butter in thin slices. Combine all ingredients except vanilla in a heavy three-quart (three-liter) saucepan. Place pan over medium heat and stir constantly with a wooden spoon until butter and all sugar crystals are dissolved. After this, stir frequently during the cooking process to prevent scorching. Just before mixture comes to a boil, after about eight minutes, wash down sides of pan with a pastry brush dipped in hot water. Lay thermometer in pan, do not clip on.

2. As mixture continues to cook, wash down sides of pan twice more. When thermometer registers 238°F and candy begins to thicken, turn heat to medium low. After this, test a sample in ice water several times to see if candy has reached proper consistency. Candy should be finished when the thermometer registers 245°F (118°C) or is at consistency you like. This takes about 30 minutes. Remove from heat, add vanilla and stir just until blended.

3. Pour into prepared pan or on marble slab. Do not scrape pan. Allow to cool and firm overnight. Butter a long sharp knife and cut with a back-and-forth movement into 3/4" (1.9cm) squares. Wrap each piece individually. Store at room temperature a few days, or in the refrigerator for up to three weeks. Yield: 64 caramels.

RUM CARAMEL KISSES

Everyone loves these delicious morsels! Creamy, rum-flavored caramel conceals the surprise of a crisp roasted almond. Cooking temperature is very important in this recipe—watch thermometer carefully!

> 1 cup (240ml or 200g) granulated sugar
>
> 1 cup (240ml) light corn syrup
>
> 1 cup (240ml) whipping cream
>
> ¼ teaspoon (1.2ml) salt
>
> 2 tablespoons (30ml or 28g) butter
>
> 6 tablespoons (90ml) evaporated milk
>
> 1 teaspoon (5ml) vanilla
>
> 1 teaspoon (5ml) rum flavoring
>
> 100 whole almonds, roasted — about 5 ounces (140g)

Before you begin, roast the almonds (Chapter 2). Line a 10" (25.4cm) square pan with foil and lightly butter the foil. Or butter a marble slab and arrange buttered metal bars to form a 10" (25.4cm) square.

1. Combine sugar, corn syrup, cream and salt in a three-quart (three-liter) heavy saucepan. Set on medium heat and stir constantly with a wooden spoon until all sugar crystals are dissolved. Just before mixture comes to a boil, about five minutes, wash sides of pan with a pastry brush dipped in hot water. Lay thermometer in pan.

2. Continue cooking, stirring occasionally, until thermometer registers 232°F (111°C). Add butter, cut in thin slices, and evaporated milk, in fourths, stirring constantly between each addition. Temperature will drop, or "slack off" to about 222°F (106°C). Wash sides of pan again. When temperature rises to 238°F (114°C) and mixture thickens, turn heat to medium-low. When thermometer registers 245°F (118°C), remove from heat. Entire cooking time will be about 35 minutes. Add flavorings, stirring just enough to blend.

3. Pour into prepared pan or on marble slab. Mixture will be about ¼" (.6cm) thick. When candy is firm, about three hours, use a sharp buttered knife to slice into ten strips, 1" (2.5cm) wide. Butter a scissors and cut each strip into 1" (2.5cm) squares. Place an almond on a square and roll between your palms into a little cylinder, covering almond completely. Place each candy on a piece of wax paper or cello-

phane, roll to cover and twist ends to seal. Store at room temperature for several days, or in refrigerator for up to three weeks. Yield: 100 kisses.

TO VARY THIS RECIPE

For rum caramels, omit almonds and pour cooked candy into a 6" (15.2cm) square pan lined with foil and buttered. Or pour onto buttered marble slab with metal bars arranged to form a 6" (15.2cm) square. Let set overnight and slice into 3/4" (1.9cm) squares. Yield: 64 caramels.

WILTON CARAMEL FOR DIPPING

This rich delicious caramel is especially formulated for dipping marshmallows and apples, or for making "Turtles". The coating will stay soft and creamy for weeks.

- 1⅓ cups (320ml) sweetened, condensed milk
- ½ cup (120ml or 100g) granulated sugar
- ⅓ cup (80ml or 56g) light brown sugar, firmly packed
- ¾ cup (180ml) light corn syrup
- ¼ cup (60ml or 56g) butter
- 1½ teaspoons (7.5ml) vanilla

1. Combine milk, sugars and corn syrup in a heavy three-quart (three-liter) saucepan. Set over medium heat and stir constantly with a wooden spoon until all sugar crystals are dissolved. Wash down sides of pan with a pastry brush dipped in hot water, then lay thermometer in pan. Stir frequently as caramel cooks, washing down sides of pan twice more. At about 236°F (113°C), start testing for consistency by dropping a little into ice water. Caramel should form a soft but firm ball. At 242°F (117°C), or correct consistency, remove from heat.

2. Stir in butter, cut in thin slices, and vanilla. Allow to cool, *undisturbed* for about ten minutes, before using to dip marshmallows or apples. Leftover carmel coating may be refrigerated in a covered container for up to two weeks—then softened in a double boiler over simmering water to be used again. For directions for dipping marshmallows, see Chapter 8, for Turtles, Chapter 11, for Apples, Chapter 14.

WILTON CHOCOLATE CARAMELS*

Rich, chocolate-y, chewy—a perfect chocolate caramel!

- 1⅓ cups (320ml) light corn syrup
- 1½ cups (360ml or 250g) granulated sugar
- 1⅓ cups (320ml) sweetened, condensed milk
- 2 cups (480ml) whipping cream
- ½ cup (120ml or 112g) butter, cut in thin slices
- 3½ ounces (98g) unsweetened chocolate, chopped

Before you begin, line an 8" (20.3cm) square pan with foil and lightly butter the foil. Or lightly butter an area on your marble slab, arrange metal candy bars in an 8" (20.3cm) square and butter the inner edges of the bars. Finely chop the chocolate.

1. Combine all ingredients except chocolate in a heavy four-quart (four-liter) pan. Place over medium heat and stir constantly with a wooden spoon until all sugar crystals are dissolved and mixture is smooth. Wash down sides of pan with a pastry brush dipped in hot water. Lay thermometer in pan (do not clip on) and stir very frequently, moving thermometer as necessary.

2. When temperature reaches 225°F (107°C) (about 45 minutes) add chocolate. As mixture cooks, wash down sides of pan twice more. At about 238°F (114°C) start to test a little of the mixture in cold water. When temperature reaches 245°F (118°C), or when mixture is at the consistency you like, remove from heat. Entire cooking time is about 55 minutes.

3. Pour into prepared pan or on slab. Do not scrape pan. Let firm overnight. Butter a long sharp knife and cut the candy into 3/4" (1.9cm) squares, using a sawing motion. Wrap each square individually. Store for several days at room temperature, or refrigerate up to three weeks. Yield: 100 caramels.

*May be used as centers for dipping

BUTTERSCOTCH CARAMELS*

Delectably rich, chewy, with a smooth butterscotch flavor—these are the most caramel-y caramels of all.

    1 cup (240ml or 224g) butter
    2¼ cups (540ml or 450g) granulated
        sugar
    ¼ teaspoon (1.2ml) salt
    ½ cup (120ml) light corn syrup
    ½ cup (120ml) dark corn syrup
    1⅓ cups (320ml) sweetened, condensed
        milk
    1 teaspoon (5ml) vanilla

Before you begin, line an 8" (20.3cm) square pan with foil and butter the foil. Or butter a marble slab and arrange metal candy bars to form an 8" (20.3cm) square. Butter inner sides of metal bars.

1. Place butter in three-quart (three-liter) heavy saucepan over low heat. When butter has melted, blend in sugar and salt with a wooden spoon. Gradually add syrups, then milk, stirring constantly.

2. Turn heat to medium-low and continue stirring until mixture is almost boiling. Wash down sides of pan with a pastry brush dipped in hot water. *Lay thermometer in pan (do not clip on)* and continue cooking, stirring frequently. Wash down sides of pan twice more during cooking. When thermometer registers 238°F (114°C), start testing by dropping a little of the mixture into ice water. When thermometer registers 248°F (120°C), or is at the consistency you like, remove from heat. Entire cooking time is about 25 minutes.

3. Let stand five minutes, then blend in vanilla. Do not beat. Pour into prepared pan or on marble slab. Do not scrape pan. Allow to cool and firm overnight. Lift out of pan onto cutting board and peel off foil—or remove metal bars. Cut into 3/4" (1.9cm) squares with a long sharp buttered knife. Use a back-and-forth motion. Wrap each caramel individually. Store at room temperature for several days or for up to three weeks in the refrigerator. Yield: about 100 pieces.

NUT BUTTERSCOTCH CARAMELS

For an even richer candy, stir in one cup (240ml or 150g) crisped chopped nuts along with the vanilla.

ORANGE CARAMELS*

Add the fresh tangy flavor of orange to a rich caramel mixture and you'll create a superlative candy! Be sure to use a four-quart (four-liter) pan for cooking — this candy foams up as it heats.

    2 cups (480ml) warmed whipping cream
    2 cups (480ml or 400g) granulated sugar
    1 cup (240ml) light corn syrup
    ⅓ cup (80ml or 90g) butter
    ¼ teaspoon (1.2ml) salt
    1 tablespoon (15ml) dried grated
        orange peel

Before you begin, line an 8" (20.3cm) square pan with foil and lightly butter the foil. Or butter an area on your marble slab, arrange metal bars in an 8" (20.3cm) square and butter inner surfaces of bars.

1. Place *one cup* of the cream in a small saucepan and heat just until warm. Combine sugar, corn syrup, butter (cut in thin slices) and salt in a heavy four-quart (four-liter) saucepan. Add the one cup of warmed cream and set on medium heat. Stir constantly with a wooden spoon until all sugar crystals are dissolved, butter is melted and mixture is smooth. Wash down sides of pan with a pastry brush dipped in hot water. Lay thermometer in pan. (Do not clip on.)

2. Meanwhile, warm second cup of cream. When mixture in large pan reaches 180°F (83°C), slowly pour second cup of warmed cream into it, stirring as you pour. Continue cooking at medium heat, washing down sides of pan twice more. Stir frequently. At 236°F (113°C), start testing a little of the mixture in ice water. When thermometer registers 245°F (118°C), or mixture is at the consistency you like, remove from heat. Entire cooking process will take about 35 to 45 minutes.

3. Blend in grated orange rind and pour into prepared pan or on marble slab. Do not scrape pan. Allow to firm and cool overnight. Cut into 3/4" (1.9cm) pieces with a long, buttered sharp knife, using a sawing motion. Wrap individually. Store at room temperature for several days. Or store in the refrigerator for up to three weeks.
Yield: about 100 pieces.

HOW TO FORM
A CARAMEL-COVERED LOG

Caramel-covered logs are deservedly popular forms of candy. Fudge, nougat or divinity is formed into a cylinder or log, then covered with caramel and rolled in nuts or coconut.

A log is a perfect gift candy—it's easy to wrap, the covering keeps the center fresh and moist, and there's always the surprise of the toothsome interior when the candy is sliced to serve.

Any nougat, traditional or fondant fudges, or divinity may be used for the center of the log. Divinities are light and delicate, and must be formed very quickly.

Any caramel recipe in this chapter, *except* Wilton Caramel for Dipping, may be used for covering a log. (Dipping temperature of this recipe is too high.) Omit nuts or coconut from the caramel.

Caramel-coated logs may be made ahead, wrapped closely in plastic wrap and refrigerated for up to three weeks. Freezing will not impair their quality.

1. Make caramel, pouring it into a 10" (25.4cm) square pan lined with foil and buttered. Or pour onto a buttered marble slab with metal candy bars arranged in a 10" (25.4cm) square. When firm, refrigerate.

2. Form the log center, following directions given in Chapter 5 for fudge, Chapter 7 for divinity or nougat.

3. Meanwhile, cut caramel in half, making two 10" x 5" (25.4cm x 12.7cm) rectangles. Place on separate sheets of foil. Warm one in oven set at lowest temperature for about three minutes to soften. Unwrap a log center, place on softened caramel and roll to cover completely. Do same for second log.

4. Place crisped, chopped nuts or coconut on square of wax paper. You will need one cup of nuts or coconut for two logs. Brush each log with light corn syrup, then roll in nuts, pressing firmly. Wrap closely in plastic wrap and store in refrigerator for up to three weeks. To serve, bring to room temperature. Heat a long sharp knife in hot water, butter it, and cut the log into ¼" (.6cm) slices, using a back and forth motion. Yield: about 36 slices from each log.

STRAWBERRY COCONUT
CARAMELS*

New and just fabulous! Coconut gives a special chewy, yet tender texture—set off by the fresh fruity flavor.

    ¾ cup (180ml or 150g) granulated sugar
    2 tablespoons (30ml) water
    1 cup (240ml) light corn syrup
    ¼ cup (60ml or 56g) butter
    ¾ cup (180ml) evaporated milk
    ½ teaspoon (2.5ml) salt
    2 drops oil of strawberry
    3 drops red liquid food color
    1 cup (240ml or 84g) flaked coconut

Before you begin, line a 6" (15.2cm) pan with foil and lightly butter the foil. Or butter an area of your marble slab and arrange metal candy bars to form a 6" (15.2cm) square. Butter inner surfaces of bars. Cut butter in thin slices.

1. Combine sugar, water and syrup in a two-quart (two-liter) heavy saucepan. Set over medium heat and stir constantly with a wooden spoon until all sugar crystals are dissolved. When mixture is almost boiling, wash down sides of pan with a pastry brush dipped in hot water. At boiling point, add butter, stirring constantly.

2. When mixture comes to a boil the second time, pour in the milk very slowly, stirring as you pour. Lay thermometer in pan. From this point on, stir frequently. When thermometer registers 238°F (114°C), start testing for consistency in ice water and lower heat. When candy is at correct consistency, or at 245°F (118°C), remove from heat. Entire cooking time is about 40 minutes.

3. Blend in food color, flavoring and coconut. Pour into prepared pan or on marble slab and allow to cool and firm overnight. Do not scrape pan. Cut into 3/4" (1.9cm) squares, using a long, sharp buttered knife and a sawing motion. Wrap individually. Store at room temperature for several days or in the refrigerator for up to three weeks. Yield: 64 caramels.

*May be used as centers for dipping

Chapter 7

DIVINITIES AND NOUGATS...
EXCITING VARIATIONS ON A THEME

If you thought divinity was just a somewhat bland white candy, and nougats were only the centers for dipped chocolates, this chapter will open your eyes! The picture at right shows just a sampling of the delicious possibilities of these candies. Crown airy divinity with fruit or chocolate, flavor it with subtle liqueur, enrich it with crunchy nuts. Form nougat into luscious candy logs or twirl it into pinwheels, sweeten it with honey or refresh it with fruit. Divinity and nougat may well be the stars of your candy repertoire.

Divinity and nougat are made in a similar fashion. A hot cooked syrup is beaten into whipped egg whites. By varying the temperature and quantity of ingredients, this simple procedure results in the firm, delicately chewy nougat or the light-as-air divinity.

Your thermometer and electric mixer make these candies very easy to turn out. Pay close attention to the temperature as the syrup cooks. Correct temperature will result in the proper consistency of the finished candy. A table model mixer is most convenient to use as you beat the stream of hot syrup into the whipped egg whites—but if you have a helper to pour the syrup, a hand-held mixer will do the job. It may be necessary to finish the last minute or two of beating by hand. Use the large bowl of your table model mixer, or a four-quart (four-liter) bowl with a hand-held mixer.

Be sure to have everything ready before you start to cook the candies—ingredients measured, pans for firming prepared and mixer set up conveniently. Once you start to combine the syrup with the egg whites, the candies will thicken very rapidly. And use Grade A Large eggs for correct proportion. A rubber scraper is handy for scraping candy from bowl to pan for firming.

Always test divinities for finished consistency. Drop a little of the whipped candy on wax paper. If the mound looks glossy and holds its shape, the candy is finished. If it does not hold its shape, beat a little longer, and test again.

At right, clockwise from top left: Chocolate Nut, Tropical and Butterscotch Caramel logs, Wilton Snow White and Chocolate Divinity Puffs, Cherry and Grasshopper Divinity, Lemon Coconut Nougat, Nougat Caramel Pinwheels, Pistachio Nougat, Chocolate-dipped nougats.

WILTON SNOW WHITE DIVINITY PUFFS*

Light and airy as a cloud, these puffs seem to float off the plate! They're crisp on the outside and creamy on the inside.

- 2½ cups (600ml or 500g) granulated sugar
- 1 cup (240ml) light corn syrup
- ⅓ cup (80ml) water
- 2 egg whites, room temperature
- ¼ cup (60ml or 24g) confectioners' sugar, sifted
- ¾ cup (180ml or 84g) chopped walnuts, crisped
- 1 teaspoon (5ml) clear vanilla

Before you begin, crisp the nuts. Line two cookie sheets with wax paper. Place egg whites in large mixer bowl.

1. Combine granulated sugar, corn syrup and water in a three-quart (three-liter) heavy saucepan. Place over high heat and stir constantly with a wooden spoon until all sugar crystals are dissolved. Wash down sides of pan with a pastry brush dipped in hot water. Clip on thermometer. Continue cooking, without stirring, washing down sides of pan twice more. When temperature reaches 250°F (121°C), remove from heat. Cooking time is about ten minutes.

2. When cooked mixture starts to boil, start to beat egg whites with mixer set at highest speed. Beat to stiff peaks. Set mixer at medium speed and pour cooked mixture into beaten egg whites in a very thin stream. Do not scrape cooking pan. When all cooked mixture has been thoroughly incorporated, turn mixer to highest speed again and beat about one minute more.

3. Add confectioners' sugar and beat at lowest speed just until sugar has been incorporated. Fold in nuts and vanilla. Test by dropping a little of the candy on wax paper. If it holds its shape and is glossy, candy is finished. If not, beat a little longer.

4. Working quickly, drop by teaspoon onto prepared cookie sheets. Allow to firm for one to two hours at room temperature. Serve the day the candy is made, or store for several weeks at room temperature in a sealed container. Yield: about 90 puffs.

WILTON CHOCOLATE ALMOND DIVINITY PUFFS*

You'll enjoy the creamy texture of this classic—and very deluxe—divinity, given a subtle touch of chocolate

- 2½ cups (600ml or 500g) granulated sugar
- 1 cup (240ml) light corn syrup
- ⅓ cup (80ml) water
- 2 egg whites, room temperature
- 2½ ounces (70g) unsweetened chocolate, chopped
- ½ teaspoon (2.5ml) clear almond extract
- ¾ cup (180ml or 115g) chopped almonds, crisped

Before you begin, crisp the nuts and chop the chocolate. Line two cookie sheets with wax paper. Place egg whites in large bowl of electric mixer.

1. Combine sugar, syrup and water in a three-quart (three-liter) heavy saucepan. Stir constantly with a wooden spoon until all sugar crystals are dissolved. Wash down sides of pan with a pastry brush dipped in hot water, then clip on thermometer. Continue cooking, without stirring, until temperature reaches 250°F (121°C). Remove from heat. Cooking time is about ten minutes.

2. When cooked mixture starts to boil, start beating egg whites with mixer set at highest speed. Beat to stiff peaks. Turn mixer to medium speed and pour cooked mixture in a very thin stream into beaten egg whites. Do not scrape cooking pan. Turn mixer to highest speed and beat about one minute more.

3. Add chopped chocolate and almond extract and beat at lowest speed just long enough to incorporate chocolate. Fold in nuts. Test candy by dropping a little on wax paper. If it holds its shape and is glossy, candy is finished.

4. Working quickly, drop by teaspoon onto prepared cookie sheets. Allow to firm for one to two hours at room temperature. Serve the day the candy is made, or store in a tightly sealed container for several weeks at room temperature. Yield: about 90 puffs.

*May be used as centers for dipping

DEEP CHOCOLATE DIVINITY*

This is a new and very unusual member of the divinity family—so chocolate-y it's almost a fudge, but with a much lighter, more delicate texture.

2 cups (480ml or 400g) granulated sugar
½ cup (120ml) water
½ cup (120ml) light corn syrup
pinch of salt
2 egg whites, room temperature
3 ounces (84g) unsweetened chocolate,
1 teaspoon (5ml) vanilla

Before you begin, place egg whites in large mixer bowl. Line an 8" (20.3cm) square pan with foil and lightly butter the foil. Chop chocolate and place in upper pan of a one-quart (one-liter) double boiler. Fill lower pan with very hot water, then place top pan in position and cover. Chocolate will be melted when it is time to use.

1. Combine sugar, water, syrup and salt in a heavy three-quart (three-liter) saucepan. Set over medium-high heat and stir constantly with a wooden spoon until all sugar crystals are dissolved. Wash down sides of pan with a pastry brush dipped in hot water. Cook, without stirring, until thermometer reaches 252°F (122°C), about 15 minutes. Wash down sides of pan twice more during cooking period.

2. Start to beat egg whites just before mixture above comes to a boil. Beat at high speed to soft peaks. When cooked mixture reaches 252°F (122°C), remove from heat and pour into beaten egg whites in a very thin stream, as you beat at high speed. Do not scrape cooking pan. When mixture begins to thicken, in about five minutes, add melted chocolate and vanilla. Continue beating about two minutes longer. Test for consistency by dropping a small spoonful on wax paper. If it is glossy and holds its shape, candy is finished.

3. Scrape into prepared pan, pressing with buttered hands or a buttered spatula to level. Allow to cool and firm about an hour at room temperature. Cut into 1" (2.5cm) squares with a sharp buttered knife. *Note:* this candy may be dropped by dessert-spoon into puffs on wax paper. To store for several weeks, wrap uncut candy closely in foil or plastic wrap and refrigerate. Yield: 64 delicious pieces.

BUTTERSCOTCH-PECAN DIVINITY*

Light and airy as all divinity, but with an intriguing butterscotch flavor and delicate beige tint. Try forming into a log, covering with caramel and chopped nuts.

2 cups (480ml or 400g) granulated sugar
½ cup (120ml) water
½ cup (120ml) dark corn syrup
pinch of salt
2 egg whites, room temperature
½ teaspoon (2.5ml) butterscotch flavoring
½ cup (120ml or 70g) chopped pecans, crisped

Before you begin, crisp the nuts (Chapter 2). Place egg whites in large mixer bowl. Line an 8" (20.3cm) square pan with foil and lightly butter the foil.

1. Place sugar, water, syrup and salt in a heavy three-quart (three-liter) saucepan. Set pan over medium-high heat and stir constantly with a wooden spoon until all sugar crystals are dissolved. Wash down sides of pan with a pastry brush dipped in warm water, then clip on thermometer. Now cook, *without stirring,* until thermometer registers 252°F (122°C), about 17 minutes. Remove from heat. Wash down sides of pan twice more during cooking period.

2. Start to beat the egg whites just before the mixture above comes to a boil. Beat at high speed to soft peaks. Pour cooked mixture into beaten egg whites in a very thin stream, while beating at high speed. Continue beating about six minutes, adding flavoring as you beat. Mixture will be glossy and thicken rapidly. If necessary, beat by hand about two minutes longer, adding nuts as you beat. Test for consistency by dropping a small spoonful on wax paper. If it holds its shape and remains glossy, candy is finished.

3. Scrape into prepared pan. Butter a spatula and press to level candy. Allow to cool and firm about one hour at room temperature. Cut into 1" (2.5cm) squares with a sharp buttered knife. To store, wrap uncut candy closely in plastic wrap and refrigerate for several weeks. Yield: 64 pieces.

PRIZE WINNING
CHERRY DIVINITY*

This candy won a prize for its fresh, fruity taste and smooth creamy texture. It could win a beauty prize, too. The delicate pink divinity is set off by a crown of sparkling scarlet cherries.

　　3 cups (720ml or 600g) granulated sugar

　　¾ cup (180ml) light corn syrup

　　¾ cup (180ml) water

　　2 egg whites, room temperature

　　3 ounce package (84g) cherry flavored gelatin

　　1 cup (240 ml or 225g) chopped candied cherries

Before you begin, line an 10" (25.4cm) square pan with foil and lightly butter the foil. Chop and measure the cherries. Place egg whites in large bowl of mixer.

1. Combine sugar, corn syrup and water in a three-quart (three-liter) heavy saucepan. Set over high heat and stir constantly with a wooden spoon until all sugar crystals are dissolved. Wash down sides of pan with a pastry brush dipped in hot water. Clip on thermometer and cook, without stirring, to 252°F (122°C), about 35 minutes. Wash down sides of pan twice more as mixture cooks. Remove from heat.

2. As mixture is cooking, beat egg whites with mixer set at highest speed. When peaks form, sprinkle gelatin over egg whites and continue beating until well blended. Scrape sides of bowl frequently.

3. Pour hot cooked syrup over beaten egg white mixture in a thin stream as you continue beating at high speed. Do not scrape bottom of pan. Test by dropping a bit of candy on wax paper. If it is glossy and holds its shape, candy is finished.

4. Scrape into prepared pan with a rubber scraper. Swirl from center to sides of pan to level. If necessary, dip a spatula in hot water and press lightly to smooth. Sprinkle cherries evenly over surface of candy and press with spatula dipped in cold water. Cool until firm at room temperature, about four hours. Dip a long sharp knife in cold water and cut into 1" (2.5cm) squares. Store, uncut and closely covered with foil or plastic wrap, in the refrigerator for up to three weeks. Yield: 100 pieces.

GRASSHOPPER DIVINITY*

Creamy texture, the subtlest, softest hint of mint and a crown of chocolate make this new divinity just irresistable.

　　2 cups (480ml or 400g) granulated sugar

　　½ cup (120ml) water

　　¼ cup (60ml) light corn syrup

　　pinch of salt

　　2 egg whites, room temperature

　　1 tablespoon (15ml) Creme de Menthe

　　3 drops green liquid food coloring

　　6 ounces (168g) semi-sweet chocolate morsels

Before you begin, line an 8" (20.3cm) square pan with foil and lightly butter the foil. Place egg whites in large bowl of mixer.

1. Place sugar, water, syrup and salt in a heavy three-quart (three-liter) saucepan. Set pan over medium-high heat and stir constantly with a wooden spoon until all sugar crystals are dissolved. Wash down sides of pan with a pastry brush dipped in warm water, then clip on thermometer. Cook, *without stirring,* until thermometer registers 260°F (127°C), about 17 minutes. Remove from heat. Wash down sides of pan twice more during cooking period.

2. Start to beat the egg whites when the mixture above comes to a boil. Beat at highest speed to stiff peaks. Pour cooked mixture into beaten egg whites in a very thin stream, beating at highest speed. Continue beating about six minutes, adding Créme de Menthe and food coloring as you beat. Mixture will be glossy and thicken rapidly. If candy becomes too heavy for mixer to function, use a wooden spoon instead, and beat about two minutes longer. Test for consistency by dropping a small spoonful on wax paper. If it holds its shape and remains glossy, candy is finished.

3. Scrape into prepared pan. Butter a spatula and press to level candy. Sprinkle chocolate morsels on top and press lightly into divinity. Allow to cool and firm about 30 minutes at room temperature. Cut into 1" (2.5cm) squares with a sharp, buttered knife. To store, wrap uncut candy closely in foil or plastic wrap and refrigerate for several weeks. Yield: 64 pieces.

May be used as centers for dipping

WILTON VANILLA NOUGAT*

This is the smooth, firm, delicately chewy classic nougat. Confectionery coating makes it set up very quickly.

- 2 cups (480ml) light corn syrup
- ¾ cup (180ml or 150g) granulated sugar
- ⅓ cup (80ml) water
- 2 egg whites, room temperature
- 5 ounces (140g) white confectionery coating, chopped, or 5 ounces of wafers
- 1 teaspoon (5ml) clear vanilla

Before you begin, line an 8" (20.3cm) square pan with foil and lightly butter the foil. Place egg whites in large bowl of electric mixer. Chop the coating.

1. Combine corn syrup, sugar and water in a three-quart (three-liter) heavy saucepan. Stir constantly with a wooden spoon until all sugar crystals are dissolved. Wash down sides of pan with a pastry brush dipped in hot water. Clip on thermometer.

2. When above mixture comes to a boil, set mixer at highest speed and beat egg whites to stiff peaks. When cooking mixture reaches 250°F (121°C), about 15 minutes, take out 1/2 cup (120ml) of it in a metal measuring cup. Set mixer at lowest speed and slowly pour the half cup of hot syrup into the beaten egg whites.

3. Allow mixer to remain at lowest speed while remaining syrup continues to cook to 280°F (138°C), about 24 more minutes. Remove from heat.

4. Turn mixer to medium speed and pour remaining syrup in a thin stream into egg white mixture. Do not scrape pan. When syrup is thoroughly incorporated, turn off mixer, add chopped coating and vanilla and stir by hand until well blended. Do not beat. Pour into prepared pan and refrigerate until firm, about one to two hours. Slice into ¾" x 1¼") 1.9cm x 3.2cm) bars with a sharp knife and a sawing motion. In tightly sealed box, keeps for a week at room temperature. Or wrap uncut candy closely in foil or plastic wrap and refrigerate for up to three weeks. Yield: about 64 pieces.

PISTACHIO NOUGAT

Fold one cup (240ml or 125g) pistachios into Wilton Vanilla Nougat after coating has been stirred in.

LEMON COCONUT NOUGAT*

Gelatin makes this new, light nougat foolproof and very easy to put together. You'll like the delicate tint, fruity taste and the surprise of coconut. Try dipping this nougat in dark chocolate—it's fantastic!

- 3 cups (720ml or 600g) granulated sugar
- ¾ cup (180ml) light corn syrup
- ¾ cup (180ml) water
- 2 egg whites, room temperature
- 3-ounce package (84g) lemon flavored gelatin
- 2 or 3 drops yellow liquid food coloring
- 1½ cups (360ml or 112g) flaked coconut

Before you begin, line a 10" (25.4cm) square pan with foil and butter the foil. Put egg whites into large bowl of mixer.

1. Combine sugar, corn syrup and water in a three-quart (three-liter) heavy saucepan. Place over high heat and stir constantly with a wooden spoon until all sugar crystals are dissolved. Wash down sides of pan with a pastry brush dipped in hot water, then clip on thermometer. Continue cooking, without stirring, until thermometer registers 252°F (122°C), washing down sides of pan twice more. Remove from heat. Cooking process will take about 12 to 15 minutes.

2. Start to beat egg whites when syrup mixture comes to a boil. Beat at highest speed until soft peaks form. Sprinkle gelatin over beaten egg whites, then beat again until stiff peaks form. Turn off mixer.

3. Pour hot syrup mixture over egg white mixture in a thin stream, beating constantly at highest speed. Add food coloring while beating. After all hot syrup has been incorporated, test candy by dropping a little on wax paper. If it holds its shape, candy is finished. The beating will take only four or five minutes. Fold in coconut.

Use a rubber scraper to spread candy in prepared pan. If necessary, level the surface with a clean scraper dipped in hot water. Allow to firm for one hour in the refrigerator, or about an hour and a half at room temperature. Cut in 1" (2.5cm) squares, using a long sharp knife dipped in hot water. Serve immediately, or wrap the uncut candy closely in plastic wrap and refrigerate for up to three weeks. Yield: 100 pieces.

FRENCH ALMOND NOUGAT*

One of the finest nougats—just slightly chewy, with a delicate almond flavor. For real luxury, dip in light or dark chocolate.

1½ cups (360ml or 250g) granulated sugar

1 cup (240ml) light corn syrup

¾ cup (180ml) water

2 egg whites, room temperature

4 drops pink liquid food coloring

½ teaspoon (2.5ml) salt

½ teaspoon (2.5ml) butter

½ teaspoon (2.5ml) clear vanilla extract

½ teaspoon (2.5ml) almond extract

¾ cup (180ml or 115g) chopped almonds, crisped

Before you begin, crisp the nuts. Line an 8" (20.3cm) square pan with foil and butter the foil. Place egg whites in large mixer bowl.

1. Combine sugar, corn syrup and water in a three-quart (three-liter) heavy saucepan. Stir constantly with a wooden spoon until all sugar crystals are dissolved. Wash down sides of pan with a pastry brush dipped in hot water. Clip on thermometer. Continue cooking, without stirring. Wash down sides of pan twice more as mixture cooks.

2. When temperature of cooked mixture reaches 240°F (116°C), set mixer at highest speed and beat egg whites to stiff peaks. Turn off mixer.

3. Continue cooking mixture until thermometer registers 275°F (135°C). Remove from heat. Entire cooking time is about 15 minutes. Turn mixer to highest speed as you pour hot cooked mixture in a thin stream into beaten egg whites. Do not scrape cooking pan. Add food coloring and butter while beating. When candy is very thick and glossy, turn off mixer. This will take about five minutes. Fold in salt, flavoring and nuts with a rubber scraper. Scrape out of bowl into prepared pan. Level surface with a spatula dipped in hot water. Allow to firm about two hours at room temperature. Cut into ¾" x 1" (1.9cm x 2.5cm) bars and place in candy cups. Store for several days at room temperature in sealed box. To store for up to three weeks, wrap uncut candy closely in plastic wrap or foil and refrigerate. Yield: about 80 pieces.

ITALIAN TORRONE*

This colorful version of nougat is rich in nuts and fruit and flavored with the flowery sweetness of honey. Its tender texture makes it especially good when formed into a log and dipped in chocolate. Be sure to cook in a four-quart (four-liter) pan. The mixture foams up at boiling point.

½ cup (120ml) honey

3 cups (720ml or 600g) granulated sugar

⅔ cup (160ml) hot water

2 egg whites, room temperature

⅔ cup (160ml or 80g) chopped walnuts, crisped

⅔ cup (160ml or 150g) chopped candied cherries

Before you begin, crisp the nuts (Chapter 2). Chop and measure the cherries. Line a 10" (25.4cm) square pan with foil and lightly butter the foil. Place egg whites in large mixer bowl. Have a metal measuring cup with handle at hand.

1. Combine honey, sugar and water in a four-quart (four-liter) heavy saucepan. Stir constantly with a wooden spoon until all sugar crystals are dissolved. Then clip on thermometer.

Meanwhile, beat egg whites at high speed until stiff peaks form. When cooking mixture reaches 230°F (110°C) take out 2/3 cup (160ml) of it, using a metal measuring cup with handle. Pour this in a thin stream into the whipped egg whites as you beat at highest speed. Turn off mixer.

2. Continue cooking the honey mixture to 265°F (129°C), then remove from heat. Wash down sides of pan twice more as mixture cooks. Entire cooking time is about 20 minutes.

3. Pour hot cooked mixture in a thin stream into egg white mixture, as you beat at highest speed. Do not scrape cooking pan. When mixture begins to thicken, stop mixer and fold in nuts and cherries. Remove from bowl with a rubber scraper and press into prepared pan. Refrigerate overnight. Cut into 1¼" x 3/4" (3.2cm x 1.9cm) pieces. Place pieces in fluted paper candy cups, pack closely in box, cover with plastic wrap and put lid on box. Store for a week at room temperature. To store for up to three weeks, wrap uncut candy closely in plastic wrap and refrigerate. Yield: about 100 pieces.

WILTON
FIRM CHOCOLATE NOUGAT*

A classic, mild-flavored nougat with a chewy but tender texture. This is delicious dipped in dark chocolate, but very good "as is".

    2 egg whites, room temperature
    2 cups (480ml) light corn syrup
    ⅓ cup (80ml) water
    ¾ cup (180ml or 150g) granulated sugar
    5 ounces (140g) milk chocolate, chopped
    1 teaspoon (5ml) vanilla

Before you begin. This candy firms very fast at the end, so be sure to have your mixer set up near the stove and everything you need at hand ahead of time. Chop chocolate finely as possible. Line an 8" (20.3cm) square pan with foil and butter the foil. Place egg whites in large bowl of mixer.

1. Combine corn syrup, water and sugar in a heavy three-quart (three-liter) saucepan. Place over high heat and stir constantly with a wooden spoon until all sugar crystals are dissolved. Wash down sides of pan with a pastry brush dipped in hot water. Clip on thermometer.

2. Continue cooking, without stirring, until mixture reaches 240°F (116°C). Set mixer at highest speed and beat egg whites to stiff peaks, then set mixer at lowest speed. When mixture reaches 250°F (121°C), take about a half-cup of it from pan and slowly pour it into beaten egg whites. (Use a half-cup metal measuring cup with handle.)

3. Continue to cook remaining mixture in pan, allowing mixer to continue to beat at low speed. When temperature reaches 280°F (138°C), remove from heat. This will take just a few minutes. Turn mixer to medium speed and slowly pour remaining hot mixture in a thin stream into egg white mixture. Do not scrape cooking pan. Just as soon as it is thoroughly incorporated, just a minute or two, turn off mixer. Entire cooking and mixing time will be about 16 to 18 minutes.

4. Immediately stir in chocolate and vanilla with a wooden spoon. Mixture will set up quickly. Remove from bowl with a rubber scraper and press into prepared pan. Dip scraper in hot water and press to level if necessary. Allow to cool and firm at room temperature about an hour and a half. Cut into 3/4" x 1" (1.9cm x 2.5cm) bars with a buttered knife and a sawing motion. Set each bar in a paper candy cup, pack closely in a box, cover with plastic wrap and cover the box. Keep at room temperature for several days. Or refrigerate, uncut, for several weeks, wrapped closely in foil or plastic wrap. Yield: about 80 pieces

NOUGAT CARAMEL PINWHEELS

Rich, smooth, mellow and absolutely delicious! Everyone loves these cute little pinwheels made of chewy nougat and buttery caramel.

    1 recipe Wilton Caramel for Dipping (page 61)
    1 recipe Wilton Vanilla Nougat (page 69)

Before you begin, line a 12" (30.5cm) square pan with foil and lightly butter the foil. Or butter your marble slab and arrange metal candy bars on it to form a 12" square. Butter inner surfaces of bars.

1. Make the caramels according to recipe directions and firm in prepared pan or on marble slab.

2. Prepare nougat recipe. When finished beating, spread over cooled and firmed caramel, leaving about 2" (5.1cm) at one end of caramel uncovered. Press with buttered spatula. Allow to firm and cool several hours or overnight.

3. Turn candy out of pan, or remove from marble slab. Lightly butter a smooth surface and your hands, and roll into a tight cylinder, starting with end covered with nougat. Lengthen the cylinder by rolling it with your hands near the center and gradually moving them out toward the ends. Cut the cylinder in two as it lengthens, and roll each half individually. When the cylinders are about 1" (2.5cm) in diameter, slice into ½" (1.3cm) pieces, using a sharp knife and a sawing motion. Put each slice in a fluted paper candy cup, pack into a box, cover with plastic wrap and place lid on box. It will keep for up to two weeks at room temperature. Or wrap the uncut cylinders tightly in foil or plastic wrap and refrigerate for a month or more. Yield: 100 pieces.

*May be used as centers for dipping

HOW TO FORM DIVINITY AND NOUGAT LOGS

Both of these candies are perfect for making centers or logs. Here's the easy way to form them.

Divinities are delicate and must be handled carefully. Any divinity in this chapter makes a good log center.

1. Cool and firm the candy as recipe directs. Cut the finished block of candy in half, reserving one half to cut in squares for serving. Cut remaining half in two, making two squares. Work with one square at a time.

2. Lightly butter a smooth surface or your marble slab. With buttered hands, knead the square very lightly, just enough to roll into a cylinder about 9½" (24.2cm) long. If you plan to dip the logs in confectionery coating or chocolate, cut each in two. For covering with caramel, do not cut. Wrap each log in buttered wax paper, smoothing after it is wrapped. Put logs in freezer for ten minutes before dipping or covering with caramel.

3. For dipping in confectionery coating, consult Chapter 3. For dipping in chocolate, consult Chapter 11. Chapter 6 tells how to cover the logs in caramel, then coat them with crisp chopped nuts. A half-recipe of divinity makes two generous 10" (25.4cm) logs or four 5" (12.7cm) logs.

Nougats make perfect log centers.
1. When you have finished beating the candy, turn out on buttered cookie sheet or buttered marble slab. Allow to cool slightly for a few minutes.

2. With a sharp buttered knife, cut the candy in four roughly equal pieces. With buttered hands, knead each piece on a lightly buttered surface, then roll into a cylinder about 12" (30.5cm) long, 1" (2.5cm) in diameter. Cut each log in two, press ends to flatten and wrap tightly in wax paper. Refrigerate until ready to dip or cover in caramel. A nougat recipe makes eight logs, each about 6" (15.2cm) long. If you prefer, turn half of the recipe into a 6" (15.2 cm) square pan for cutting and serving —make four logs from the other half. Consult Chapter 6 for covering with caramel, Chapters 3 and 11 for dipping in coating or chocolate.

Finished logs store very well because the covering keeps the center fresh. Wrap logs tightly in foil or plastic wrap. Logs dipped in chocolate or coating may be kept in a cool place for up to a month. Caramel-covered logs may be stored for a week at room temperature, for three weeks in the refrigerator, or frozen for months.

HOW TO FORM CENTERS FOR DIPPING FROM DIVINITY OR NOUGAT

For divinity centers, cut the firmed candy in ½" (1.3cm) or ¾" (1.9cm) squares. Or you may dip divinity puffs to create casually shaped candies. Make puffs a little smaller than usual.

For nougat centers, cut firmed candy in bars, about ½" x 1" (1.3cm x 2.5cm).

Dip centers in confectionery coating, as Chapter 3 directs. Or dip in chocolate, Chapter 11.

Here are a few suggestions for mouth-watering log combinations. You'll invent many more.

CHOCOLATE NUT NOUGAT LOG

Center: ½ recipe Wilton Firm Chocolate Nougat, room temperature.

Dip in: 2 pounds (908g) of milk chocolate. See Chapter 11.

Final touch: 8 ounces (227g) chopped walnuts, crisped. Place nuts in shallow pan. Deposit freshly dipped log in nuts, heap nuts on log and press lightly.

BUTTERSCOTCH CARAMEL DIVINITY LOG

Center: ½ recipe Butterscotch Pecan Divinity.

Cover with: 1 recipe Rum Caramel Kisses, almonds omitted. See Chapter 6.

Final touch: 8 ounces (227g) chopped pecans, crisped. Place nuts on square of wax paper. Brush log with corn syrup, then roll in nuts, pressing firmly.

TROPICAL NOUGAT LOG

Center: ½ recipe Lemon Coconut Nougat. Use pineapple flavored gelatin instead of lemon gelatin. Omit yellow food coloring and substitute ten drops of orange liquid food coloring.

Dip in: 2 pounds (908g) of white confectionery coating, chopped, or 2 pounds wafers. See Chapter 3.

Final touch: 14 ounces (398g) flaked coconut. Deposit freshly dipped log in coconut, heap coconut over log and press lightly.

Chapter 8

MARSHMALLOWS AND JELLIES

These candies are among the most creative you can make! After you've made a few of each, and seen how easy it is, put your imagination to work to vary the recipes. Marshmallows and jellies depend on gelatin (or pectin) for their texture. Marshmallows are beaten with an electric mixer to achieve their characteristic fluffiness. Both are light enough for summer, bright enough for holidays.

Marshmallows made at home have very little resemblance to the purchased variety. They're light and fluffy as clouds! Flavors can be almost as varied and enticing as your imagination dictates—add your favorite extract, fold in crisp chopped nuts or bits of dried or candied fruits, cover them with toasted coconut or caramel or dip molded shapes in colorful confectionery coating or rich chocolate. Marshmallows have a bonus for weight watchers, too. Each luscious 1'' (2.5cm) cube contains only 20 calories!

A mixer takes the work out of making marshmallows—use either a hand-held or a table model. If you are making a cooked marshmallow and using a hand-held mixer, have a helper pour the hot syrup as you control the mixer.

Marshmallows are firmed on unglazed paper. A clean, cut-open brown paper bag is ideal. When dampened, the paper peels off easily. Dust the candies with a mixture of cornstarch and confectioners' sugar.

Jellies are a very traditional form of candy and one of the easiest to make. Their clear sparkling colors and distinct flavors are fascinating. You may firm jellies on unglazed paper, like marshmallows, but it is easier to finish the candies in a lightly oiled pan. Dust jellies with a mixture of cornstarch and confectioners' sugar for a soft glowing look, or with superfine sugar for sparkle. You may dip jellies in confectionery coating or chocolate (Chapters 3 and 11), first dusting off excess sugar—but most candy lovers prefer them unadorned.

At left, a box of Candy Stripes. In the jar, Coconut Covered Marshmallows, Caramel Marshmallows and Cherry Marshmallows. On the plate, Strawberry Turkish Delight, Walnut Cranberry Squares and Orange Jellies.

QUICK APRICOT MARSHMALLOWS*

The easiest of all to make and perhaps the most delicious—these marshmallows have a fresh, fruity flavor, a pretty pastel color and a heavenly, melt-in-your mouth texture.

2 three-ounce (84g each) packages apricot-flavored gelatin

⅓ cup (80ml) cold water

⅔ cup (160ml) light corn syrup

½ cup (120ml or 112g) finely chopped dried apricots

¼ cup (60ml or 25g) confectioners' sugar

¼ cup (60ml or 32g) cornstarch

Before you begin, fit a piece of clean porous paper in the bottom of an 8" (20.3cm) square pan. Chop and measure apricots.

1. Combine gelatin and cold water in top pan of a one-quart (one-liter) double boiler. Let stand five minutes, or until gelatin is firm. Bring water in lower pan to a simmer, set top pan in position and stir until gelatin is clear, just a few minutes.

2. Put gelatin and corn syrup in large mixer bowl. Beat at highest speed for about twelve minutes. Marshmallows are finished when mixture climbs sides of beaters and when ribbons fall off the beaters and hold their shape on surface of mixture. Fold in apricots. Spread into prepared pan with rubber scraper. Swirl from center to edges of pan to level. Refrigerate overnight.

3. Next morning, blend confectioners' sugar and cornstarch, then sift into a cookie sheet with 1" (2.5cm) sides. Loosen sides of marshmallow with a small spatula dipped in cold water. Turn out onto cookie sheet. Place a folded towel wrung out of cold water on top of the paper. In just a few minutes the paper will be moist enough to peel off easily. Heap cornstarch mixture on marshmallow, then cut into 1" (2.5cm) strips with a long serrated knife. Dip the knife in cold water to prevent sticking. Tumble the strips in cornstarch mixture, then cut each into 1" (2.5cm) squares with a scissors dipped occasionally in cold water. Tumble the squares in the cornstarch mixture and allow to remain on cookie sheet about an hour to dry. Brush with a clean dry pastry brush. Store in a tightly closed container or plastic bag for up to three weeks at room temperature. Yield: 64 marshmallows.

TO VARY THIS RECIPE
Use your favorite flavor of gelatin—all are delicious. Substitute chopped candied cherries, chopped nuts or crushed peppermint candy for the apricots.

FLUFFY UNCOOKED MARSHMALLOWS*

These go together so quickly and easily you'll be amazed. In less than half an hour you'll have a tempting batch of tender marshmallows cooling—ready for you to cut the next morning.

2 tablespoons (30ml or 14g) unflavored gelatin

⅓ cup (80ml) cold water

½ cup (120ml or 100g) granulated sugar

⅔ cup (160ml) light corn syrup

1 teaspoon (5ml) vanilla extract

¼ cup (60ml or 25g) confectioners' sugar

¼ cup (60ml or 32g) cornstarch

Before you begin, fit a piece of clean porous paper in an 8" (20.3cm) square pan.

1. Combine gelatin and cold water in top pan of a one-quart (one-liter) double boiler. Let stand five minutes or until gelatin is firm. Bring water in lower pan to a simmer, set top pan in position and stir until clear and syrupy. Add sugar and stir until sugar crystals are dissolved—just a minute or two.

2. Pour gelatin mixture into large mixer bowl. Add corn syrup and flavoring, then beat at highest speed of mixer. Test after twelve minutes. If mixture is very light and fluffy and ribbons dropped from beaters hold their shape on the surface of mixture, candy is finished. Remove from bowl with a rubber scraper and spread into prepared pan. Swirl from center to edge of pan to level. Refrigerate overnight.

3. Next morning, blend cornstarch and confectioners' sugar and sift onto a cookie sheet with 1" (2.5cm) sides. Loosen sides of marshmallow with a small spatula dipped in cold water. Invert onto cookie sheet. Moisten paper with a towel wrung out of cold water and peel off. Heap cornstarch mixture over surface of marshmallow. Remove to cutting board and cut into long 1" (2.5cm) wide strips with a serrated knife dipped in cold

water. Tumble strips in cornstarch mixture, then cut each into 1" (2.5cm) squares with a scissors dipped in cold water. Tumble squares in cornstarch mixture and allow to dry on cookie sheet for about an hour. Brush with a clean dry pastry brush. Store in a tightly closed container or plastic bag for three weeks at room temperature. Yield: 64 marshmallows.

WILTON BASIC COOKED MARSHMALLOWS*

Marshmallows made using this cooked-syrup method are a little firmer than the preceding recipes for uncooked marshmallows—but equally light and delicious.

  2 tablespoons (30ml or 14g) unflavored gelatin
  ½ cup (120ml) cold water
  2 cups (480ml or 400g) granulated sugar
  ¾ cup (180ml) light corn syrup
  ¾ cup (180ml) hot water
  2 teaspoons (10ml) vanilla
  ¼ cup (60ml or 25g) confectioners' sugar
  ¼ cup (60ml or 32g) cornstarch

Before you begin, line the bottom of an 8" (20.3cm) square pan with porous paper. Or lay paper on marble slab and arrange metal candy bars in an 8" (20.3cm) square.

1. Combine gelatin and ½ cup (120ml) cold water in large mixer bowl. Let stand while you cook syrup.

2. Combine sugar, corn syrup and 3/4 cup (180ml) hot water in a three-quart (three-liter) heavy saucepan. Place over high heat and stir constantly with a wooden spoon until all sugar crystals are dissolved. Wash down sides of pan with a pastry brush dipped in hot water, then clip on thermometer. Cook without stirring to 245°F (118°C), about ten minutes. Wash down sides of pan twice more while mixture cooks. Remove from heat.

3. Set mixer at highest speed. Slowly pour hot syrup in a thin stream over gelatin in bowl. Continue beating for about 15 minutes, or until ribbons dropped off the beater retain their shape on the surface of the mixture. Add vanilla toward end of beating. Use a rubber scraper to remove mixture from bowl into prepared pan or slab. Swirl from center to edges of pan to level. Let firm overnight at room temperature.

4. Blend cornstarch and confectioners' sugar, then sift into a cookie sheet with 1" (2.5cm) sides. Loosen sides of marshmallow with a small spatula dipped in cold water and turn out onto cookie sheet. Lay a damp folded towel on paper for a few minutes, then peel off paper. Heap cornstarch mixture on square of marshmallow, then cut in eight 1" (2.5cm) strips with a serrated knife dipped in cold water. Roll strips in cornstarch mixture, then cut each into eight 1" (2.5cm) squares with a scissors dipped in cold water. Tumble squares in cornstarch mixture and let stand for about an hour to dry. Brush with a clean dry pastry brush. Store at room temperature in an airtight container for up to three weeks.

COCONUT COVERED MARSHMALLOWS

Turn marshmallows into a crunchy caramel-flavored treat in just a few minutes! We recommend using purchased marshmallows — the homemade version is too tender.

  ½ cup (120ml) dark corn syrup
  ½ teaspoon (2.5ml) butter
  30 marshmallows
  1 cup (240ml or 85g) flaked coconut, toasted

Before you begin, toast coconut (Chapter 2). Place in shallow bowl or pan.

1. Combine syrup and butter in a small saucepan and stir over low heat just until heated through. Place six or eight marshmallows in a small heat-proof bowl and pour hot syrup over them. Tumble with a fork to coat, then drop into coconut. Tumble, then press to secure coconut and place on wax paper to harden.

2. Keep syrup over lowest heat as you work. Store in a tightly closed container or plastic bag for up to three weeks at room temperature. Yield: 30 candies.

*May be dipped in coating or chocolate

CHERRY MARSHMALLOWS*

This pale pink confection tastes just as good as it looks. Color Flow Mix gives a creamy but firm texture.

- ¾ cup (180ml) light corn syrup
- 2 teaspoons (10ml or 4g) Wilton Color Flow Mix
- 1 tablespoon (15ml) cold water
- 2 tablespoons (30ml or 14g) unflavored gelatin
- ⅓ cup (80ml) cold water
- 1 cup (240ml or 200g) granulated sugar
- ⅓ cup (80 ml) hot water
- ½ teaspoon (2.5ml) oil of cherry
- ½ cup (120ml or 112g) finely chopped candied cherries
- ¼ cup (60ml or 32g) cornstarch
- ¼ cup (60ml or 25g) confectioners' sugar

Before you begin, line bottom of an 8" (20.3 cm) square pan with porous paper. Or lay paper on marble slab and arrange metal candy bars in an 8" (20.3cm) square. Chop and measure cherries.

1. Put corn syrup in large mixer bowl. Combine Color Flow Mix with one tablespoon (15ml) cold water and add to corn syrup. Beat at low speed about 30 seconds. Combine gelatin with ⅓ cup (80ml) cold water and pour over corn syrup mixture.

2. Combine sugar and ⅓ cup (80ml) hot water in a heavy two-quart (two-liter) pan. Place over high heat and stir constantly until all sugar crystals are dissolved. Wash down sides of pan with a pastry brush dipped in hot water, then clip on thermometer. Continue cooking to 243°F (117°C), about ten minutes. Wash down sides of pan twice more as syrup cooks. Remove from heat.

3. Pour hot syrup in a thin stream into mixture in bowl as you beat at highest speed. Continue beating until a ribbon dropped from beater retains its shape on the surface of the mixture, about ten minutes. Add flavoring and food color toward end of beating. Fold in cherries. Spread in prepared pan or slab with a rubber scraper, swirling from center to edges to level surface. Allow to firm overnight at room temperature.

4. Blend cornstarch and confectioners' sugar, then sift onto cookie sheet with 1" (2.5cm) sides. Loosen sides of marshmallow with a small spatula dipped in cold water and turn out onto cookie sheet. Remove paper by moistening with a folded damp towel, then peeling off. Sift cornstarch mixture over marshmallow and cut in 1" (2.5cm) strips with a serrated knife dipped in cold water. Roll strips in cornstarch mixture, then cut each into eight 1" (2.5cm) squares with a scissors dipped in cold water. Tumble squares in cornstarch mixture, then allow to dry in cookie sheet about an hour. Brush with a clean dry pastry brush. Store in an airtight container for up to three weeks at room temperature. Yield: 64 marshmallows.

MOLDING MARSHMALLOWS

Dip light, tender marshmallow in colorful confectionery coating for holiday treats.

1. Prepare marshmallow as recipe directs. Wilton Basic Cooked Marshmallow or Fluffy Uncooked Marshmallow are good choices. Add food color and flavoring as you beat — lemon for yellow coating, mint for green, raspberry or cherry for pink, almond for white or chocolate flavored coating. If you like, fold in chopped nuts or candied fruits.

2. Large shapes, such as eggs or hearts, are best when molded first, then dipped in confectionery coating. Spray molds with non-stick pan release, then dust thoroughly with cornstarch. Spoon marshmallow mixture into mold, leveling top. Slightly underfill the mold, do not allow marshmallow to mound. Let firm overnight, then unmold. For a two-piece mold, such as a three-dimensional egg, mold each half separately. After unmolding, brush flat surface of one half with water, then lay second molded half on it. Dip in confectionery coating (Chapter 3).

If you wish the sharp details of the mold to show, first mold a hollow shape in confectionery coating. (See the shells in the picture at right). Spoon in marshmallow, then seal bottom of mold with coating. Marshmallows, in their pillowy square shapes, are good dipped in confectionery coating, too. Just follow directions in Chapter 3. To dip in chocolate, see Chapter 11.

3. For names, dots and other line decoration use tube 1 and contrasting coating. For larger trims, use tube 4. Use buttercream and tubes 23 or 225 to pipe blossoms on wax paper. When dry, attach with a dot of melted coating and add tiny leaves.

*May be dipped in coating or chocolate

CANDY STRIPES

A box of this gaily colored candy makes a cheery gift! Make it in a two-step method — first jelly, then marshmallow.

RASPBERRY JELLY LAYERS

  3 cups (720ml or 600g) granulated sugar

  ¼ cup (60ml) fresh lemon juice

  ⅔ cup (160ml) hot water

  4 tablespoons (60ml or 28g) unflavored gelatin

  ½ cup (120ml) cold water

  5 drops oil of raspberry

  6 drops red liquid food color

Before you begin, brush two 8" (20.3cm) square pans lightly with vegetable oil. Squeeze and measure the lemon juice. Sprinkle gelatin on ½ cup (120ml) cold water and set aside.

1. Combine sugar, lemon juice and hot water in a four-quart (four-liter) heavy saucepan. Set on high heat and stir constantly with a wooden spoon until all sugar crystals are dissolved. Wash down sides of pan with a pastry brush dipped in hot water, then clip on thermometer. Continue to cook, without stirring, until temperature reaches 250°F (121°C). Remove from heat.

2. Add gelatin mixture, oil of raspberry and food color and stir until well blended. Pour an equal amount of the mixture into each prepared pan. Let cool at room temperature about 30 minutes, then firm in refrigerator about an hour.

MARSHMALLOW LAYER

  ½ recipe Wilton Cooked Marshmallows (firm other half of recipe in a 6" (15.2cm) square pan)

  ½ cup (120ml or 98g) superfine sugar

1. While Raspberry Jelly is firming in refrigerator, prepare marshmallow recipe according to directions in this chapter. Pour half of completed recipe over firmed jelly layer in one pan.

2. Allow marshmallow layer to set about an hour at room temperature. Loosen firmed jelly layer in second pan and turn out on top of marshmallow layer. Allow candy to set at least two hours at room temperature.

3. Cut completed candy into 1" (2.5cm) squares with a knife dipped in cold water. Place superfine sugar in cookie sheet with 1" (2.5cm) sides and tumble squares to coat. Let candy remain in cookie sheet overnight, at room temperature, then tumble in sugar again. To store for several weeks, place each piece in a fluted paper candy cup and pack closely in a tightly sealed box. Yield: 64 pieces.

TO VARY THIS RECIPE
Use your imagination to create your own bright version of Candy Stripes. Flavor the jelly with peppermint and tint it green — or flavor with oil of lemon and tint yellow. The marshmallow layer can be tinted and flavored to your taste, too.

CARAMEL COVERED MARSHMALLOWS

These are rich, luscious, absolutely irresistible! Use purchased marshmallows — homemade marshmallows are too tender.

  1 finished recipe Wilton Caramel for Dipping (Chapter 6)

  36 purchased marshmallows, cut in half

  1 or 2 teaspoons (5 or 10ml) cream for thinning

Before you begin, cut each marshmallow in half with a scissors dipped in cold water for a shallower height. Line two cookie sheets with foil and lightly butter the foil.

1. After making the caramel recipe, allow it to stand for about ten minutes to cool. Set pan in a larger pan containing hot water. Dip the marshmallows in much the same way as you would dip a bonbon center in confectionery coating. Drop a half-marshmallow into the caramel mixture, then use a two-tined dipping fork to tumble. Lift out with fork beneath the marshmallow, and make several circling motions with the fork to allow excess caramel to drop off. Move fork to prepared cookie sheet and slide marshmallow off with tip of a paring knife. If caramel mixture becomes too thick, stir in a few drops of cream, then continue dipping.

2. Let candies firm overnight at room temperature. Place each in a fluted paper candy cup. Serve within a few hours, or wrap each candy in plastic wrap and refrigerate for up to three weeks. Yield: 72 candies.

QUICK PINEAPPLE JELLIES

Make these shimmering jels in just minutes! They're light, refreshing, not too sweet. Do not dust these candies with sugar—it will break them down.

- 4 tablespoons (60ml) or (28g) unflavored gelatin
- ⅓ cup (80ml or 67g) granulated sugar
- 2 cups (480ml) canned or bottled pine-apple juice
- 1 teaspoon (5ml) lemon extract
- 1 drop yellow liquid food color

Before you begin, brush an 8" (20.3cm) square pan lightly with vegetable oil.

1. Blend gelatin and sugar in a heatproof bowl. Bring pineapple juice to a boil, add to gelatin mixture and stir until gelatin is completely dissolved.

2. Add lemon extract and food color and stir until well blended. Pour into prepared pan and refrigerate about an hour until firm. Loosen jelly from sides of pan with a spatula and turn out onto cutting board. Dip a sharp knife in cold water and cut into 1" (2.5cm) squares. To store for several weeks, wrap uncut candy tightly in plastic wrap and refrigerate. Yield: 64 pieces.

QUICK CRANBERRY JELLIES

Just as quick and just as good as Quick Pine-apple Jellies—with an intriguing tart-sweet flavor. Do not dust with sugar—it will break them down.

- 4 tablespoons (60ml) or (28g) unflavored gelatin
- ⅓ cup (80ml or 67g) granulated sugar
- 2 cups (480ml) cranberry juice cocktail
- 1 teaspoon (5ml) lemon extract
- 4 drops red liquid food color

Before you begin, brush an 8" (20.3cm) square pan lightly with vegetable oil.

1. Blend gelatin and sugar in a heatproof bowl. Bring cranberry juice cocktail to a boil, add to gelatin mixture and stir until gelatin is completely dissolved.

2. Add lemon extract and food color and stir until well blended. Pour into prepared pan and refrigerate about an hour until firm. Loosen jelly from sides of pan with a spatula and turn out onto cutting board. Dip a sharp knife in cold water and cut into 1" (2.5cm) squares. To store for several weeks, wrap uncut candy tightly in plastic wrap and refrigerate. Yield: 64 pieces.

APPLE MINT JELLIES

Canned applesauce lends a light bubbly texture and a fresh flavor to this traditional recipe. Easy, pretty, almost foolproof.

- 3 tablespoons (45ml or 21g) unflavored gelatin
- ½ cup (120ml) cold water
- 15 ounces (425g) canned sweetened applesauce
- 2 cups (480ml or 400g) granulated sugar
- 4 drops green liquid food coloring
- 2 drops oil of peppermint
- ½ cup (120ml or 98g) superfine sugar for dusting

Before you begin, brush an 8" (20.3cm) square pan with vegetable oil.

1. Sprinkle gelatin over the cold water and set aside. Place applesauce and sugar in a two-quart (two-liter) saucepan and set on medium high heat. Stir constantly until all sugar crystals are dissolved, then wash down sides of pan with a pastry brush dipped in hot water. Clip on thermometer. Stir occasionally until thermometer registers 218°F (103°C). Continue cooking for five minutes. Mixture will hold the same temperature, and become thicker. Remove from heat.

2. Stir for about ten minutes until thermometer registers about 170°F (77°C). Add the gelatin by tablespoonfuls, stirring to thoroughly incorporate. Stir in food color and oil of peppermint.

3. Pour into prepared pan and cool at room temperature for 30 minutes. Refrigerate about two hours or until firm. Spread super-fine sugar on a cookie sheet. Loosen sides of candy and invert on cookie sheet. Heap sugar on candy. Cut into 1" (2.5cm) squares with a knife dipped in warm water. Tumble squares in sugar. Allow to stand uncovered overnight, then tumble squares to coat again. Place squares in paper candy cups and put in tightly sealed box. To store for several weeks, wrap uncut candy tightly in plastic wrap and refrigerate. Dust with sugar as described above.

WALNUT-CRANBERRY SQUARES

Serve this treat at holiday time—it's tangy. not too sweet and crunchy textured.

    1 16-ounce can (480ml) jellied cranberry
      sauce
    2 three-ounce (90ml or 85g) packages
      strawberry-flavored gelatin
    1 cup (240ml or 120g) finely chopped
      walnuts, crisped
    1 cup (240ml or 196g) superfine sugar

Before you begin, crisp the nuts (Chapter 2). Brush a 9" x 5" (22.9cm x 12.7cm) loaf pan with vegetable oil.

1. Combine cranberry sauce and gelatin in a heavy three-quart (three-liter) saucepan. Place on high heat and stir constantly until mixture comes to a full rolling boil, about eight minutes.

2. Stir in nuts and pour mixture into prepared pan. Cool in refrigerator about two hours. Spread sugar in a cookie sheet with 1" (2.5cm) sides. When firm, turn candy out of pan onto cookie sheet. Heap sugar on top of candy and cut into 1" (2.5cm) squares with a knife dipped in warm water. Tumble squares in sugar. Allow to remain overnight in sugar, then tumble to coat again. Place squares in paper candy cups, then in tightly sealed box. To store for several weeks, wrap uncut candy tightly in plastic wrap and refrigerate. Dust in sugar as described above before serving. Yield: 45 pieces.

TURKISH DELIGHT

An old-fashioned name for a refreshing jelly with the spritely tang of fresh lemon.

    2 tablespoons (30ml or 14g) unflavored
      gelatin
    ⅓ cup (80ml) fresh lemon juice
    3 tablespoons (45ml) cold water
    grated rind of one lemon
    2 cups (480ml or 400g) granulated sugar
    ⅔ cup (160ml) hot water
    5 drops yellow liquid food coloring
    ½ cup (120ml or 98g) superfine sugar for
      dusting.

Before you begin, brush a 6" (15.2cm) square pan with vegetable oil. Grate lemon rind.

1. Combine gelatin, lemon juice, cold water and lemon rind in a small bowl and let stand five minutes or more.

2. Combine granulated sugar and hot water in a heavy three-quart (three-liter) saucepan. Place over high heat and stir constantly with a wooden spoon until all sugar crystals are dissolved. Wash down sides of pan with a pastry brush dipped in hot water. Clip on thermometer and cook, without stirring to 236°F (113°C), about ten minutes. Remove from heat.

3. Stir in gelatin mixture. Place over medium heat and stir constantly until thermometer registers 224°F (107°C), only about two minutes. Remove from heat and stir in food coloring. Pour into prepared pan and let cool and firm overnight at room temperature. Spread superfine sugar in a cookie sheet. Loosen sides of candy from pan and invert on cookie sheet. Heap sugar on top of candy and cut into 1" (2.5cm) squares with a knife dipped in warm water. Tumble squares in sugar, let remain overnight in sugar, then coat again. Place in paper candy cups, then in tightly sealed box. To store for several weeks, wrap uncut candy tightly in plastic wrap and refrigerate. Yield: 36 pieces.

HOLIDAY MINT JELLY

Tender, flavorful, pretty as a picture!

    1 cup (240ml or 200g) granulated sugar
    1 cup (240ml) light corn syrup
    ¾ ounce (49g) package dry fruit pectin
    ¾ cup (180ml) cold water
    ½ teaspoon (2.5ml) baking soda
    2 drops oil of peppermint
    5 drops red liquid food coloring
    2 drops green liquid food coloring
    ½ cup (120ml or 98g) superfine sugar
      for dusting

Before you begin, lightly oil two 6" (15.2cm) square pans with vegetable oil.

1. Combine granulated sugar and corn syrup in a heavy two-quart (two-liter) saucepan. In a second two-quart saucepan, combine pectin, cold water and baking soda. Place both pans over high heat. Stir alternately until sugar mixture is at a full boil and foam has thinned from pectin mixture, about five minutes.

2. Pour pectin mixture in a thin stream into sugar mixture, stirring constantly. Boil one minute more, then remove from heat. Stir in oil of peppermint. Pour half of mixture into

another pan and stir in red food color. Tint other half with green food color. Pour into prepared pans and cool and firm at room temperature about three hours.

3. Spread superfine sugar in a cookie sheet with 1" (2.5cm) sides. Loosen candies from sides of pans and invert in cookie sheet. Heap sugar over candies, then cut in 1" (2.5cm) squares with a knife dipped in warm water. Tumble squares in sugar, then let stand in sugar overnight. Tumble again in sugar. Set each square in a paper candy cup and pack in a tightly sealed box. To store for three weeks, wrap uncut candy closely in plastic wrap and refrigerate. Yield: 36 red and 36 green candies.

ORANGE JELLIES

This candy is really good for you!

4 tablespoons (60ml or 28g) unflavored gelatin

½ cup (120ml) cold water

3 cups (720ml or 600g) granulated sugar

⅔ cup (160ml) hot water

⅓ cup (80ml) lemon juice

6 ounces (180ml) frozen concentrated orange juice, thawed

8 drops orange liquid food color

½ cup (120ml or 100g) superfine granulated sugar

Before you begin, line an 8" (20.3cm) square pan with foil and brush lightly with vegetable oil. Thaw orange juice. Sprinkle gelatin on cold water and set aside to soften.

1. Combine 3 cups (720ml or 600g) granulated sugar, hot water and lemon juice in a four-quart (four-liter) heavy saucepan. Place over medium heat and stir constantly with a wooden spoon until all sugar crystals are dissolved. Wash down sides of pan with a pastry brush dipped in hot water, then clip on thermometer. Continue to cook, without stirring, to 255°F (124°C), about 15 minutes. Wash down sides of pan twice more as mixture cooks. Remove from heat.

2. Add gelatin mixture, orange juice and food color. Stir until well blended. Pour into prepared pan and firm for several hours at room temperature.

3. Place superfine sugar in a cookie sheet with 1" (2.5cm) sides and turn out candy on it. Heap with sugar, cut into 3/4" (1.9cm) squares and tumble in sugar. Let squares remain in sugar overnight, then tumble again. To store for several weeks, wrap closely in plastic wrap and refrigerate. Cover with sugar as directed above. Yield: about 100 pieces.

Chapter 9
THE GLORIOUS TRUFFLE

Rich, silky, luxurious, with a unique melt-in-your mouth quality, the truffle is surely the ultimate in candies. At its most basic, the truffle is a simple uncooked mixture of chocolate and cream—see the Classic Chocolate Truffle in Chapter 1. The action of the chocolate on the liquid causes the mixture to stiffen. But truffles can be enriched with butter or egg yolk, perfumed by liqueurs, varied by substituting other liquids for cream—even given a pretty pastel appearance by using confectionery coating instead of chocolate.

Traditionally, the truffle is simply formed into a rough ball shape, then rolled in grated chocolate or cocoa to resemble its famous namesake. But truffles can also be enrobed in chocolate, dipped in pastel confectionery coating or rolled in coconut or chopped nuts. Truffles are a delightful treat anytime—but at their best as a sophisticated dessert with black coffee.

The recipes in this chapter have a medium firm consistency—but you can modify the texture to suit your taste. Add another ounce or two of chocolate and the truffle will become firmer—and still retain its delightful, melt-in-your mouth texture.

Unless you plan to dip your truffles in confectionery coating, we do not recommend making them in very warm weather.

CHERRY KIRSCH TRUFFLES

Melting rich with a light fluffy texture and a subtle cherry flavor! You can put this deluxe treat together in about 15 minutes.

- ¼ cup (60ml) whipping cream
- 9 ounces (252g) milk chocolate, chopped
- 2 tablespoons (30ml) kirsch
- ¼ cup (60ml or 56g) candied cherries, finely chopped

Before you begin, chop the chocolate. Chop and measure the cherries. Line a cookie sheet with wax paper.

1. Place cream in a small saucepan over medium heat and bring to boiling, stirring constantly. Remove from heat, add chopped chocolate, cover the pan and let stand three minutes to melt chocolate.

2. Stir mixture until smooth and chocolate is thoroughly blended. Stir in kirsch, a tablespoon (15ml) at a time, then blend in cherries. Refrigerate for an hour.

3. Remove pan from refrigerator and beat with a hand-held electric mixer at highest speed for three minutes. (If mixture appears to have separated while chilling, beating will bring it to an even, fluffy texture.) Take off portions with a dessert spoon and form into mounds on prepared cookie sheet. Refrigerate for 40 minutes. To store for up to three weeks, place candies in paper candy cups, then in tightly sealed box and refrigerate. Yield: about 45 truffles.

At right: an array of truffles. On upper level of server, Sour Cream Rum Truffles and Chocolate Mint Truffles. On lower level, Chocolate Almond Balls, Fresh Lemon Truffles and Orange Truffles.

ORANGE LIQUEUR TRUFFLES*

This might be your favorite truffle! It's richer than rich, perfumed with orange liqueur and flavored with the essence of fresh oranges. Just fabulous!

- 9 ounces (252g) semi-sweet chocolate, chopped
- 1½ tablespoons (23ml or 18g) super-fine sugar
- 2 tablespoons (30ml or 28g) unsalted butter
- ¼ cup (60ml) whipping cream
- 2 tablespoons (30ml) orange liqueur
- 1 tablespoon (15ml or 15g) grated fresh orange rind
- 1 egg yolk

Before you begin, chop the chocolate. Grate the skin of an orange with a small hand grater, measure and set aside. Line a 6" (15.2cm) square pan with foil, lightly butter the foil.

1. Combine chocolate, sugar, butter (cut in small pieces) and cream in the top pan of a one-quart (one-liter) double boiler. Bring 1" (2.5cm) of water in lower pan to a simmer, turn heat to low and put top pan in position. Stir with a wooden spoon until chocolate is melted and mixture is smooth. Remove from heat and take off upper pan.

2. Stirring constantly, gradually add liqueur, then grated rind. When mixture is luke-warm, stir in egg yolk and blend well. Pour into prepared pan and refrigerate about an hour, or until firm. To serve, turn out of pan, peel off foil and cut in 3/4" (1.9cm) pieces. Place each piece in a paper candy cup. To store for up to two weeks, wrap uncut candy closely in foil or plastic wrap and refrigerate. Yield: 64 pieces.

TO VARY THIS RECIPE

Form truffle balls by rolling each piece into a ball, then rolling in confectioners' sugar or cocoa.

SOUR CREAM RUM TRUFFLES

A subtle whiff of rum enhances these tangy, delectably rich confections.

- ½ cup (120ml or 65g) raisins, chopped
- 2 tablespoons (30ml) rum
- ⅓ cup (80ml or 75g) sour cream
- 9 ounces (252g) white confectionery coating, chopped, or 9 ounces wafers
- 1½ cups (360ml or 106g) flaked coconut for rolling

The day before you begin, chop raisins, place in small container, add rum and cover. Let stand at room temperature overnight. Before making truffles, line a cookie sheet with wax paper. Line a second sheet to receive the formed candies. Chop the confectionery coating finely.

1. Spread raisins on a paper towel to dry. Place sour cream in a small saucepan over low heat. Bring to a boil, stirring constantly with wooden spoon. As soon as cream reaches boiling point, remove from heat, add the chopped coating and cover the pan. Leave covered for three minutes to allow coating to melt.

2. Stir the sour cream mixture until perfectly blended and smooth. Add raisins, then place in freezer about seven minutes to cool and firm. Remove from freezer, stir to blend and drop by teaspoon (approximately 5ml) into mounds on prepared cookie sheet. Place cookie sheet into refrigerator to firm for about 45 minutes.

3. Spread coconut in a small pie tin or shallow bowl. Remove cookie sheet from refrigerator and form each truffle mound into a ball by rolling between your palms. As each ball is formed, drop into coconut and roll to coat. Place balls on prepared cookie sheet. If mixture becomes too soft, place in freezer a few minutes.

Store in refrigerator, well covered, for as long as several weeks.

Yield: about 40 3/4" (1.9cm) truffles.

*May be used as centers for dipping

CHOCOLATE ALMOND BALLS

The crunchy coating of crisp nuts contrasts with a creamy chocolate center. Heavenly!

6 ounces (168g) unsweetened chocolate, chopped

1⅓ cups (320ml) sweetened condensed milk

2 pounds (908g) white confectionery coating, chopped, or 2 pounds wafers

2 cups (480ml or 224g) finely chopped almonds, crisped

Before you begin, crisp the nuts. Chop chocolate and confectionery coating finely and place on separate sheets of wax paper. Line an 8" (20.3cm) square pan with foil.

1. Fill lower pan of one-quart double boiler with water to a depth of 1" (2.5cm). Bring to a simmer, then place top pan in position and pour in chopped chocolate. Remove from heat and stir until chocolate is melted.

2. Pour sweetened condensed milk in two-quart (two-liter) saucepan. Clip on thermometer and place over low heat. Stir constantly until thermometer registers 160°F (70°C). Remove from heat.

3. Pour melted chocolate into heated sweetened condensed milk, stirring until mixture is smooth and completely blended. Pour mixture into prepared pan and refrigerate an hour or more, or until firm. If you wish, you may leave overnight in refrigerator. While candy is cooling, line a cookie sheet with wax paper. Place nuts in small pie tin or shallow bowl.

4. Remove firm chocolate mixture from refrigerator, turn out of pan and peel off foil. Cut in 3/4" (1.9cm) squares. Working quickly, dust your hands in confectioners' sugar, and roll each piece into a ball between your palms. Place balls on prepared cookie sheet. If mixture becomes too soft, place in refrigerator to harden for a few minutes.

5. Melt confectionery coating and dip balls as described in Chapter 3. Place dipped balls in pan of nuts and roll to coat. Continue until all balls are dipped and coated. Store, well covered, for several weeks in the refrigerator. Remaining coating may be hardened on foil and saved for future use. Store leftover nuts in sealed container in refrigerator. Yield: about 100 pieces.

CHOCOLATE MINT TRUFFLES

A very traditional, very delicious truffle. A touch of mint accents the rich chocolate.

6 ounces (168g) milk chocolate, chopped

2 ounces (56g) butter

2 egg yolks

2 drops oil of peppermint

3 tablespoons (30ml) cocoa for rolling

Before you begin, chop the milk chocolate, weigh and place in top pan of a one-quart (one-liter) double boiler. Place egg yolks in a small bowl. Stir briefly with a fork, just to a smooth consistency. Cut butter in small pieces. Place cocoa in shallow bowl.

1. Fill lower pan of double boiler with hot water to a depth of 1" (2.5cm). Set on lowest heat and put top pan containing chocolate in position. Cover pan and let stand until partially melted—about two minutes. Uncover, and stir until completely melted and smooth. Remove top pan from lower pan. (Leave lower pan on lowest heat). Blend in the butter, a few pieces at a time, with a fork. Add a little of the warm chocolate mixture to the egg yolks in the bowl, then empty the bowl into the chocolate mixture.

2. Replace top pan on lower pan and stir gently for about two minutes. Stir in oil of peppermint and remove top pan. Place mixture, still in top pan, in freezer for just three minutes. Line a cookie sheet with wax paper to receive formed candies.

3. Remove pan from freezer, stir gently to smooth. Dust your palms with cocoa. Take off portions of the candy with a small dessert spoon, roll between your palms into balls and drop in cocoa. Roll to coat, then place balls on prepared cookie sheet. If mixture is too soft to form, let stand at room temperature for about 20 minutes to stiffen. Cover coated truffles loosely with wax paper overnight. Place in fluted paper candy cups to serve. Store at room temperature for a day or two. To store for up to two weeks, place in tightly sealed box and refrigerate. Bring to room temperature to serve. Yield: 20 truffles.

COFFEE AND CREAM TRUFFLES*

The name says it all—a full-bodied coffee flavor mellowed with cream.

　　2 pounds (908g) white confectionery coating, or 2 pounds wafers

　　1 cup (240ml) whipping cream

　　3 tablespoons (45ml) dry instant coffee

　　½ teaspoon (2.5ml) salt

Before you begin, line an 8" (20.3cm) square pan with foil. Chop the confectionery coating.

1. Bring water in lower pan of a two-quart double boiler just to a simmer. Turn heat to low, put top pan in position and pour in chopped coating. Stir constantly with wooden spoon until coating is almost melted. Remove from heat, leaving lower pan in position, and continue stirring until coating is completely melted.

2. In a small saucepan, heat cream to 160°F (70°C), stirring in coffee and salt.

3. Add cream mixture to melted coating, stirring just until completely blended. If mixture appears grainy and curdled, do not be concerned—it will smooth out as it cools. Pour into prepared pan. Refrigerate until firm, about 30 minutes. Droplets of moisture may form on surface while cooling. They will be absorbed as candy firms.

Cut into 3/4" (1.9cm) squares. To store for weeks in the refrigerator, wrap closely, uncut, in foil or plastic wrap. Let stand a few minutes at room temperature before cutting. Yield: about 100 pieces.

SWISS CHOCOLATE TRUFFLES

This satiny European truffle is given a traditional finish by dipping twice in chocolate.

　　1 cup (240ml) whipping cream

　　1 pound, 6 ounces (625g) semi-sweet chocolate, chopped

　　3 tablespoons (45ml) rum

　　2 pounds (908g) tempered dark chocolate for dipping (page 107)

Before you begin, chop the semi-sweet chocolate. Line a cookie sheet with wax paper.

1. Place cream in small saucepan and set over low heat. Stirring constantly, bring to a boil. Remove from heat and add the chopped semi-sweet chocolate. Stir until chocolate is melted and mixture is smooth.

Stir in rum. Place pan in refrigerator about an hour, or until mixture is stiff.

2. Remove pan from refrigerator, stir briefly and drop by teaspoon into mounds on prepared cookie sheet. Refrigerate again to harden, about 30 minutes, then form into balls by rolling between your palms. Place balls on second prepared cookie sheet. Dip immediately, or refrigerate until ready to dip.

3. To dip in chocolate, consult Chapter 11. Temper the dark chocolate, then dip each ball and deposit on wax paper. When dipped candies have hardened, dip a second time. Deposit on a coarse screen placed over a shallow pan. Roll the freshly dipped candies over the screen, then place on wax paper to harden. Place candies in paper candy cups, then in tightly sealed box. Store in a cool place for up to a month. Yield: about 65 truffles.

MOCHA CREAM TRUFFLES*

These candies have a firm texture but melt in the mouth like all truffles.

　　1 cup (240ml) whipping cream

　　2 pounds (908g) chopped confectionery coating, milk chocolate flavor, or 2 pounds wafers

　　3 tablespoons (45ml) dry instant coffee

　　½ teaspoon (2.5ml) salt

Before you begin, finely chop the confectionery coating. Line an 8" (20.3cm) square pan with foil.

1. Bring water in lower pan of a two-quart (two-liter) double boiler just to a simmer. Turn heat to low, put top pan in position and pour in chopped coating. Stir constantly until coating is almost melted. Remove from heat. Leaving top pan in position on lower pan, continue stirring until coating is completely melted.

2. Pour cream into a small saucepan. Place over low heat and clip on thermometer. Stir constantly, blending in coffee and salt. At 160°F (70°C), remove from heat.

3. Pour cream mixture into melted coating and stir just until completely blended. Pour into prepared pan and refrigerate until firm —about 30 minutes. Cut into 3/4" (1.9cm) squares. Refrigerate, uncut and closely wrapped in foil or plastic wrap for several weeks. Yield: about 100 pieces.

FRESH LEMON TRUFFLES

You'll love these sunshiny confections with the fresh flavor of lemon.

- 1½ cups (360ml or 127g) shredded coconut
- 5 drops yellow liquid food coloring
- ½ teaspoon (2.5ml) milk
- 9 ounces (252g) white confectionery coating, chopped, or 9 ounces wafers
- 1 teaspoon (5ml) freshly grated lemon rind
- ⅓ cup (80ml) whipping cream

Before you begin, tint coconut. Place coconut in a plastic bag, blend food coloring with milk in a large spoon and add to coconut. Twist bag to seal and knead until coconut is evenly tinted. Place in shallow bowl. Chop coating and grate lemond rind. Line two cookie sheets with wax paper.

1. Place cream in a small saucepan over low heat and bring to a boil, stirring constantly. Remove from heat, add chopped coating and cover the pan for three minutes to melt. Add lemon rind and stir until mixture is smooth and well blended. Place pan in freezer about seven minutes to cool and firm.

2. Remove pan from freezer and stir to blend. Drop mixture by teaspoon (15ml) into mounds on prepared cookie sheet. Place in refrigerator about 45 minutes to harden.

3. Form each mound into a ball by rolling between your palms. Drop into coconut and roll to coat. If mounds become too soft to form, place in freezer a few minutes to harden. Store, closely covered, in refrigerator for up to several weeks. Yield: about 40 truffles.

*May be used as centers for dipping

Above: Swiss Chocolate Truffles are double dipped for rough texture

Chapter 10

INDISPENSABLE FONDANT
KEY TO MANY FINE CANDIES

Do you want to build a reputation as a creator of really fine candies? Then master the art of making fondant. There are just three basic recipes for fondant—Corn Syrup, Cream of Tartar and Buttercream. The first two are interchangeable and all-purpose. Buttercream is a rich concoction to use for centers of chocolates. We're also including a new chocolate fondant that's deliciously rich. All are easy and fun to make. *Be sure to use cane sugar,* not beet sugar, in making fondant. Beet sugar foams up too much.

Versatile fondant is the base of many confections. With it you can form creamy centers in an almost endless variety of flavors—then dip them in rich chocolate, or in one of the many colors of confectionery coating. You can melt fondant and use it to dip centers for traditional pastel bonbons. Or coat cubes of cake in melted fondant to make delicious tiny petits fours. Fondant, tinted and flavored, creates elegant mints that add so much to a party.

Fondant stores very well. Make it even several months ahead, put it in an airtight container, cover it with a damp towel and seal the container. Keep it in the refrigerator and it will be ready for making mints, centers or for dipping whenever you are. Bring to room temperature before using.

What do you need to make fondant? Ideally, a marble slab about 15" x 25" (38.1cm x 63.5cm), a set of metal candy bars and a scraper. A paint scraper with a blade at least 3" (7.6cm) wide is satisfactory, but a candy scraper with a 5" (12.7cm) blade is even better. If you don't have a marble slab or metal candy bars, we'll describe an alternate method later in this chapter.

Fondant is really easy and fun to make. As you work the simple cooked syrup mixture you'll watch it change like magic—first thickening and whitening, then turning into a stiff mass. Follow the picture lesson starting on the next page as demonstrated by Norman Wilton and work some candy magic of your own.

At left, cake cubes dipped in pastel fondant make a tray as pretty as a bouquet. Decorate them with dainty piped flowers and the sparkle of piping gel. Directions are on page 100.

WILTON CORN SYRUP FONDANT
. . . A PICTURE LESSON

Here is a newly developed fondant recipe easily made in any kitchen. It's a quick method, too—in just an hour you'll produce a creamy all purpose fondant.

Here, Norman Wilton shows you, step by step, just how easy it is to make fondant. Read through the recipe, following the pictures, then make your own batch of perfect all-purpose fondant.

    2 cups (480ml) hot water

    6 cups (1.5 l 1.2kg) granulated sugar

    ¾ cup (180ml) light corn syrup

Before you begin, arrange metal candy bars on a clean marble slab. An area of about 12" x 18" (30.5cm x 45.7cm) is right for this recipe. Make sure there is at least 6" (15.2cm) of free space on all sides of the bars to allow room for working with the scraper. If you're using an electric range, turn heat unit to highest temperature.

If you have a larger marble surface, 30" x 36" (76.2cm x 91.4cm) approximately, or more, you will not need metal candy bars. Just pour the cooked syrup in the center of the marble surface.

1. Stir water and sugar together in a heavy three-quart (three-liter) saucepan. Place pan over highest heat and add corn syrup. Place pastry brush and thermometer in a container of hot tap water. When mixture comes to a boil, about 15 minutes, wash down the sides of the pan above the liquid with the wet pastry brush. Clip on thermometer. Continue cooking, without stirring, washing down sides of pan twice more. When temperature reaches 240°F (116°C) remove from heat. This will take only about seven minutes. Allow to stand a minute until bubbles subside.

2. Immediately pour the hot syrup onto the prepared marble slab. Pour the syrup *away* from you, and do not scrape pan. Now let the fondant cool, *without touching it,* to lukewarm. If you give in to curiosity and repeatedly put your finger on the fondant to test the heat, the whole batch may crystalize as it turns back to sugar.

After about 15 minutes, you will notice tiny wrinkles forming at the edges of the fondant, indicating it is cooling. Wait another 15 minutes and lightly touch the edge of the fondant. If it holds the imprint of your finger, feels lukewarm and at body temperature, the fondant is ready to work. Depending on the temperature of the room, the entire cooling process should take about 30 minutes.

3. After cooling, remove the candy bars and immediately begin to work the fondant with the scraper. Grasp the handle of the scraper with the back of your hand up. Holding the blade almost horizontal, move it under the edge of the fondant and lift it to the center. Work quickly from all sides, keeping the mass moving constantly.

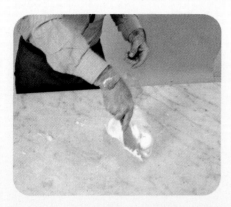

4. After about five minutes, the fondant will begin to appear white, then creamy. Continue working it until it becomes stiff and can be formed into a mound. It should be stiff enough so you can stand the scraper straight up in it.

5. Now knead the mass briefly, about three minutes, until it becomes soft and creamy. Place in a container (a plastic bowl with a cover is ideal). Dip a clean kitchen towel in cold water, wring it out until it is just damp, and cover the fondant. Seal the container.

Use immediately, or store at room temperature for several days. Or store in the refrigerator for several months. After a day or two, check the fondant. If liquid has formed on the surface, remove the towel and reseal the container. This recipe will yield enough fondant for over 300 mints or about 250 centers.

Note: fondant leftover from dipping bonbons may be refrigerated in a sealed container for weeks. *Do not use* this fondant for mints or centers—but you may melt it again for dipping bonbons or covering petits fours.

AN ALTERNATE METHOD OF WORKING FONDANT

You may use a large cookie sheet to pour the cooked fondant on to cool it. Select a heavy cookie sheet, 15" x 24" (38cm x 61cm) with 1" (2.5cm) sides. Set the cookie sheet on a cake rack to allow air to flow under it and promote even cooling.

Pour the cooked fondant on the cookie sheet. Pour *away* from you and *do not scrape pan.* Allow to cool. This will take about 20 to 25 minutes. You may test for coolness by touching the bottom of the cookie sheet. When it feels lukewarm the fondant is ready to work. Work it with the scraper just as described in the Picture Lesson at left. Knead and store just as described in the recipe for Wilton Corn Syrup Fondant.

HOW TO MAKE A "BOB" FROM WILTON CORN SYRUP FONDANT

Here is a shortcut method to increase your store of fondant. Since fondant is used in so many ways to make candy, this is a good timesaver. *Use only the corn syrup fondant recipe for a "bob".*

1. Make a recipe of Wilton Corn Syrup Fondant. Work the cooled fondant on the marble slab until it is stiff, just as described in the Picture Lesson at left.

2. Make a second recipe through Step 1. Remove pan from heat and add the finished, worked fondant you made before. Break the finished fondant into lumps with a wooden spoon and stir constantly until the mixture lightens and becomes perfectly smooth. You may now pour the mixture into a container, allow to cool, then cover tightly to store. Or you may use the "bob" while it is still liquid to drop mints.

Vary the quantity of the "bob" as you wish. Just remember to add an equal amount of finished, worked fondant to the same amount of newly cooked fondant.

WILTON
CREAM OF TARTAR FONDANT

This is just as easily made as Wilton Corn Syrup Fondant, page 92. Cream of tartar is used to keep the sugar from crystallizing.

It's important to cook this mixture as rapidly as possible—the cream of tartar does its work during the cooking period and if that is too long, the cream of tartar will make the fondant soft. That is why *hot* water is used, and an electric range is preheated.

We recommend using this recipe for mints because of its superior gloss. This quality makes it perfect for dipping, too.

   2 cups (480ml) *hot* water

   6 cups (1.5 liter or 1.2kg) granulated cane sugar

   ½ teaspoon (2.5ml) cream of tartar

Before you begin, arrange metal candy bars on marble slab to form an area about 12" x 18" (30.5cm x 45.7cm). Or prepare a large heavy cookie sheet as described in the Alternate Method, page 93. If your range is electric, turn a heat unit to high. Place pastry brush and thermometer in container of hot water.

1. Combine hot water and sugar in a heavy four-quart (four-liter) saucepan. Place pan on high heat and add cream of tartar. When mixture starts to boil, wash down sides of pan with a pastry brush dipped in hot water. Clip on thermometer. Wash down sides of pan twice more as mixture cooks. Do not stir. When temperature reaches 240°F (116°C), remove pan from heat and immediately pour out on slab or prepared cookie sheet. Entire cooking time should be about ten minutes or less.

2. Cool the fondant just as for Wilton Corn Syrup Fondant, page 92. When mixture is cool, remove bars and work vigorously with a metal scraper. In about five minutes, the fondant will become stiff. Knead briefly, just until soft and creamy. You may use immediately, or place in container, cover with a damp cloth and tightly cover the container. Keep at room temperature for several days, or store in the refrigerator for several months. Yield: enough to make about 250 centers or over 300 mints.

WILTON
BUTTERCREAM FONDANT

Here is the aristocrat of fondants, rich in butter and milk with a smooth creamy flavor and texture. Buttercream Fondant is used for centers of dipped candies only—never for dipping itself. Like Wilton Corn Syrup and Cream of Tartar Fondants, it can be varied in countless ways. With it you can make simple but deluxe chocolate creams or chocolates studded with nuts or fruit. Tint it any delicate color you like, flavor it with extracts or add the perfume of a distinguished liqueur—even use it to stuff dried or candied fruits.

To gain a reputation as a creator of truly exquisite candies, be sure to add this fondant to your repertoire of recipes. It's just as quick and easy to make as the other Wilton fondants. Please note: *medium*, rather than high, heat is needed for this recipe to prevent scorching.

   2½ cups (600ml or 500g) granulated cane sugar

   1 cup (240ml) milk

   2 tablespoons (30ml or 30g) butter

   ¼ teaspoon (1.2ml) cream of tartar

Before you begin, arrange metal candy bars on marble slab to form an area about 12" x 18" (30.5cm x 45.7cm). Or prepare a large heavy cookie sheet as described in the Alternate Method, page 93. Since this is a rather small recipe, as you pour out cooked syrup, it will seek its own level and flow to a rather thin depth. This will make the fondant cool more rapidly to be ready for working. Place pastry brush and thermometer in container of very hot water and set near stove.

1. Combine sugar, milk and butter (cut in small pieces) in a heavy three-quart (three-

liter) saucepan. Place on medium heat and add cream of tartar. Stir constantly with a wooden spoon until all sugar crystals are completely dissolved and mixture is almost at boiling point. It will foam up as it heats. Wash down sides of pan with wet pastry brush, then clip on thermometer. Continue cooking without stirring, washing down sides of pan twice more. When temperature reaches 236°F (113°C), immediately remove pan from heat. Entire cooking process will take about 15 minutes or less.

2. Pour out onto slab, or into prepared cookie sheet. Let cool to approximately body temperature, about 15 minutes, then work with a scraper just as the Picture Lesson, page 92, shows. Very soon the mixture will begin to whiten, then thicken. Continue working until it is very stiff and can be formed into a firm ball. Kneading is not necessary. You may form centers at once. To store for months, place in container with a tight cover, cover with a damp cloth and then seal cover. Keep refrigerated. Yield: about 55 centers for dipping.

NEW WILTON CHOCOLATE CREAM FONDANT

A new fondant, especially developed for chocolate lovers! This fondant is really an adaptation of Wilton Corn Syrup Fondant, page 92, and just as easy to make. It's smooth, rich and creamy—makes marvelous fudg-y centers and can be used for dipping, too.

    1⅓ cups (320ml) hot water

    4 cups (960ml or 800g) granulated cane sugar

    ½ cup (120ml) light corn syrup

    3 ounces (85g) unsweetened chocolate

    2 tablespoons (30ml or 28g) butter

Before you begin, bring water in lower pan of one-quart (one-liter) double boiler to a simmer, place chocolate in top pan and set on lower pan. Stir constantly until chocolate is almost melted. Remove from heat. Replace hot water in lower pan with cold water and continue stirring chocolate until

smooth and completely melted.

Arrange metal candy bars on marble slab to form a 12" x 18" (30.5cm x 45.7cm) rectangle. (Or prepare a cookie sheet to receive fondant, page 93.) If your stove is electric, turn heat unit to highest temperature.

1. Stir hot water and sugar together in a three-quart (three-liter) heavy saucepan. Place over high heat and stir constantly until all sugar crystals are dissolved. Clip on thermometer and continue cooking without stirring, to 240°F (116°C), washing down sides of pan twice more as mixture cooks. Remove from heat. Entire cooking process takes about twelve minutes.

2. As soon as bubbles subside, pour mixture onto marble slab, or prepared cookie sheet. Allow to cool, *undisturbed*, until fondant holds the imprint of your finger and feels lukewarm. This takes about eight minutes. Cut butter in small pieces and scatter over surface of fondant. Pour melted chocolate over fondant. Remove metal candy bars.

3. Now work the fondant with a scraper, just as the Picture Lesson, page 92, shows. When the fondant is stiff enough to hold the scraper straight up, it is finished. Knead briefly and place the ball of fondant in a container. Cover with a damp cloth, then put the cover on the container. Store in the refrigerator for up to three weeks. The fondant may be used at once. Yield: enough fondant for 200 centers.

TO VARY THIS RECIPE

Make a butter fondant, using the same procedures. Omit the chocolate and just work the butter into the fondant as described in paragraphs 2 and 3. If you like, you may add a teaspoon of any clear flavoring extract and a few drops of liquid food coloring along with the butter.

Fondant centers for dipped chocolates are the most important use of fondant. To read just how you can vary your basic fondants by adding fruits, nuts, flavoring and tints, please turn the page.

95

CENTERS MADE FROM WILTON CREAM OF TARTAR OR CORN SYRUP FONDANT

Fondant is such a versatile substance you can vary it in almost as many ways as you can dream up. Here are just a few delicious suggestions for fondant centers. *All are based on one-quarter recipe* of Wilton Corn Syrup or Cream of Tartar Fondant.

To dip centers in fondant, see page 100. To dip in confectionery coating, see page 22; to dip in chocolate, see Chapter 11.

1. To start, dust marble slab or counter with cornstarch. Cut off approximately one-fourth of the finished fondant. If fondant has been refrigerated, bring to room temperature. Dust your hands with cornstarch and knead briefly on prepared work surface to form in a rough circular shape. Make a depression in the center.

2. Put flavoring, chocolate, food color or other additions in the depression, then knead vigorously until all ingredients are evenly distributed. If fondant is too soft, dust with a little cornstarch—if too stiff, dip your fingers in cool water and knead to pliable consistency. Form into centers as described on page 97.

3. Yield for each variation is about 60 or more centers for dipping.

Rosewater centers have a delicate flavor. Knead ½ teaspoon (2.5ml) rosewater and one drop of red food color into one-quarter recipe of fondant. Dip in pale pink fondant or pink confectionery coating.

Nut butter centers, crunchy and rich. Crisp ¼ cup (60ml or 30g) of finely chopped nuts (page 16). Cut one tablespoon (15ml or 15g) of chilled butter into tiny pieces. Working quickly so as not to melt butter, knead in butter and one-third of the nuts into one-quarter recipe fondant. Continue kneading as you add remainder of nuts. Dip in light or dark chocolate.

Peppermint patty centers. Cut one tablespoon (15ml or 15g) of chilled butter in tiny pieces. Dip a toothpick in oil of peppermint and apply to one-quarter recipe of fondant. Add one drop of red or green food color and butter. Knead all together. Dip in either light or dark chocolate.

Chocolate centers for the real chocolate lover! Melt and cool 1½ ounces (45g) of unsweetened chocolate. Add to one-quarter recipe of fondant and knead until evenly colored. Dip in dark chocolate.

Fruit centers. Add ¼ cup (60ml or 50g) of finely chopped dried or candied fruit to one-quarter recipe of fondant. Use dried dates, apricots, prunes or raisins, or candied cherries, pineapple or peel—or use mixed fruits. Knead well. Dip in light or dark chocolate, pastel fondant or confectionery coating. *Note:* Do *not* use maraschino cherries—fondant will become runny.

Pastel centers. Add one drop of liquid food color to one-quarter recipe of fondant. To flavor, add ¼ teaspoon (1.2ml) of clear extract—vanilla, almond, cherry, raspberry, rum or the flavor of your choice. Or add one teaspoon (5ml) of liqueur. Use kirsch, cointreau, rum, creme de menthe, brandy or any well flavored liqueur. Knead well. Dip in confectionery coating or chocolate.

Maple-walnut centers. Knead ¼ teaspoon (1.2ml) of maple flavoring and ¼ cup (60ml or 30g) crisped walnuts, finely chopped, into one-quarter recipe of fondant.

CENTERS MADE FROM WILTON BUTTERCREAM FONDANT

These centers are richer and even more delicious than those made from Wilton Cream of Tartar or Corn Syrup Fondant. Unadorned Buttercream Fondant makes a very good center for dipped chocolates, with a creamy mellow flavor. For variety, add crisped chopped nuts, chopped dried or candied fruits, and flavorings and tints as you desire. The procedure for preparing the fondant is similar to that used for Wilton Cream of Tartar and Corn Syrup Fondants.

1. Dust your work surface liberally with cornstarch, and dust your hands with cornstarch too. Remove chilled fondant from refrigerator, cut off one-half of the amount and place on dusted surface.

2. Working quickly, knead the fondant briefly, adding nuts, fruit, flavoring and food color in the same amounts as directed for Cream of Tartar or Corn Syrup Fondant centers. Use one or two drops of *oil based* flavoring, not extract, as desired.

Return kneaded fondant to refrigerator to firm before forming into centers. A half-recipe of Wilton Buttercream Fondant will yield about 50 centers for dipping.

FONDANT CENTERS MADE FROM WILTON CHOCOLATE CREAM FONDANT

This fondant makes a luscious center just as it is, but you can dress it up for really luxurious candies.

Prepare the fondant just as for Wilton Cream of Tartar or Corn Syrup Fondant, first bringing it to room temperature. Be sure to dust your hands and work surface liberally with cornstarch. *All the variations below are based on one-quarter recipe* of Wilton Chocolate Cream Fondant.

Yield for each variation is about 50 centers for dipping.

Chocolate almond centers. Knead ¼ cup (60ml) of chopped almonds, crisped, and 2 drops of oil of almond into one-quarter recipe of fondant. Form into centers and dip in milk chocolate.

Chocolate coconut centers. Knead ¼ cup of flaked coconut into one-quarter recipe of fondant. Form into centers and dip in dark chocolate.

Chocolate mint centers. Knead one drop of oil of peppermint into one-quarter recipe of fondant. Dip in green confectionery coating.

Chocolate orange centers. Knead two drops of oil of orange and ¼ cup (60ml) of finely chopped candied orange peel into one-quarter recipe of fondant. Dip in dark chocolate.

Chocolate cherry centers. Knead two drops of oil of almond and ¼ cup (60ml) chopped candied cherries into one-quarter recipe of fondant. Dip in pink confectionery coating.

HOW TO FORM FONDANT CENTERS

Use this method for making evenly sized centers to dip in chocolate or the various tints of confectionery coating.

1. *For centers made from Wilton Cream of Tartar or Corn Syrup Fondants.* Dust work surface lightly with sifted cake flour or cornstarch. After you have kneaded the nuts, fruit or other additions into the fondant, cut the mass of fondant in two and form each into a ball. Roll the ball on the floured work surface into a cylinder about 1" (2.5 cm) in diameter. Cut the cylinder into 3/4" (1.9cm) pieces. Roll each piece into a ball. Place balls on a cookie sheet covered with wax paper and lightly dusted with flour. Allow to slightly crust, about 30 minutes.

2. *For centers made from Wilton Buttercream Fondant.* The procedure is the same as for Cream of Tartar or Corn Syrup Fondants, but be sure the kneaded fondant is well chilled before forming the centers. Dust your work surface and hands with plenty of cake flour.

3. *For cut-out fondant centers, use either* Wilton Cream of Tartar or Corn Syrup Fondant. This method is usually used for chocolate covered mints. Bring one cup of the fondant to room temperature and knead in one or two drops of oil-based flavoring and a few drops of liquid food coloring. Dust work surface and rolling pin lightly with sifted cake flour and roll out the fondant just like cookie dough. Roll to a thickness of about ¼" (.6cm). Dip cutter in flour and cut out shapes. Scraps may be rerolled. Transfer cut-outs to a cookie sheet lined with wax paper and very lightly dusted with flour. Allow to crust about ten minutes, then turn over to allow bottoms to crust. Yield: about 20 round cut-outs, 2" (5.1cm) in diameter.

4. Dip centers in confectionery coating, page 22, or in chocolate, Chapter 11.

5. *Chocolate Easter eggs.* Use any of the fondant center variations. To form eggs, cut off about 4" (10.1cm) from your cylinder. Dust your palms with sifted cornstarch or cake flour and roll the portion of fondant into an egg shape. Allow to crust, then dip in chocolate or confectionary coating. Decorate with names piped in contrasting chocolate (page 113) or confectionary coating (page 30).

MINT PATTIES . . . EASY TO MAKE FROM FONDANT

Perfect mint patties have a glossy finish, an even, delicate color and a creamy texture. The temperature to which you bring the melted fondant is very important for all of these qualities. If it is too high, the patties will be dull, may develop white spots and have a slightly grainy texture. They will still taste good, however, and the family will enjoy them.

Speed in dropping the patties is necessary, too. If you go too slowly, the fondant will cool and harden in the funnel. Should that happen, put the fondant back in the top of the double boiler and gently re-heat to 140°F (60°C). Be sure to warm the funnel and stick, too. With just a little practice, you will be turning out perfect mint patties.

One-fourth of a recipe of Wilton Corn Syrup or Cream of Tartar Fondant is the most practical amount to use.

If you have skill as a decorator, mint patties are perfect to display it. Trim the finished patties with spirals, initials, scrolls or hearts piped with a tiny round tube and royal icing. Bouquets of tiny drop flowers are pretty, too.

> ¼ recipe of either finished Wilton Corn Syrup or Cream of Tartar Fondant
>
> 1 drop oil of peppermint
>
> 1 drop red liquid food color

Before you begin, cover a counter or table top with wax paper.

Set mint patty funnel and stick in a container of very hot water to warm.

1. Place finished fondant in top pan of a one-quart (one-liter) double boiler. Bring water in lower pan to a simmer and put top pan over it. Break up fondant with a wooden spoon and stir constantly until melted.

As soon as fondant becomes liquid, clip on thermometer and continue stirring until temperature reaches 140°F (60°C). Watch carefully—it is very important not to overheat the fondant. This will cause white spots and a dull finish. Add flavoring and food color as you stir.

2. Remove top pan of boiler from lower pan. Carefully dry funnel and stick and put stick in position within funnel. Pour melted fondant into funnel. (It's best to have someone hold funnel upright as you pour.)

Now drop the patties on prepared counter. Hold funnel upright with your left hand, about an inch above surface. With your right hand, lift stick, then push down to drop a patty. Work quickly so fondant does not harden. After you have dropped a few patties, you will achieve a rhythm in lifting and pushing down the stick so patties will be uniform, each about the size of a 50¢ coin. Continue until all fondant is dropped.

The patties will set up very quickly—in five or ten minutes. As soon as they are firm, turn them over and allow the underside to dry. Pack the finished patties in a box between sheets of wax paper. Close the box and put it in a tightly sealed plastic bag to keep for several days. Yield: about 70 patties.

TO VARY THIS RECIPE

Flavor and *tint* the fondant in any way you wish for variety. Try lemon extract in yellow patties, almond extract in delicate green, vanilla in white. Be sure you use clear flavorings—deep colored ones may discolor the patties.

HOLIDAY MINT PATTIES

It's fun to dress up a tray of homemade mint patties for Christmas. The candies will add a festive touch to any holiday party.

Tint fondant in Christmas colors and form into mints as directed at left. Make a paper decorating cone (page 26), cut about ¼" (.6cm) off the point and drop in tube 1. Make a recipe of Wilton Royal Icing (page 103). Place small portions in separate containers and tint with liquid food coloring.

Half-fill the cone with tinted icing and pipe the designs on the mints, doing all trim in one color on all mints at one time. The flowers, mistletoe and holly berries are just dots. The leaves are two touching elongated shells. Form points on holly leaves by pulling out with a toothpick.

Centers made from uncooked mixtures may also be used for dipping in confectionery coating, chocolate or fondant. They're very quick and easy to put together and most acceptable substitutes for the classic cooked fondants.

CHEWY COCONUT CENTERS

A delightful center, delicately chewy, not too sweet, with a mild true coconut flavor. Be sure to use desiccated (sometimes called macaroon) coconut.

¾ cup (180ml) light corn syrup

6 purchased marshmallows, quartered

½ teaspoon (2.5ml) vanilla

2¼ cups (540ml or 168g) desiccated coconut

Before you begin, cut marshmallows into quarters with a scissors dipped in cold water. Line a cookie sheet with wax paper and lightly dust with flour.

1. Place syrup and marshmallows in a one-quart (one-liter) saucepan over medium heat. Stir constantly until marshmallows are melted and mixture is very hot—about five minutes. Remove from heat, stir in vanilla, then thoroughly blend into the coconut. Allow to set until cool enought to handle— about ten minutes.

2. Lightly dust your work surface with flour and flour your hands. Form into logs or cylinders. Put one-fourth of mixture on floured work surface, pat into long shape, then roll into a cylinder about 8½" (21.6cm) long. Cut cylinder into twelve equal portions with a sharp knife. Roll each portion between your palms into a ball, and place on prepared cookie sheet. Repeat to form centers from remaining mixture.

3. You may dip the centers immediately into melted fondant, chocolate or confectionery coating. Or set close together on a tray and cover tightly with plastic wrap or foil—then refrigerate for up to three weeks. Bring to room temperature before dipping. Yield: 48 centers.

UNCOOKED BUTTER FONDANT

A rich and delicious fondant for centers that can be put together in about 15 minutes. This pliable mixture can be very easily formed into centers, or rolled out to be cut into shapes.

- ⅓ cup (80ml or 90g) butter
- ¼ teaspoon (1.2ml) salt
- ⅓ cup (80ml) light corn syrup
- 1 teaspoon (5ml) clear vanilla
- 1 pound (454g) sifted confectioners' sugar (approximate)

Before you begin, line a cookie sheet with wax paper. Lightly dust with flour.

1. Whip butter and salt in electric mixer set at medium speed until fluffy. Use large bowl of mixer. Add corn syrup in thirds, whipping after each addition. Add vanilla.

2. Add sugar, all at once, and stir with a wooden spoon until mixture holds together. Turn out on a surface very lightly dusted with flour. Knead until mixture is perfectly smooth and can be formed into a ball.

3. Divide fondant into fourths and work with one portion at a time. Lightly dust a smooth surface with flour and form each portion into a cylinder about 11" (27.9cm) long. Cut into 3/4" (1.9cm) pieces, then roll between your palms into balls. Set centers on prepared cookie sheet as you form them. You may dip at once, or cover cookie sheet tightly with plastic wrap and refrigerate for one or two days before dipping. To store for two weeks, wrap ball of fondant tightly in two layers of plastic wrap and refrigerate. Bring to room temperature to form centers. Yield: about 60 centers.

HOW TO DIP
CLASSIC PASTEL BONBONS
IN FONDANT

It's easy to dip centers in fondant—and the glossy, translucent pastels of the finished candies are especially pretty.

Centers to use. Choose a center that is not too sweet—divinity, coconut or marzipan centers are good choices. The centers should be light in color. Dark centers will show through the fondant coating.

- 2 cups (480ml or 800g) finished fondant, either Wilton Corn Syrup or Cream of Tartar, pages 92 and 94 (approximate)
- 2 or 3 drops liquid food coloring
- 1 teaspoon (5ml) clear flavoring extract
- 4 or 5 teaspoons (20 or 25ml) water
- 50 centers for dipping (approximate)

Before you begin. Dipping in fondant is just like dipping in confectionery coating or chocolate. Set up your work area just as described on page 22. If fondant has been refrigerated, bring to room temperature.

1. Fill lower pan of one and a half quart (one and a half liter) double boiler with water. Break up fondant and place in upper pan. Set over lowest heat and stir constantly with a wooden spoon.

2. As fondant melts, add flavoring and food coloring and one or two teaspoons of water. Check with thermometer. When fondant is at 105°F (40°C), it is ready for dipping. Remove from heat. Keep top pan over lower pan while dipping.

3. Dip centers just as described on page 23. Stir the fondant as much as possible as you dip to avoid crusting. If fondant becomes too thick, stir in a little more water. Check the temperature from time to time. It should remain at 105°F (40°C). If temperature drops, set double boiler over lowest heat and stir until fondant comes back to 105°F, then continue dipping centers.

4. Centers will set up in ten minutes or less. Set bonbons in paper candy cups, then in a closed box. Store at room temperature for up to a month. Leftover fondant may be stored in tightly sealed container in the refrigerator for months—then used again for dipping (not for making centers). Yield: about 50 bonbons.

Fondant leftover from dipping centers may be refrigerated in a tightly sealed container to be used again for *dipping only.* Do not use for mints or for forming centers. Melt just as explained above, adding a teaspoon or two (5ml or 10ml) of water, as necessary.

At right: Classic Bonbons ringed with Aloha Kisses and Coconut Snowdrifts make an appealing candy tray.

NEAPOLITAN SQUARES

In southern Italy, sweets are often layered in various tints and flavors. Make these delightful candies to add color and variety to a tray or gift box.

> ¾ recipe of either Wilton Corn Syrup (page 92) or Cream of Tartar Fondant (page 94), divided in thirds
>
> ¼ cup (60ml or 30g) finely chopped pecans, crisped
>
> 1 tablespoon (15ml or 15g) chilled butter, cut in tiny pieces
>
> red and green liquid food coloring
>
> cherry, vanilla and almond extracts (use clear variety)

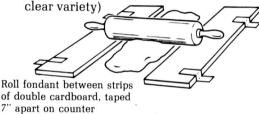

Roll fondant between strips of double cardboard, taped 7" apart on counter

Before you begin, form strips of double corrugated cardboard to serve as guides for thickness of fondant as you roll it. Tape two pieces of cardboard, each 4" x 12" (10.1 cm x 30.5cm), together and wrap in wax paper. Repeat for second strip. Tape the two strips to counter, long sides about 7" (17.8cm) apart. Crisp the nuts.

1. To one third of the fondant, add two drops of green color and ¼ teaspoon (1.2ml) almond extract and knead. In second portion, knead in nuts, butter and ½ teaspoon (2.5 ml) vanilla extract. In third portion, knead in two drops of cherry extract and one or two drops of red food color. Keep all portions closely wrapped in plastic.

2. On counter prepared with cardboard strips, first roll green-tinted fondant. Form fondant into a rough rectangle. Place length of wax paper between strips, dust with cornstarch, then lay fondant on paper and lightly dust. Cover fondant with second sheet of wax paper. Roll out to a rectangle 7" x 10" (17.8cm x 25.4cm), letting ends of rolling pin rest on cardboard strips. Strips will assure uniform thickness of fondant. See diagram.

Remove top sheet of wax paper and place rolled fondant, still on lower sheet, on cookie sheet.

3. Roll out white fondant just as you did

green fondant. Remove top sheet of paper and carefully place rolled fondant on top of green fondant on cookie sheet. Remove wax paper. Do the same with pink fondant, leaving wax paper covering on top.

4. Place a sheet cake pan on top of wax paper-covered layers. Set several food cans in pan to weight fondant. Place in freezer for 30 minutes or refrigerator about two hours. Peel off top paper, trim rough edges and cut into 3/4" (1.9cm) squares with a sharp knife. Fondant will be sticky, but will air dry in about ten minutes. To store for several weeks, wrap uncut candy closely in plastic wrap and refrigerate. Yield: about 70 squares.

ALOHA KISSES

Use Wilton Buttercream Fondant (page 94) to create this new and delightful treat.

> ½ recipe Wilton Buttercream Fondant
>
> ½ teaspoon (2.5ml) pineapple extract
>
> ⅔ cup (160ml or 100g) macadamia nuts, chopped very coarsely
>
> ⅔ cup (160ml or 150g) candied pineapple, chopped finely
>
> 1 pound (454g) milk chocolate, chopped*

Before you begin, line two cookie sheets with wax paper. Chop and measure the nuts and pineapple. Chop chocolate.

1. Bring water in lower pan of 1½-quart (1½-liter) double boiler to a simmer. Put fondant in upper pan and place in position on lower pan. Break up fondant with a wooden spoon and stir constantly until fondant is smooth and liquid—about the consistency of catsup. Remove from heat and stir in pineapple extract.

2. Remove top pan from lower pan and fold in nuts and pineapple. Drop candy from tip of dessert spoon into high mounds onto prepared cookie sheet. If mixture becomes too stiff, place pan over hot water and stir to soften. If it is too liquid, stir until it becomes stiffer. Allow candy to firm about twenty minutes, then turn over to dry bottoms, about ten minutes.

3. Temper chocolate for dipping as described in Chapter 11. Hold each piece of candy by the top and dip halfway into chocolate, leaving top half exposed. Place on cookie sheet to set at room temperature. Or place in refrigerator about five minutes, then allow to complete setting up. Yield: about 40 candies.

COCONUT SNOWDRIFTS

Use your Wilton Buttercream Fondant (page 94) to make this quick candy. It's just as pretty as it is delicious.

½ recipe Wilton Buttercream Fondant

1½ cups (360ml or 128g) flaked coconut

½ teaspoon (2.5ml) almond extract

1 pound (454g) pink confectionery coating, chopped, or 1 pound wafers

Before you begin, line two cookie sheets with wax paper. Chop coating.

1. Bring water in lower pan of 1½-quart (1½-liter) double boiler to simmer. Put fondant in upper pan and place in position on lower pan. Break up fondant with a wooden spoon and stir constantly until fondant is smooth and liquid, about the consistency of catsup. Remove from heat.

2. Stir in coconut and almond extract. Remove top pan from lower pan and drop candy from tip of dessert spoon into high mounds onto prepared cookie sheet. Allow to firm about twenty minutes, then turn candy over to dry bottoms, about ten minutes.

3. Melt confectionery coating for dipping as described on page 22. Hold each piece of candy by the top and dip halfway into coating, leaving top half exposed. Place on cookie sheet to set. Yield: about 36 candies.

DAINTY PETITS FOURS COVERED WITH FONDANT

These delicious, bite-size cakelets have a stylish Continental flair. See them on page 90. Use your favorite pound cake recipe.

2 cups (480ml or 800g) finished fondant, either Wilton Corn Syrup (page 92) or Cream of Tartar (page 94)

2 or 3 drops liquid food coloring

1 teaspoon (5ml) clear almond extract

4 or 5 teaspoons (20ml or 25ml) water

50 pound cake cubes 1" (2.5cm) high

¾ pound (340g) dark chocolate flavored confectionery coating, chopped, or ¾ pound wafers

Wilton Royal Icing and piping gel for decorating

*You may substitute confectionery coating in light chocolate flavor for the chocolate. Follow dipping directions on page 22.

Before you begin, trim off crusty edges of cake and cut in 1" (2.5cm) cubes. Set cake cubes on cake rack. Line a cookie sheet with wax paper.

1. Melt fondant as directed for Classic Pastel Bonbons, page 100. Add food coloring, flavoring and water as you stir.

2. Pour fondant over cake cubes, touching up any bare spots with a small spatula. If fondant becomes too thick for easy pouring, add a little more water and warm over simmering water until it thins and temperature is 105°F (40°C). Let cakes set up at room temperature, about 20 minutes.

3. Rewarm the remaining fondant to 105°F (40°C) and pour the cakes a second time. Thin fondant as necessary with water. Let cakes set up, about 20 minutes.

4. Melt confectionery coating as described on page 22. Holding cake cubes with your fingers, dip lower part of each in melted coating. This will seal the petits fours and keep them fresh for up to three weeks.

5. To decorate the cakes, cut about ¼" (.6cm) off the point of a paper decorating cone (page 26) and drop in tube 1. Half-fill the cone with Wilton Royal Icing, fold to seal securely and pipe outlines of a flower shape on each cake. Tint about 1/3 cup (80ml) of piping gel with liquid food coloring. Place gel in a paper decorating cone, seal securely and snip just a tiny opening from point. Squeeze cone gently to fill in the flower outlines.

WILTON ROYAL ICING

4 teaspoons (20ml or 20g) Wilton Meringue powder

2 cups (480ml or 200g) sifted confectioners' sugar

3 tablespoons (45ml) warm water

¼ teaspoon (1.2ml) cream of tartar

1 teaspoon (5ml) light corn syrup

Place all ingredients except corn syrup in small bowl of electric mixer. Blend at low speed, then turn speed to high and beat seven to ten minutes or until light and fluffy. Blend in corn syrup.

This icing dries very quickly, so keep bowl covered with a damp cloth while using. Store in tightly sealed container in the refrigerator for several months. Bring to room temperature and rebeat to re-use. Yield: 1¾ cups.

Chapter 11

CHOCOLATE CROWN JEWEL OF CANDY

America's favorite flavor—and the preferred flavor all over the world! There's a fascinating history behind this wonderful food. The story of chocolate starts with the discovery of America in 1492. When Columbus showed his treasure trove of wonderful things from the New World to King Ferdinand of Spain, among them were a few dark brown, insignificant beans. These were cacao beans—the source of all our chocolate. When Cortez conquered Mexico, the Aztec emperor Montezuma served a chocolate drink to his Spanish guests, a drink reserved for royalty and considered fit for the gods. It was the Spaniards who got the idea of sweetening chocolate with sugar to make it more palatable for European tastes. By the 17th century, drinking chocolate was the rage of Europe.

A milestone in the history of chocolate occurred in 1876 when Swiss Daniel Peter developed a way to produce solid chocolate for eating. In a very real way, this discovery marked the start of modern candy making. When most people say candy, they mean a confection dipped or molded in chocolate.

Chocolate is a pure natural food. From the time of its harvesting from the cacao tree to the final product of refined chocolate, a great deal of care is taken in its processing. Did you know that the cacao tree flourishes only in rainy, tropical areas 20° north or south of the equator? After initial harvesting, fermentation and drying on the plantation, the beans are shipped to manufacturers for the painstaking process of roasting, grinding, adding sugar, milk and other ingredients and finally forming into the bars used in candy making. During all these operations, the chocolate undergoes many tests for quality—the most important being tests for purity.

Chocolate is nutritious. In comparison to fruits, nuts and confections usually used as snacks, chocolate is an outstanding source of food energy, protein, minerals and vitamins. There has been a study made that shows that chocolate actually inhibits tooth decay! But of course, most of us love chocolate just because it is so delicious!

What chocolate to use for candy making? This is a matter of taste. Each manufacturer offers a chocolate that varies slightly from others in flavor and texture. As you begin your adventures in dipping and molding, purchase chocolate in 8-ounce bars at your food market. Experiment with different brands to find the one you like the best. As you gain experience, you'll want to buy 10-pound blocks of chocolate to have on hand.

Chocolate must be tempered before it is used for dipping or molding. Tempering is a process of raising and lowering the temperature of chocolate so the finished candies will harden properly and have a handsome soft sheen. *A low-temperature thermometer is a must* for tempering chocolate. With this simple tool, you'll have success in your very first attempt at chocolate molding or dipping. And you'll feel a true sense of accomplishment in creating luxurious *real chocolate* candies!

One word of caution. Chocolate has a very low melting point. Therefore, confine your chocolate projects to times when the weather is not hot or humid. The ideal temperature for dipping or molding chocolate is 68°F, or even lower.

Don't confuse chocolate with confectionery coating. Some of the techniques for dipping and molding the two substances are very similar—but the temperature controls needed for working with chocolate are completely different from those used for confectionery coating. Read the pages that follow on dipping and molding chocolate, rely on your thermometer, and be sure of success!

TEMPERING CHOCOLATE FOR MOLDING

Before you can mold elegant chocolates or enchanting dimensional figures you must first temper the chocolate. Tempering may be compared to tempering metal to make it strong—it enables the chocolate to set up and harden properly so it will retain the fine details of the mold. Tempering is really a process of temperature control combined with vigorous stirring.

For your first adventure in tempering chocolate, use one pound (454g) of *either milk or dark chocolate.* Your most important tool is a low-temperature thermometer. These usually register from 30°F to 120°F (-1°C to 49°C). Proper temperature is the key to tempering chocolate—so make sure your thermometer is at hand.

1. Chop the chocolate with a long sharp knife on a cutting board. The finer it is chopped, the quicker it will melt.

2. Fill lower pan of a one-quart (one-liter) double boiler with hot water at about 140°F (60°C). (Take from tap or heat water on stove.) Use your thermometer to check temperature.

3. Put about one-fourth of the chopped chocolate in top pan of double boiler and set in position on lower pan. Stir the chocolate *vigorously* as it melts, scraping the sides and bottom of the pan. A rubber scraper is the most convenient tool for this. The idea is to keep the entire mass of chocolate at the same temperature. When the chocolate in the pan is almost melted, add a second fourth of chopped chocolate. Stir vigorously, just as before, until the chocolate is nearly melted. Continue adding chocolate, stirring as it melts until all the chocolate is melted and smooth.

At all times, make very sure *no water gets into chocolate.* Wipe the outside of the upper pan with a dry towel every time you remove it from lower pan. Even a small amount of water will cause the chocolate to stiffen and become useless for molding.

4. When chocolate is completely melted, pour out warm water in lower pan, and replace it with cold water at about 65°F (19°C). Stir the chocolate vigorously to cool it. Check the temperature. When chocolate is at 85°F (29°C), pour out the cold water in lower pan and replace it with water at 100°F (37°C)—just lukewarm.

5. Stir chocolate again until temperature registers 89°F (31°C)—*never any higher.* Now it is ready to mold. To hold the chocolate at this temperature, fill lower pan with 90°F (32°C) water.

MOLDING SOLID CHOCOLATES IN ONE-PIECE MOLDS

Review the molding directions for confectionery coating on page 24. Now that the chocolate has been properly tempered, the technique is similar and just as easy.

For your first adventure in molding chocolate, we recommend using a clear plastic mold containing a number of fancy bonbon shapes. Be sure the mold is clean and polished and at room temperature.

1. *Test the chocolate* by dropping just a bit on wax paper. It should appear shiny and start to set up immediately. Spoon the chocolate into the mold cavities. Hold filled mold an inch or two above surface and drop sharply once or twice to eliminate air bubbles.

2. Set mold in freezer. Check frequently to see if mold has a frosty appearance, indicating chocolate has hardened—then remove immediately. Small bonbon shapes will harden in about eight minutes. Invert mold over table covered with a towel. Flex mold gently and candies will drop out.

TEMPERING CHOCOLATE FOR FORK DIPPING

For dipping chocolates with a dipping fork, just as for molding chocolate, the chocolate must first be tempered. The process is very similar to tempering chocolate for molding —the only difference is the degree of temperature the chocolate is brought to for dipping. Follow the steps carefully and keep your low-temperature thermometer at hand. Use one pound (454g) of *either milk or dark chocolate* for your first adventure in dipping.

1. Follow the directions for chopping and melting the chocolate through Step 3 on the opposite page.

2. Replace the hot water in the lower pan of the double boiler with cold water. Make sure not even a drop of water gets into chocolate. Now stir the chocolate vigorously until the temperature of the chocolate is cooled to 83°F (28°C).

3. Replace the cold water in the lower pan with water at 85°F (29°C). Check with thermometer. Leave the upper pan over the lower pan to hold the chocolate at dipping temperature. Now the chocolate is ready for dipping. Test by dipping the tip of a knife blade into the chocolate. Place knife in refrigerator for just one minute. Chocolate should be set up and look glossy.

HOW TO FORK-DIP CHOCOLATES

Dipping centers with a dipping fork in chocolate is really fun—and easy. If you've had the experience of dipping centers in confectionery coating (page 22) you'll be surprised at how much easier it is to dip in chocolate. The tempered chocolate has a heavier consistency that seems to cling readily to the center. For round or oval centers, use a loop-type dipping fork. For square centers, use a two-tined fork.

1. *Prepare centers.* A firm center such as marzipan, fudge, coconut or fondant is easiest to dip. Set 40 to 50 centers in neat rows on a cookie sheet covered with wax paper and very lightly dusted with sifted flour. Allow centers to come to room temperature and lightly crust.

2. Set up your work area on a counter. At left place the cookie sheet containing centers. In the center, you will place your pan of tempered chocolate. At right, set a second cookie sheet covered with wax paper. This will receive the dipped chocolates.

3. *Dip the centers.* With your left hand, drop a center into the pan of chocolate. With your right hand, tumble with the fork to completely cover, then lift it out with the fork under it. Tap the stem of the fork sharply on the side of the pan so excess chocolate will drop off. Move your hand to the prepared cookie sheet and give a quick turn of your wrist so the dipped center will drop off, *upside down.* Now make a decorative swirl on the candy with the thread of chocolate clinging to the fork.

Once the dipped center has been deposited on the cookie sheet, *do not move it.* This would cause the covering of chcolate on the bottom of the candy to become thin, or even form a hole. If this happens, serve the chocolate within a few days, as the chocolate covering will not be airtight.

4. Work quickly and rhythmically. Stir the chocolate with the fork from time to time to keep all of it at a uniform temperature.

5. After you've completed dipping the centers, slide the cookie sheet into the refrigerator for *five minutes only.* This will give a final "snap" to the chocolate covering and help give it a nice sheen. Place candies in paper candy cups, then in a closed box. They will keep for six weeks or more at a temperature of 68°F (20°C) or less.

THE ADVENTURE OF HAND DIPPING CHOCOLATES

Once you have had the fun of working with chocolate, and have dipped chocolates with a dipping fork, you'll enjoy learning the time-honored method of hand dipping.

In older days, all fine chocolates were hand-dipped. Now this skill has virtually disappeared and purchased candies are almost always enrobed in chocolate by machine.

Follow this picture lesson to learn the satisfying art of hand dipping chocolates. As you move and handle the chocolate, you'll soon become familiar with subtle changes it undergoes as it is cooled and tempered. Each finished candy will have your own individual touch.

BEFORE YOU BEGIN

Prepare your centers for dipping. It's easiest to use centers you have made before and refrigerated. You may use any of the recipes marked with an asterisk in this book—but if you are a novice at dipping, we suggest you use a firm center such as a coconut, marzipan or stiff fondant mixture. Cover the back of a cookie sheet with wax paper, taping at ends to secure. Dust very lightly with sifted cake flour and set the centers out in neat rows. You will need about 50. While you are making other preparations the centers will come to room temperature and slightly crust. It's important that the centers be at room temperature.

Set up your work area. Select any convenient table or surface at which you can sit comfortably. The center of the table will be the dipping area. Place your marble slab here. Marble is an ideal surface for cooling and working chocolate—but if you don't have a slab, a formica surface will do. At the left side set your cookie sheet holding the centers. Cover the back of a second cookie sheet with wax paper and set it at the right. This will be used to receive the dipped chocolates. Get out a paint scraper with a blade about 3" (7.6cm) wide.

Chop the chocolate. Start with about a pound and a half (681g). You won't need all of it to dip 50 centers, but any leftover chocolate may be saved and used again. Use a large cutting board and a long sharp knife. Try to chop the chocolate into pieces about ½" (1.2cm) or less in diameter. The finer it is chopped, the quicker it will melt.

1. *Melt the chocolate.* Select a double boiler of one and a half to two-quart (1½ to two-liter) capacity. One with a heavy porcelain top pan is ideal because it heats evenly, but an aluminum or enamel pan is satisfactory. Put water in lower pan. Put chopped chocolate in upper pan and set over lower pan. Using *lowest heat,* bring water to 140°F (60°C). Stir the chocolate vigorously with a wooden spoon as it melts. This will keep all of it at a uniform temperature and help it melt evenly. When the first cup has almost melted and just a few lumps remain, add a second cup as you stir. Continue until all the chopped chocolate has melted and mixture is smooth. Remove from heat. Melting will take about 25 minutes.

2. *Chocolate is ready to temper.* Remove top pan and pour about half of the chocolate onto your marble slab or work surface. (*Important:* Make very sure *no* water gets into the chocolate. Wipe outer surface of top pan completely dry before pouring chocolate.) Set top pan back on lower pan to keep warm.

Now for the fun! Tempering chocolate is almost like finger painting. Move the chocolate around vigorously with your right hand, keeping all of it in motion. Use your hand almost like a scraper, with edge of palm and little finger against marble. Keep your left hand clean and away from chocolate.

3. *From time to time,* move chocolate into a central puddle or pool, using the scraper in your left hand—then continue working it with your right hand.

When the chocolate thickens, becomes heavy and loses its warmth, test by touching a little to your upper lip. If it feels distinctly cool, it's tempered and ready for dipping. This will take about ten minutes of working.

4. *Start to dip.* With your clean left hand, pick up a center and drop it into the pool of chocolate. Pinch it slightly as you pick it up to flatten top and bottom.

5. *Tumble the center* in the chocolate to coat it completely.

6. *Then pick it up,* holding it on your first two fingers. Shake to remove excess chocolate.

7. *Move your hand* to the prepared cookie sheet, turn your hand over and deposit the dipped chocolate on the sheet.

8. *As you lift your hand* up from the chocolate, a little thread or string of chocolate will cling to your finger. Make a quick curving motion of your finger to form a design on top of the chocolate. At first make just an "O" or a "C" shape. As you become adept at dipping, you can put almost any letter on the chocolate to identify flavor.

9. *When your pool of chocolate depletes*, pour the remaining chocolate from the double boiler onto the slab. (Don't let your supply of chocolate get down too far before adding more—you should still have a pool remaining on the slab.) Again *be sure to wipe dry the top pan* as you remove it from the lower pan so no water has a chance to get into chocolate. Temper the chocolate just as before until it thickens slightly and feels cool when touched to your lip. Now complete dipping the centers.

10. *Work rythmically.* As your left hand is picking up a center and dropping it into the pool of chocolate, your right hand is moving a dipped center to the cookie sheet.

11. Here is a close-up of the finished chocolates, each with a nice sheen and proudly crowned with a "W". It will take about 30 minutes at room temperature, about 68°F (20°C) for them to completely set up and harden.

12. Scrape up the remaining chocolate from the slab back into the top pan. Now use a rubber scraper to remove all of the chocolate from the pan to a length of foil. Let the chocolate harden completely (it will take up to eight hours) then cover it with foil and place in a tightly closed plastic bag. You may use it for your next dipping or molding adventure—or in any recipe. Store at room temperature (68°F or 20°C) or cooler for months. Before you dip or mold with it, it must be completely tempered again.

MORE CHOCOLATE MOLDING TECHNIQUES

Molding with chocolate is just as easy and very similar to molding with confectionery coating. Just be sure the chocolate is tempered as described on page 106, and that you work in a cool, dry atmosphere. 68°F (20°C) is ideal

Molds to use. *Clear plastic molds* are the easiest to use. You may hold the filled mold above eye level to check for air bubbles. It's also easy to tell if the chocolate has hardened sufficiently by the frosty appearance of the outside of the mold.

Metal molds are ideal, if you are fortunate enough to own them. Metal chills more rapidly than plastic, so the time needed for the chocolate to harden will be shorter.

Care of molds. Wash by swishing through warm suds and rinsing with warm water. (Hot water may cause plastic molds to warp.) Dry and polish carefully with a soft cloth. Any mark or scratch on the mold will show up on the finished candy.

Amounts of tempered chocolate needed are the same as for confectionery coating molds. See the chart on page 35 to estimate how much chocolate to chop and temper.

MOLDING CHOCOLATE IN TWO-PIECE MOLDS

Review the directions on page 27. The techniques will be the same, except you will be using tempered chocolate instead of confectionery coating.

For solid candies, align mold and clip together securely. Improvise a stand to hold mold upright and set clipped mold in stand upside down. Fill mold with tempered chocolate, drop stand sharply on surface to eliminate air bubbles, then set in freezer to harden. Approximate time needed is on page 35. *Do not leave in freezer longer then necessary.* Unmold and trim seam.

For hollow candies, fill clipped mold completely with tempered chocolate, just as for solid candies. Place filled mold in freezer for just a few minutes to harden the outside of the mold. Pour out the still-soft chocolate onto foil, then replace mold in freezer to completely harden—just a few minutes. Unmold and trim seam. Seal opening with tempered chocolate applied with a spatula. Let harden at room temperature.

HOLLOW CHOCOLATE CANDIES IN ONE-PIECE MOLDS

Use this technique for the liqueur glasses and dessert boxes on page 114—or for any other shape you wish to be hollow.

1. Fill mold cavities completely with tempered chocolate. Place in freezer for just two or three minutes until chocolate has hardened just on the outside. Remove mold from freezer and invert over foil to empty excess chocolate. Return to freezer for just a few minutes to completely harden. Unmold on a towel-covered surface.

2. For filled hollow molds, see page 26. Make sure filling is at room temperature.

HOW TO STORE MOLDED CHOCOLATE CANDIES

These candies will keep for months under proper conditions. Be sure the candies are well wrapped so they will not pick up any foreign odors. 68°F (20°C) is an ideal temperature for storage—but the candies will keep well at a temperature of up to 75°F (24°C). *Place small candies* in paper candy cups, then in a box. Cover with wax paper or plastic wrap and cover the box.

Wrap larger candies in clear plastic wrap, or cover with thin foil.

ADD TRIMS TO YOUR MOLDED OR DIPPED CHOCOLATES

Add your own decorative touches to chocolate candies—they'll look very special—even better than expensive purchased candies.

Chocolate cut-outs. Make these the same way as confectionery coating cut-outs, page 30. Spread a thin layer of tempered chocolate (page 106) on a sheet of foil taped to the back of a cookie sheet. Allow the chocolate to set up at room temperature, but not completely harden. This will take just a few minutes. Use small truffle cutters or the small end of a large round tube to cut the shapes. When chocolate has hardened, cut tape to release foil and run your hand under the foil. Cut-outs will pop up. Attach cut-outs to candies with dots of chocolate. Save the scraps to retemper.

Chocolate leaves. These make beautiful trims for dipped chocolates. Carefully wash and dry fresh, nonpoisonous leaves. Mint or rose leaves are good choices. Cover a cookie sheet with wax paper. Using a small spatula, spread a $1/8$" (.3cm) thickness of tempered chocolate (page 106) over the back of the leaf. Place on prepared cookie sheet. When chocolate has been spread on all leaves, put the cookie sheet into the refrigerator for just five minutes. Carefully peel the leaf away from the chocolate by pulling the stem. Result: a perfect reproduction of the leaf with every vein visible.

Flavoring chocolate. You may add *oil-based flavoring* to tempered chocolate for an intriguing taste. Stir in about four drops of the flavoring per pound (454g) of chocolate near the end of the tempering process. Oil of peppermint or oil of orange add delicious accents to chocolate.

PIPING WITH TEMPERED CHOCOLATE

Contrasting tones of milk and dark chocolate offer a good opportunity to personalize your candies with names, or dress them up with flowery decorations. You'll find piping with chocolate easy and enjoyable.

1. Make a parchment paper decorating cone (page 26). Cut about ¼"(.6cm) off the point and drop in tube 1.

2. Temper about 12 ounces (340g) of either milk or dark chocolate as directed on page 106. Stir in just ¼ teaspoon (1.2ml) of light corn syrup. Fill your decorating cone about half-full with this chocolate and fold top to seal securely. Now pipe your names or decorations. Just a very light squeeze of the cone will release a ribbon of chocolate. It's most efficient to trim a number of molds at one time in assembly line fashion .

Some of the most popular and most delicious candies are based on tempered chocolate. They make fabulous treats or gifts.

WALNUT MINT BARK

An all-time favorite among chocolate lovers, this candy gives lots of scope for creativity. You can vary it in many ways. We recomment you firm the candy in a pan for neat, even pieces.

2 pounds (908g) dark chocolate, tempered for molding (page 106)

5 drops oil of peppermint

1 cup (240ml or 112g) broken walnuts, crisped

Before you begin, crisp the nuts. Line a 9" x 13" (22.9cm x 33cm) sheet cake pan with foil. Chop the chocolate.

1. Temper the chocolate as for molding. Directions are on page 106. When chocolate is at molding temperature, stir in oil of peppermint and nuts.

2. Pour candy into prepared pan, using a rubber scraper. Level surface with scraper. Allow to firm at room temperature just until set, but not completely hardened. Run the tines of a fork over the surface of the candy to give a bark-like texture. Score into 1½" (3.8cm) squares with a sharp knife. Continue firming at room temperature until candy has hardened, about two hours. Break into squares to serve. To store for several months, wrap uncut candy tightly in plastic wrap. Keep at about 68°F (20°C). Yield: about 48 generous pieces.

TO VARY THIS RECIPE

Substitute any type of crisp nuts for the walnuts. Use the *oil-based* flavoring of your choice. Try milk chocolate almond bark— it's a real winner!

DELUXE ROCKY ROAD

Easy and absolutely delicious! Few confections have remained so popular for so many years as Rocky Road. A recipe of this candy makes a fabulous gift for anyone who adores chocolate.

If you are inexperienced in working with chocolate, this easy-to-make candy is a good project to start with.

You may substitute confectionery coating in light chocolate flavor for the milk chocolate in this recipe, (see page 22) but the taste and texture just won't be as good. For warm summer days, however, confectionery coating will give you Rocky Road.

  1 pound (454g) milk chocolate, tempered for molding (page 106)

  12 large marshmallows

  6 ounces (approximately 170g) pecan halves, crisped

Before you begin, cut the marshmallows in quarters with a kitchen scissors. If they stick, dip the scissors in cold water. Crisp the nuts (Chapter 2). Chop the chocolate into small pieces on a cutting board. Line an 8" (20.3cm) square pan with foil.

1. Temper the chocolate for molding as described on page 106.

2. Pour about half of the tempered chocolate into the prepared pan. Scatter the marshmallows evenly over the chocolate, then sprinkle with the nuts.

Stir the remaining chocolate well, and drizzle it over the nuts and marshmallows. It won't cover completely, but will offer a tantalizing glimpse of the nuts and marshmallows. Let stand at room temperature, about 68°F (20°C), until chocolate is set but not completely hardened. Score into 1¼" (3.2cm) squares with a sharp knife. Allow to harden completely. Turn out of pan and peel off foil. Break into chunks. Wrap each individually in wax paper. For gift-giving, wrap the entire block in clear plastic wrap, then dress it up with ribbon and trims.

Store in a cool place for several weeks, closely wrapped and uncut. Yield: 36 pieces.

TO VARY THIS RECIPE

Substitute any dried fruit for the nuts, or use crisped walnuts, peanuts or cashews instead of the pecans. The original Rocky Road is still the favorite, though!

PECAN CARAMEL TURTLES

Here's a candy that's become a classic! Crunchy pecans combine with rich chocolate with the surprise of caramel inside. If you like the purchased version of turtles, just make a batch at home. They're fantastic!

  1 pound (454g) pecan halves, roasted

  1 recipe Wilton Caramel for Dipping, page 61

  1 pound (454g) milk chocolate, tempered for dipping, page 107 (approximate)

Before you begin, roast the pecans (page 16). Line two cookie sheets with foil.

1. Spread nuts on prepared cookie sheets. Pat to distribute in an even layer. If caramel is not freshly made, heat in a double boiler over simmering water until pourable.

2. Drop circles of caramel about the size of a half dollar on nuts. Leave about an inch (2.5cm) of space between each circle. The best way to do this is to pour the caramel into a mint patty funnel—then drop the circles just as you would drop mint patties (page 98). If you prefer, you may drop the circles with a spoon. Allow caramel to firm as you prepare chocolate.

3. Spoon tempered chocolate over the caramel circles, covering them completely. Hold cookie sheet an inch or two above table and drop sharply to level the chocolate. Chocolate will set up at room temperature in about 20 minutes. When firm, pick up each turtle, shaking off extra nuts and place in a paper candy cup. Store in a covered box in a cool place for up to three weeks. Yield: about 50 turtles.

Note: Refrigerate leftover nuts and caramel in sealed containers. Allow excess chocolate to harden, then store in sealed plastic bag in a cool place.

At left: for an elegant ending to dinner, serve liqueur in chocolate glasses or dessert in chocolate boxes. Page 111 tells how to mold the glasses and boxes.

Chapter 12

MARZIPAN.

VERSATILE, DELICIOUS, FUN!

Marzipan is one of the oldest sweets—mention of it is found in centuries-old writings. Modern candy makers love it for its rich mellow taste and especially for its versatility.

After you have blended and kneaded together the simple ingredients that make marzipan, it becomes a substance as pliable as modelling clay.

You can roll out marzipan and cut it into flower and geometric shapes to trim confections and cakes. Marzipan can be modelled into miniature fruits and vegetables that look fresh-picked. Add some of these to a gift box of candy for color and variety—or present a basket heaped with a marzipan harvest. You can even fashion quaint little marzipan people and animals for children to marvel at—and later consume. Marzipan is also the main ingredient in delicious centers to dip in confectionery coating, chocolate or fondant. And don't miss our collection of recipes for delectable marzipan candies. They're on pages 126 and 127.

WILTON BASIC MARZIPAN

Make this easy recipe for modelled fruits, vegetables and figures, for rolled cut-outs or to make centers.

- 8 ounces (227g) almond paste
- 2 egg whites, unbeaten
- ½ teaspoon (2.5ml) vanilla or rum flavoring
- 3½ cups (840ml or 350g) sifted confectioners' sugar (approximate)

1. Crumble almond paste in a large mixing bowl. Add egg whites and flavoring and knead until thoroughly mixed. Now add the sugar, a cup at a time and knead very thoroughly after each addition until no lumps remain. Add enough sugar to the mixture so that marzipan has the texture of heavy pie dough. The entire process will take about 20 minutes.

2. Wrap closely in plastic wrap, then put in a tightly closed container and store for months in the refrigerator. When ready to use, bring to room temperature and knead again. If marzipan is too stiff, knead in a drop or two of warmed corn syrup until original consistency is restored. Yield: 1 1/3 pounds or enough for about 38 fruits or about 100 ½" (1.2cm) centers for dipping.

At left, baskets heaped with miniature marzipan vegetables and fruits. Directions for modelling them are on pages 118 and 119.

BASIC MARZIPAN TECHNIQUES

Tint marzipan in two ways. Break off a portion of the batch and knead in liquid food color, a drop at a time, until you reach the tint desired. To tint brown, knead in cocoa. For a rich, appetizing tan, knead in dry instant coffee powder.

Or make a prepared tint to paint on pieces. Put about two teaspoons (10ml) of kirsch or any white liqueur in a small container. Add liquid food color a drop at a time. Test for color by brushing a little on a piece of white paper. Brush the color on the completed marzipan piece with a small artist's brush. The alcohol in the liqueur will make the color dry in a few minutes. Mix color this way to add a pretty blush to peaches, pears or apples.

To roll out marzipan, dust work surface and a small rolling pin with a sifting of confectioners' sugar. Roll out just like cookie or pie dough. Cut the rolled marzipan with small cookie cutters or gum paste cutters.

To attach one piece of marzipan to another, dip or brush egg white on one piece and attach to second piece with a turning motion.

Always glaze completed fruits or figures as soon as they have dried enough to hold their shapes. Besides giving the pieces an attractive gloss, the glaze will keep the marzipan fresh and moist.

CORN SYRUP GLAZE

 ½ cup (120ml) light corn syrup

 1 cup (240ml) water

Combine syrup and water and heat to boiling in a small saucepan. Brush on marzipan pieces while hot. Allow pieces to dry at room temperature, about 20 minutes. This will give a soft shine.

For a shinier finish, substitute just one tablespoon of water for the one cup of water in the recipe.

MODELLING MARZIPAN FRUIT AND VEGETABLES

The creative candy maker will find this work easy and lots of fun! It takes just a little practice to turn out miniature fruits and vegetables that look just like they were picked from a garden. See picture, page 116.

All pieces start the same way. Cut off about a third of finished Wilton Basic Marzipan. (Keep remainder well covered.) This amount will make ten or more of any one variety of the fruits or vegetables. Knead in liquid food color until you reach the tint you desire. Dust a cutting board or marble slab with confectioners' sugar. Now roll the tinted marzipan with your hands into a basic cylinder about 1" (2.5cm) in diameter. Cut the cylinder into 1" (2.5cm) pieces and form balls by rolling between your palms. Now add the details that distinguish each fruit or vegetable.

For tools, all you will need is an orange stick with one pointed end, a small artist's brush and a small sharp knife. As fruits are modelled, place on wax paper-lined tray to harden for an hour or two.

Oranges are made from orange-tinted marzipan. Push in a clove for the stem end and roll the fruit over a grater for texture.

Peaches start with a yellow ball. Groove one side with the dull side of the knife. Indent stem end with the round end of the stick. Cut off the "blossom" from a clove and push in for stem. Dip an end of a clean damp cloth into prepared red tint (opposite page) and rub over one side of the peach for a natural blush.

Apples are made from red or light green marzipan. For red apples, just indent and push in a clove stem. For green apples, add a blush, just as you did for peach.

Tomatoes are formed with a red ball. Slightly flatten the ball by pressing with your palm, indent in center and make several grooves from the indentation with the stick. Pinch off a tiny piece of green marzipan, roll between your fingers, flatten and cut off to about 3/8" (1 cm) length.

Arrange five of these tiny pieces around indentation, attaching with egg white. Roll a tiny piece of green marzipan between your fingers into a stem and attach in center.

Potatoes are made from untinted marzipan. Form ball into a rough oval, indent for eyes with stick, then roll in cocoa.

Cucumbers start with untinted balls. Roll on surface to a cylinder about 2" (5.1cm) long with tapered ends. Paint with green prepared tint. When color dries, go back and repaint with lengthwise strokes for deeper color stripes.

Bananas are formed from yellow marzipan balls in a similar way to cucumbers. Pinch the cylinder for pointed ends, then paint stripes and flecks with brown prepared tint. Add a touch of green at ends.

Carrots. Roll an orange ball on surface to a long cylinder, tapering to a point at one end. Make grooves down the length with the dull side of the knife. Indent stem end. For stems, cut a tiny rectangle from green thinly rolled marzipan. At one short end, make three cuts like fringe. Roll and insert in indentation. Brush a little green prepared tint at stem end of carrot.

Onions are modelled from untinted marzipan. Flatten the ball and deeply indent. Make stripes on side with a length of coarse cotton thread. Paint about 1½" (3.8cm) in center of thread with green prepared tint. Hold painted thread against onion from indentation to bottom center. Roll tiny cylinders about 1" (2.5cm) long between your

fingers. Press three together at base, dip in egg white and attach at indentation. Paint light green.

Cabbages and lemons are formed from larger and smaller sized marzipan balls.

For cabbages, cut a 2" (5.1cm) piece from your basic cylinder of green marzipan. Form into a ball, then give texture by pressing with a leaf mold, or the side of the stick. Thinly roll a small piece of green marzipan and cut out three circles with a 1½" (3.8cm) round cutter. Thin the edges by pressing with your fingers, then add texture as you did the ball. Paint lower third of these leaves with egg white and wrap around central ball.

Lemons begin with a 3/4" (1.9cm) length cut from basic cylinder of yellow marzipan. Form into a ball, then elongate into oval. Pinch ends to points, then roll over grater. Touch ends with green prepared tint.

Flower and leaves are cut from thinly rolled marzipan. Use a tiny flower-shaped cutter for the flowers, then attach ¼" (.6cm) yellow balls in the centers. Cut leaves with a small leaf-shaped cutter, or cut pointed ovals ½" x ¾" (1.2cm x 1.9cm), with a knife. Groove for veins with a knife, then attach to stem ends of peaches and apples.

Let all pieces harden an hour or two on wax paper, then brush with Corn Syrup Glaze.

HOW TO MODEL CUTE MARZIPAN FIGURES

Basic tools are an orange stick, a sharp knife and a small rolling pin. Small cutters and decorating tubes are handy for details.

First estimate the amount of marzipan you will need and divide and tint it all at once. It's easier to make at least two figures at once. Any four of the figures shown in our color picture require one recipe of Wilton Basic Marzipan, page 117.

Santa and Mrs. Santa are good examples for estimating amounts of tinted marzipan. Make a recipe of Basic Marzipan. Form into a large cylinder. Cut off about 2/3 of it to tint red. From the remaining piece, cut off 1/3. Leave half of this untinted, tint the other half brown. Divide the rest of the marzipan in two, tint half flesh color and the other half blue. Be sure to keep the tinted marzipan you are not working with well wrapped in plastic wrap. Store remaining marzipan for future use.

Basic shapes form all figures as diagram shows. *Noses and eyes are tiny balls. For hands,* flatten two ends of arms and cut into mitten shapes. *Shoes* are made extra-large to balance the figure.

Most trims are cut from rolled marzipan. Cut buttons or cheeks with tube 10 or 12. Always dip cutters or tubes in confectioners' sugar before cutting.

Form parts and assemble figures in orderly progression, using egg white as glue.

1. *A day ahead,* form ball for head and insert toothpick. Model cone for body. On underside, carve out hollow to receive legs for standing figure. Roll cylinder for legs and curve. Model feet.

2. *The next day,* assemble feet, legs and body. Cut trims from rolled gum paste and attach. Roll cylinder for arms, flatten ends and cut hands. Add cuffs, if needed. Attach arms at top of body, a little to the rear. Curve in position. Form a little disc about ½" (1.2cm) in diameter and attach for neck. Or cut a collar from rolled marzipan. Insert toothpick on head through neck or collar, arms and body. Now your basic figure is complete.

3. Add the finishing touches. For hair, cut a flower shape from rolled marzipan with a cutter about 1" (2.5cm) in diameter. Or cut a circle and fringe all around. Model tiny balls for eyes and nose and attach. Cut cheeks with tube 10. For mouth roll a bit of marzipan between your fingers to a string, and curve into a smile.

4. Set figure on wax paper to dry. After an hour or so, paint with Corn Syrup Glaze. Dry thoroughly. You've created a beguiling little personality!

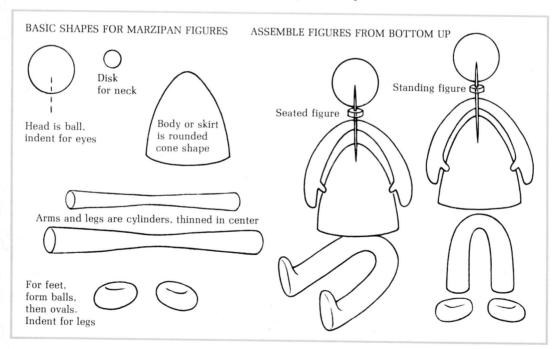

BASIC SHAPES FOR MARZIPAN FIGURES

Disk for neck

Head is ball, indent for eyes

Body or skirt is rounded cone shape

Arms and legs are cylinders, thinned in center

For feet, form balls, then ovals. Indent for legs

ASSEMBLE FIGURES FROM BOTTOM UP

Standing figure

Seated figure

Above: pliable marzipan makes it easy to create jolly little people. For detailed directions for modelling each figure, please turn the page.

Follow the basic techniques and directions on pages 118 and 120, then model these winsome little people. You'll think of many more personalities to create for special occasions. Insert toothpicks in all heads.

ANGEL is 3" (7.6cm) high. Leave space behind hands for taper

Head is 1" (2.5cm) ball, hair 1" (2.5cm) flower shape. Roll marzipan string into halo

Small disc for neck

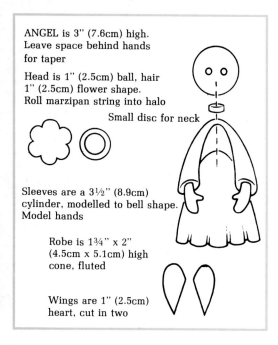

Sleeves are a 3½" (8.9cm) cylinder, modelled to bell shape. Model hands

Robe is 1¾" x 2" (4.5cm x 5.1cm) high cone, fluted

Wings are 1" (2.5cm) heart, cut in two

FISHERMAN, 4" (10.1cm) tall, holds 4" (10.1cm) wire brushed with egg white, covered with marzipan. Make bench first, assemble pants and boots on it and dry before putting together rest of figure

Head 1" (2.5cm) ball. Hat is grooved 1" (2.5cm) circle plus arc. Ears are half-circles. ½" (1.2cm) disc for collar 3" (7.6cm) cylinder, cut in half forms arms

Body is cone 1¼" x 1½" (3.2cm x 3.8cm) high

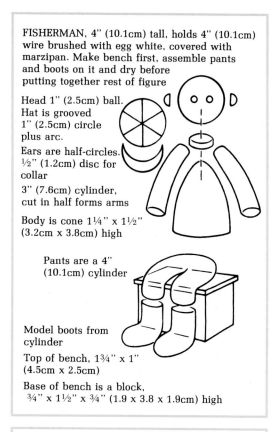

Pants are a 4" (10.1cm) cylinder

Model boots from cylinder

Top of bench, 1¾" x 1" (4.5cm x 2.5cm)

Base of bench is a block, ¾" x 1½" x ¾" (1.9 x 3.8 x 1.9cm) high

3" (7.6cm) ESKIMO holds a fish! Fur trim is made from ¼" (.6cm) "string" grooved with knife

1" (2.5cm) ball for head. Hair is ¾" (1.9cm) circle, fringed. Hood is 1" (2.5cm) circle, ¼" (.6cm) thick, grooved and wrapped over back of head

4" (10.1cm) cylinder forms arms
Body is cone, 1¾" x 2" (4.5cm x 5.1cm) high

5" (12.7cm) cylinder for legs, turn up at ends

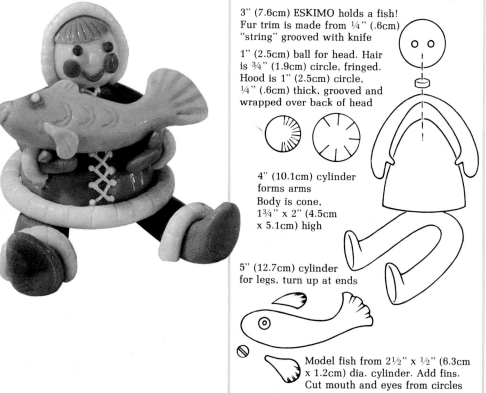

Model fish from 2½" x ½" (6.3cm x 1.2cm) dia. cylinder. Add fins. Cut mouth and eyes from circles

SANTA stands 4¾" (12.1cm) high.
For beard, cut 1" (2.5cm)
flower shapes in half and
attach, starting at bottom

Hat is ¾" (1.9cm) ball, cut off.
Make head same way

Small disc for neck

Roll 4" (10.1cm) cylinder
for arms

Body is cone, 2"
(5.1cm) wide at
base, 1¾" (4.5cm)
high. Hollow out space
at bottom for legs

4" (10.1cm) long
cylinder for legs

Model boots
from balls

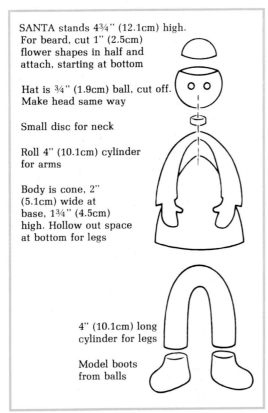

MRS. SANTA is 4" (10.1cm) high.
For apron, cut center hole in 3"
(7.6cm) rolled circle.
Cut circle in half.
1" (2.5cm) ball for head

1" (2.5cm) circle, wedge
cut out, for collar

1" (2.5cm) flower shape
for hair

Arms from 3"
(7.6cm) cylinder.

Model hands

Bodice is cone ¾" x 1"
(1.9cm x 2.5cm) high

Skirt is 2" x 1¾"
(5.1cm x 4.5cm) high cone,
flattened at top,
fluted with stick

Flattened ovals for feet

Plate is 1" (2.5cm)
circle, arc cut out

Cut doughnuts with
tube 12, holes tube 4

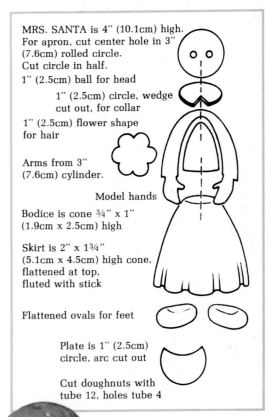

FLOWER GIRL, 3½" (8.9cm) high, holds
a bouquet cut with tiny flower
cutter. Stems from strings of marzipan

Head is 1" (2.5cm) ball,
hair is 1" (2.5cm) circle,
fringed

Collar is 1" (2.5cm)
flower shape

Dress is 1¾" x 1¾"
(4.5cm x 4.5cm) cone,
fluted. Attach ½" (1.2cm)
balls for sleeves

Arms are two 1½"
(3.8cm) long cylinders

2½" (6.3cm)
cylinder forms legs

Feet are 1" (2.5cm)
long ovals

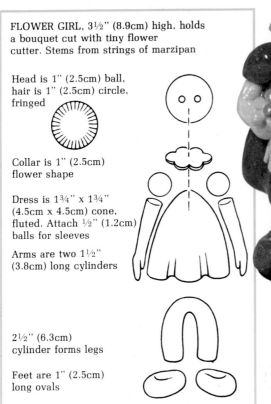

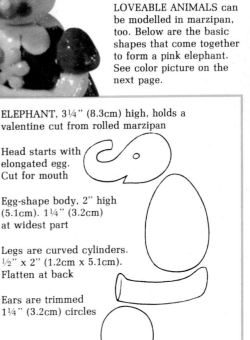

LOVEABLE ANIMALS can
be modelled in marzipan,
too. Below are the basic
shapes that come together
to form a pink elephant.
See color picture on the
next page.

ELEPHANT, 3¼" (8.3cm) high, holds a
valentine cut from rolled marzipan

Head starts with
elongated egg.
Cut for mouth

Egg-shape body, 2" high
(5.1cm). 1¼" (3.2cm)
at widest part

Legs are curved cylinders.
½" x 2" (1.2cm x 5.1cm).
Flatten at back

Ears are trimmed
1¼" (3.2cm) circles

MARZIPAN PETS, FUN TO MODEL

Marzipan can make the sweetest pets a child ever fell in love with! Make a recipe of Wilton Basic Marzipan (page 117), read the general instructions on pages 118 and 120, then create these cute little creatures from basic shapes. One recipe will make one of each animal pictured—to make just the lion and elephant you will need a half-recipe. One pig, one cat and one bunny take a fourth-recipe. Most heads are secured with toothpicks. (Directions for making elephant are on page 123.)

ONE-PIECE PIG has almond ears, almond slivers for legs. Curly string tail

Body is bottle shape, 2½" x 1¼" (6.3cm x 3.2cm). Flatten end and cut for mouth.

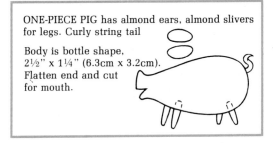

A CUTE BUNNY is made with just two main pieces plus a shaped ball for tail

Head is a pointed egg 1½" (3.8cm) high. Split for ears

Body a modified egg 1⅝" (4.1cm) long.

Model tail

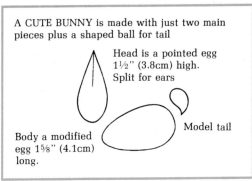

BEGUILING PUPPY, 2¼" (5.7cm) high has almond ears, tiny red tongue

Head, 1½" (3.8cm) high x 1" (2.5cm)

side view   front view

Body a squat egg, 1½" x 1½" (3.8cm x 3.8cm)

Front legs, 1½" x 2¼" (3.8cm x 5.7cm) cylinder, thinned in center and curved

Tail, 2½" (6.3cm) string

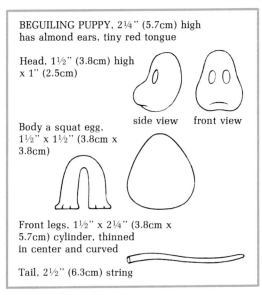

LOVEABLE LION sits 3" (7.6cm) high

Mane is a curved, tapered cylinder, 4" (10.1cm) long. Score with knife

Head and body, a curved tapered oval, 2½" (6.3cm) high

Muzzle a 1" (2.5cm) kidney bean shape Model ears, ½" (1.2cm) wide

Front legs a 2¾" (6.9cm) cylinder, curved to "U". Back legs, 1¾" (4.5cm) cylinders, flattened at back

Tail is a 2½" (6.3cm) string, fringed

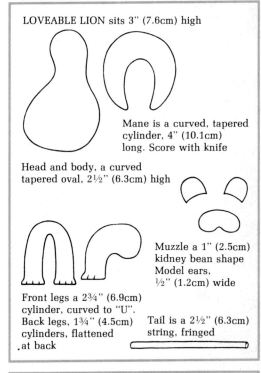

BABY BEAR is 2½" (6.3cm) high. Cut bow from rolled marzipan

Pear-shaped head is 1¼" x ⅞" (3.2cm x 2.3cm). Cut for mouth

Model ears

Legs are 1⅞" x ½" (4.8cm x 1.2cm) cylinders. Flatten at back and curve

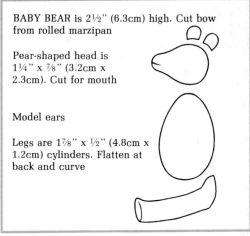

PLAYFUL KITTEN, 2½" (6.3cm) long. Teardrop eyes, ball nose

Body is tapered cylinder about 3" (7.6cm) long. Curve and cut for legs

Tapered tail, 1½" x ¼" (3.8cm x .6cm.)

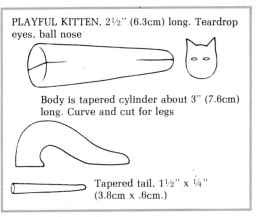

ELEGANT MARZIPAN CENTERS

Marzipan makes a rich flavorful center for dipping when dressed up with fruit, nuts or coconut. For a variety of centers, divide a batch of Wilton Basic Marzipan (page 117) or Continental Marzipan into fourths, then knead in flavoring and additions of your choice. Marzipan centers are especially easy to dip. For bonbons, dip in pastel fondant or confectionery coating. Dip in dark or light chocolate for rich delicious chocolates.

Make them ahead of time, place in pan or tray, cover well with plastic wrap and store in refrigerator for months. Bring to room temperature before dipping. Yield is about 25 centers for each variety.

Fruit centers. Knead $\frac{1}{4}$ cup (60ml or 56g) mixed, finely chopped, candied pineapple and cherries and one teaspoon (5ml) of kirsch into $\frac{1}{4}$ recipe marzipan.

Coconut centers. Knead $\frac{1}{4}$ cup (60ml or 22g) flaked coconut and one teaspoon (5ml) rum into $\frac{1}{4}$ recipe marzipan.

Apricot centers. Knead $\frac{1}{4}$ cup (60ml or 56g) finely chopped dried apricots and one teaspoon (5ml) cointreau into $\frac{1}{4}$ recipe marzipan.

Double almond centers. Knead $\frac{1}{4}$ cup (60ml or 30g) finely chopped, toasted almonds and one teaspoon (5ml) almond liqueur into $\frac{1}{4}$ recipe marzipan.

Chocolate centers. Knead $1\frac{1}{2}$ ounces (45g) melted, cooled, unsweetened chocolate and $\frac{1}{2}$ teaspoon (2.5ml) vanilla into $\frac{1}{4}$ recipe marzipan.

FLAMED MARZIPAN

Here's an unusual and very delicate continental sweet with an intriguing flavor.

1 recipe of Wilton Basic Marzipan (page 117) or Continental Marzipan

2 teaspoons (10ml) rosewater

1 egg yolk

1 teaspoon (5ml) water

1 pound (454g) dark chocolate, tempered for dipping (page 107)

Before you begin, line a cookie sheet with foil. Dust counter or marble slab with sifted confectioners' sugar.

1. On prepared counter or slab, knead the rosewater thoroughly into the marzipan.

2. Working with one quarter of the marzipan at a time (keep remainder well wrapped in plastic), roll it into a long cylinder, about 1" (2.5cm) in diameter. Break off a piece and roll on surface with your fingers into a pencil-size rope about 3/8" (1cm) thick. Cut off 4" (10.1cm) and form it into a spiral, figure "8", rosette or twist. Place on prepared cookie sheet. Continue until you have formed all the marzipan. Allow to dry, uncovered, overnight.

2. Stir egg yolk and water together and lightly brush the candies with this mixture. Set broiler at 400°F (204°C) and place cookie sheet with brushed candies about 6" (15.2cm) below heat. Watch very carefully until candies are a delicate brown, about four minutes. Cool to room temperature.

3. Line a cookie sheet with wax paper. Dip the candies in the tempered chocolate, covering lower third only, and set on prepared cookie sheet to harden. Store in a cool place in tightly sealed box, for up to a month. Yield: 75 to 80 candies.

CONTINENTAL MARZIPAN

This marzipan is especially suited for incorporating in candies. For modelling, use Wilton Basic Marzipan (page 117).

8 ounces (227g) almond paste

4 ounces (113g) finished fondant, either Wilton Corn Syrup (page 92) or Cream of Tartar (page 94)

1. Crumble marzipan into large mixing bowl. Melt fondant in top pan of double boiler over simmering water, stirring constantly. Add to marzipan and knead until well mixed and like heavy pie dough. Kneading takes about 20 minutes.

2. Wrap tightly in plastic wrap, then put in tightly closed container and refrigerate. It will keep for months. When ready to use, bring to room temperature and knead again. If too stiff, knead in a drop or two of warmed corn syrup. Yield: enough for about 90 centers.

CHOCOLATE ALMOND SLICES

A delightful European treat that combines the flavor of marzipan with the melting richness of chocolate truffle. Very sophisticated, fun and easy to put together.

    1 recipe Classic Chocolate Truffles, page 8
    1 recipe Continental Marzipan
    2 tablespoons (30ml) sifted confectioners' sugar
    2 drops green liquid food coloring
    2 tablespoons (30ml) light corn syrup
    1 pound (454g) dark chocolate, tempered for dipping, page 107

Before you begin, make a paper decorating cone (page 26), snip about ¼" (.6cm) from point and drop in tube 12.

1. Make Classic Truffles through step 3 and refrigerate while you prepare Continental Marzipan. Blend the food coloring into the marzipan as you knead.

2. Sift confectioners' sugar over work surface and rolling pin. Roll out the marzipan into a rectangle about 8" x 10" (20.3cm x 25.4cm). Trim edges and cut into three strips about 2½" x 10" (6.3cm x 25.4cm).

3. Remove truffle mixture from refrigerator and beat with hand mixer, just until smooth and creamy. Put into paper cone and pipe a long line on each marzipan strip, about 3/4" (1.9cm) from one long side. With a pastry brush, moisten the marzipan strips on either side of the truffle line with corn syrup. Roll the marzipan strip over the truffle line, starting with long side farthest from the line. Press lightly to seal and turn roll over so seam is at the bottom. Refrigerate for about an hour, or overnight if you desire.

4. Bring rolls to room temperature. Place each on a separate sheet of wax paper. Brush chocolate over each roll with pastry brush, starting with seam and turning roll to completely cover. Refrigerate five minutes, then bring to room temperature for chocolate to harden completely. Cut into ½" (1.2cm) slices and set each slice in a paper candy cup. Pack snugly in a tightly sealed box and refrigerate for up to two weeks. Yield: about 60 slices.

Note: If any truffle remains, pipe in mounds into paper candy cups. Allow leftover chocolate to harden to use again.

RAINBOW MARZIPAN

Liqueurs give a subtle mellow flavor, dominated by the almond of the marzipan.

    1 recipe Wilton Basic Marzipan, vanilla flavored, page 117
    1 ounce (30g) unsweetened chocolate
    1 teaspoon (5ml) rum
    1 teaspoon (5ml) cointreau
    1 teaspoon (5ml) kirsch
    5 drops red liquid food color
    1 egg white, lightly stirred

Before you begin, tape cardboard strips to work surface, just as you did for Neapolitan Squares, page 102. This will assure even thickness of rolled marzipan. If refrigerated, bring marzipan to room temperature. Melt and cool chocolate.

1. Divide marzipan evenly into three portions. Knead chocolate and rum into one portion. Knead cointreau into second portion. In third portion, knead kirsch and red food color. As you finish kneading each portion, form into rough rectangle, wrap closely with plastic wrap.

2. Roll chocolate marzipan between two sheets of wax paper dusted with confectioners' sugar on prepared surface. Let ends of rolling pin rest on cardboard strips. As you roll try to form a rough rectangle about 7" x 12" (17.8cm x 30.5cm). Remove top paper and place rolled marzipan on cookie sheet. Roll untinted marzipan the same way. Brush chocolate marzipan with egg white, then peel off top paper from untinted rolled marzipan and place on chocolate marzipan. Roll pink marzipan and place on untinted marzipan, brushed with egg white.

3. To serve, trim off rough edges to form a neat rectangle and cut into 3/4" (1.9cm) squares to reveal the perfect layered colors. To store for months, wrap uncut candy closely with plastic wrap and refrigerate. Rainbow Marzipan improves with age as the flavors ripen. If cut squares will be exposed to air for more than an hour or two, brush each with Corn Syrup Glaze, page 118. Yield: about 80 squares.

Chapter 13

FRUIT AND NUT CANDIES

Enticing is the best word to describe these candies. Nature's bounty of fruit, nuts and other natural foods is combined to create candies as appealing as they are wholesome.

As you browse through the recipes in this chapter, you'll discover the enormous variety of fruit and nut candies. You'll find confections as simple and straightforward as Caramel Apples and Peanut Clusters, as decorative as Candied Roses, as sophisticated and subtle as Vienna Compotes. And don't miss Florenettes, a delightful adaptation of a European favorite — or Holiday Brandied Cherries, the easiest way ever to create the most popular of all candies.

All of the techniques needed to create these candies have been taught in previous chapters of this book. You'll discover many possibilities for originality, too. (Your-Way Candies are a good example.) So step into the kitchen and have fun creating your own versions of enticing — and wholesome — fruit and nut sweets.

YOUR-WAY CANDIES

Here's a creative candy combining wholesome fruit and nuts with the rich natural goodness of chocolate. Use your own imagination to select the fruit and nut combination most appealing to you.

    1 pound (454g) milk or dark chocolate, tempered for dipping, page 107

    dried fruits, cut in wedges or pieces

    whole roasted nuts

Before you begin, line one or two cookie sheets with wax paper.

1. Cut point from a paper decorating cone (page 26) and drop in tube 12. Half-fill with the tempered chocolate and pipe tongue shapes, about 2" x ¾" (5.1cm x 1.9cm), on prepared cookie sheet. Before chocolate hardens, center each "tongue" with a piece of fruit.

2. On either side of the fruit, place a roasted nut. If chocolate "tongue" has hardened, dip nuts in chocolate, then set in position. Let chocolate set up at room temperature, about 68°F (20°C). Yield: about 40 candies.

SUGGESTED COMBINATIONS

Roasted hazel nuts with pitted prunes

Roasted cashews with several raisins

Roasted walnut halves with dried bananas

Roasted pine nuts with dates

Roasted peanuts with dried apricots

At right: center of tray, Pineapple Fancies surrounded by Vienna Compotes. At outer edge of tray, Your-Way Candies

Candied peels are a delicious and decorative confection. Use them to garnish desserts, as an accent with after-dinner black coffee, as a pretty candy trim or as an ingredient in a candy recipe. And there's no more welcome gift than a dainty box of mixed candied peel!

The peel of grapefruit, oranges or lemons may be used interchangeably in the recipes that follow. For the peel of four medium-to-large oranges, substitute peel of two large grapefruits or six lemons.

For a more flavorful candied orange peel, reserve some of the water in which the peel was boiled and substitute it for the water in Honey Sweet Peel. Do not reserve water in which grapefruit or lemons were boiled. It is too bitter.

You can dress up peel in several ways. Just see our pretty Grapefruit Candy Jars! Here are some other methods.

Superfine sugar is a good finish for any peel. After peel has been cooked in syrup, lift out with tongs and deposit in a shallow pan filled with 3/4 cup (150g) superfine sugar. Roll strips of peel to coat, then lay on baking rack placed over cookie sheet to dry and harden overnight.

Crystal sugar (sugar in large crystal form) gives sparkle! Roll peel in this sugar just as for superfine sugar, above.

Coconut makes a fine fluffy trim and tastes delicious. Follow the method for coating peel in superfine sugar, substituting 3/4 cup (65g) flaked coconut.

Chocolate-dipped peel is deluxe! Dark chocolate tastes best on lemon and grapefruit peels, milk chocolate on orange peel. After unsugared peel has dried on rack overnight, dip in *tempered* chocolate (page 107). You'll need about 3/4 pound (340g) of chocolate. Hold strip of peel by one end and dip other end in chocolate. Let harden by setting undipped ends of peel between wires of a baking rack.

Store peel, coated with sugar or coconut in a tightly sealed jar in the refrigerator for several weeks. Store chocolate dipped peel in a tightly sealed jar in a cool place —68°F (20°C) or below.

Use syrup leftover from cooking peel for poaching apples, pears and other fresh fruit. It will lend a subtle flavor.

CANDIED GRAPEFRUIT CUPS

Show off your candied fruits in glossy little jars made of grapefruit! They're perfect for lovingly homemade gifts, too.

> 2 medium-size grapefruit, free from
>   blemishes
> 1 teaspoon (5ml) salt
> 5 cups (1.2 l or 1kg) granulated sugar
> 5 cups (1.2 l) hot water
> 2 drops green liquid food coloring

Before you begin, set out four narrow juice glasses or small vases, upside down, on a cookie sheet. You'll use these to set the jars and their lids on for drying.

1. Wash the grapefruit and cut a slice from the stem end of each for a lid. Using a serrated grapefruit knife, cut out the pulp from the grapefruit, leaving a shell about ¼" (.6cm) thick. Use a metal spoon to remove the last of the pulp from the shells. Remove pulp from lids.

2. Place shells and lids in a four-quart (four-liter) saucepan, cover with cold water and add salt. Bring to boil and allow to boil ten minutes. Drain. Repeat process two more times, omitting salt. Trim any ragged ends of white membrane from shells and lids.

3. Combine sugar, hot water and food color in a four-quart (four-liter) heavy saucepan. Set over medium heat and stir constantly with a wooden spoon until all sugar crystals are dissolved. Clip on thermometer and add grapefruit shells and lids. Spoon liquid into shells to fill them. Continue cooking, turning shells and lids several times with two wooden spoons. When shells are upright, keep filled with syrup. When thermometer registers 220°F (104°C), remove from heat. Allow shells and lids to remain in syrup overnight, keeping shells filled with syrup.

4. The next day, place pan over medium heat. Turn shells and lids several times while cooking. When lids appear clear and transparent, remove from syrup with a slotted spoon and set on glasses to dry. When temperature reaches 232°F (111°C), and shells appear clear, about 40 minutes, remove from heat. Lift out shells with two spoons and place upside down over glasses to drain and dry overnight. To add little handles to lids, dip a curly piece of candied orange rind in syrup and attach. Store, lightly covered with wax paper, for a week at room temperature.

HONEY-SWEET PEEL

4 perfect thick-skinned oranges, medium size

pinch of salt

2 tablespoons (30ml) honey*

1 cup (240ml or 200g) granulated sugar

½ cup (120ml) hot water

3 drops red liquid food coloring

Sugar, coconut or tempered chocolate for finishing

1. Wash oranges, With a sharp knife cut through skin into lengthwise quarters. Pull off skin. Place peel in a two-quart (two-liter) saucepan, cover with cold water and add salt. Place over medium heat, bring to boil and keep water at a low boil for about ten minutes, or until peel is tender. Drain peel. Pour cold water over peel and drain again. Scrape white membrane from peel with a paring knife and cut into ¼" (.6cm) strips with a scissors.

2. Combine sugar, honey and hot water in a heavy two-quart (two-liter) saucepan. Place over high heat and stir constantly with a wooden spoon until all sugar crystals are dissolved. Stir in food coloring, then clip on thermometer. Continue cooking, without stirring, to 232°F (110°C), about ten minutes. Add strips of peel, pushing it under surface of syrup. Adjust heat so that temperature remains at 220°F (104°C). Boil gently until peel becomes translucent, about ten minutes. Remove from heat.

3. Lift peel from syrup with tongs and place in prepared pan of sugar, or coconut, or place on baking rack over foil covered cookie sheet if you plan to dip in chocolate or use in recipes. Dry sugar or coconut coated peels on baking rack. Allow all peels to dry several hours or overnight. Yield: about 65 strips.

*You may substitute 2 tablespoons (30ml) light corn syrup.

Below: Candied Grapefruit Cups hold a variety of candied peels

CANDIED ROSES

It's fun to make these shimmering translucent roses! Use them as the centerpiece of a candy tray, or as cake decorations.

1 large perfect orange
2 perfect lemons
2 cups (480ml or 400g) granulated sugar
1 cup (240ml) hot water
¼ cup (60ml) light corn syrup
4 drops yellow liquid food color

Before you begin, wash and dry fruit. Clean eight or ten corsage pins or long needles in boiling water.

1. Make roses. Cut a slice almost through stem end of lemon, then peel in one continuous strip, about ½" (1.2cm) wide. Remove some of the white membrane along with the peel. Twirl peel into a spiral, using stem end as base of rose. Secure with two pins. Make second rose from lemon the same way. Make two roses from orange, peeling to center, then starting at other end.

2. Place roses in a heavy two-quart (two-liter) saucepan and cover with cold water. Place over high heat, bring to boil and boil for ten minutes. Drain, then repeat boiling process. Drain again.

3. Combine sugar, hot water and corn syrup in the same saucepan. Place over medium heat and stir constantly with a wooden spoon until all sugar crystals are dissolved. Stir in food color. Wash down sides of pan with a pastry brush dipped in hot water, then gently place roses in pan. Lower heat to simmer, and cook for 25 minutes, turning roses occasionally. Remove from heat and cool in syrup for 30 minutes. Remove roses from syrup with a slotted spoon and place on baking rack set over shallow pan. Dry overnight, then remove pins. Yield: two yellow roses and two orange roses!

TRUFFLED PRUNES

Turn the humble prune into a gourmet treat by stuffing it with truffle!

1 recipe Cherry Kirsch Truffles (page 84)
40 prunes
1 cup (240ml or 200g) superfine sugar

Before you begin, cover a cake rack with paper toweling. Cut a slit on one side of each prune with a sharp knife and open prunes. Lay prunes on prepared cake rack.

1. Make truffle recipe through step 2 and refrigerate.

2. Cover a second cake rack with paper toweling. Remove truffle from refrigerator and beat with a hand-held electric mixer at highest speed for three minutes. Fill each prune with about a half-teaspoon (2.5ml) of truffle, using a dessert spoon. Close prunes around truffle.

3. Roll prunes in sugar, then place on prepared cake rack to air-dry for several hours. Place in paper candy cups. To store for up to two weeks, refrigerate in tightly sealed box. Yield: 40 candies.

Note: drop leftover truffle in mounds by teaspoon into paper candy cups.

LIQUEUR CANDIED PEEL

A five-step method of cooking makes this mixed peel soft, tender and delicious.

3 perfect thick-skinned lemons
3 perfect thick-skinned oranges
2½ cups (600ml or 500g) granulated sugar
¼ cup (60ml) orange liqueur
4 drops yellow liquid food coloring
Sugar, coconut or tempered chocolate for finishing

1. Wash fruit and cut through peel in lengthwise quarters. Place in two-quart (two-liter) saucepan and cover with enough cold water so surface is at least 1" (2.5cm) above peel. Bring to boil over medium heat and allow to boil five minutes. Drain and repeat boiling process twice more. Trim white membrane from peels and cut into ¼" (.6cm) strips. Place in cold water, bring to boil and boil five minutes again. Drain well.

2. Place strips of peel in a 10" (25.4cm) heavy frying pan. Add sugar and place over low heat. Stir occasionally and cook for an hour and a half. Stir in liqueur and food coloring and cook for 30 minutes more.

3. Remove from syrup with tongs. Roll in sugar and place on rack for several hours to dry. Or dry on baking rack and dip in tempered chocolate. Yield: about 75 strips of candied peel.

DATES STUFFED WITH ORANGE MARZIPAN

You'll enjoy this new version of stuffed dates. The not-too-sweet marzipan filling is enlivened with candied orange peel. For best flavor, use your own homemade peel.

  ½ recipe Continental Marzipan
    (page 126)
  ¼ cup (60ml or 56g) Honey Sweet Peel,
    chopped (page 131)
  40 pitted dates

Before you begin, snip peel into very small pieces with a scissors.

1. Knead peel into marzipan until evenly distributed. If marzipan is too stiff to knead easily, soften with a few drops of warm light corn syrup.

2. Cut marzipan into four equal portions. Roll each portion into a log about 7½" (19cm) long. Cut each log into ¾" (1.9cm) pieces. Roll pieces between your palms into ovals. Insert ovals in dates, then garnish by pressing a small piece of peel into marzipan. Place each date in a paper candy cup. To store for up to six weeks, place dates in a tightly sealed box and refrigerate. Yield: 40 stuffed dates.

Note: Store remaining half-recipe of marzipan in a tightly sealed plastic bag in the refrigerator. Use for centers or as ingredient in candy.

SALTED PEANUT CLUSTERS

Anyone who loves peanuts will find these candies irresistible. Form the candies in miniature muffin pans for an after-dinner treat, or use tartlet circles for a more substantial lunch box surprise.

  ⅔ cup (160ml) light corn syrup
  ½ cup (120ml or 100g) granulated sugar
  2 tablespoons (30ml or 28g) butter
  8 ounces (227g) dry roasted salted
    peanuts

Before you begin, butter miniature muffin pans. Or cover a cookie sheet with foil and lightly butter the foil. Butter inside surfaces of tartlet circles and set on cookie sheet.

1. Combine corn syrup, sugar and butter, (cut in thin slices) in a one and a half quart (one and a half liter) heavy saucepan. Place over medium heat and stir constantly until all sugar crystals are dissolved. Wash down sides of pan with a pastry brush dipped in hot water, then clip on thermometer. Continue cooking, stirring occasionally, until thermometer registers 238°F (114°C). Remove from heat.

2. Stir in peanuts. Spoon into muffin cups or tartlet circles. Allow to firm at room temperature. Smaller candies will be firm in about an hour and a half—larger ones will take about two hours. Loosen sides of candies with a small spatula and take out of pans or circles. Wrap larger candies in squares of plastic wrap. Place smaller candies in paper candy cups, then in tightly sealed box. Store at room temperature for up to a month. Yield: about 35 small candies, or 20 larger clusters.

SPICED FILBERTS

Crisp and delicately spicy, these nuts make a fine addition to a sweet table—or serve them with coffee after dessert.

  1 pound (454g) shelled filberts
  2 tablespoons (30ml or 28g) butter
  1 teaspoon (5ml) cinnamon
  ¼ teaspoon (1.2ml) allspice
  ¼ teaspoon (1.2ml) nutmeg
  2 egg whites
  Dash of salt
  1 cup (240ml or 200g) granulated sugar

Before you begin, remove most of the brown skin from the nuts. Spread them on a cookie sheet and toast in a 350°F (177°C) oven for ten minutes. Empty onto a clean tea towel and rub between your hands to remove skins. Place nuts in mixing bowl.

1. Melt butter in a small saucepan, then stir in cinnamon, allspice and nutmeg. Pour mixture over nuts and stir to coat thoroughly. Cool thoroughly.

2. Beat egg whites with electric mixer. When foamy, add salt. When soft peaks form, gradually add sugar as you continue beating until mixture is stiff and shiny. Fold into nuts. Spread evenly on cookie sheet and bake in a 300°F (149°C) oven for about 35 minutes until coating has dried. Stir nuts occasionally as they bake. Cool at room temperature. Store in a tightly covered container in refrigerator for several weeks.

SUPER FRUIT CAKES

Fruit cake was never so delicious! A layer of rich dark chocolate covers the lavish fruit-nut mixture. You may make this candy several days ahead, then cover it with chocolate when you are planning to mold chocolate candies.

>½ cup (120ml or 112g) pitted prunes
>
>½ cup (120ml or 112g) dried apricots
>
>1 cup (240ml or 130g) golden raisins
>
>½ cup (120ml or 70g) ground, blanched almonds
>
>1 cup (240ml or 200g) granulated sugar
>
>¼ cup (60ml) light corn syrup
>
>pinch of salt
>
>¼ cup (60ml) water
>
>½ teaspoon (2.5ml) almond extract
>
>½ pound (227g) dark chocolate, tempered for molding (page 106)

Before you begin, chop the prunes and apricots as finely as possible. Line a 6" (15.2cm) square pan with foil and butter the foil.

1. Mix prunes, apricots, raisins and ground almonds in a bowl. Set aside.

2. Combine sugar, corn syrup, salt and water in a one-quart (one-liter) heavy saucepan. Place over medium heat and stir constantly with a wooden spoon until all sugar crystals are dissolved. Wash down sides of pan with a pastry brush dipped in hot water, then clip on thermometer. Continue to cook, without stirring, washing down sides of pan twice more. When mixture reaches 238°F (114°C), remove from heat. Entire cooking process takes about ten minutes.

3. Allow hot mixture to cool ten minutes. Beat just until creamy, about five minutes. Mixture will set up quickly. Stir in almond extract and fruit mixture, then spread in prepared pan. Refrigerate about three hours, or until firm.

4. Bring candy to room temperature and spread with the tempered chocolate, using a spatula. When chocolate has set but not completely hardened, lift out of pan and cut into 1" (2.5cm) squares with a sharp knife. Let chocolate harden at room temperature. Place each square in a paper candy cup, then in a tightly covered box. Store in a cool place for up to a month. Yield: 36 candies.

PINEAPPLE FANCIES

Set off the tropical sweetness of pineapple with a double dip of creamy fondant and dark chocolate. A new recipe, a new way to delight your family and friends.

>6 candied pineapple rings
>
>1 cup (240ml or 400g) Wilton Fondant, either Cream of Tartar (page 94) or Corn Syrup (page 92)
>
>1 teaspoon (5ml) clear vanilla
>
>12 ounces (340g) tempered dark chocolate (page 107)

Before you begin, line two cookie sheets with wax paper. Cut each pineapple ring in eighths to form wedges. Use a paring knife dipped in cold water. Insert a toothpick in narrow end of each wedge.

1. Melt fondant in top pan of double boiler as page 100 directs. As fondant melts, stir in vanilla. When fondant is of dipping consistency, remove double boiler from heat, but leave top pan in position. Holding pineapple wedges by toothpicks, dip each in fondant, leaving pineapple exposed at top. If necessary, tilt pan by placing folded towel under one edge. Stir fondant frequently. Set wedges on one prepared cookie sheet to dry, about ten minutes. When fondant is dry, turn wedges on sides to dry bottoms.

2. Temper chocolate as directed on page 107. Holding wedges by toothpicks, dip in chocolate, not quite as deeply as in fondant, so edge of fondant shows. Stir chocolate frequently while dipping. Place on second prepared cookie sheet. Place in refrigerator for two or three minutes, then allow chocolate to set completely at room temperature, just a few minutes. Hold candies with tip of knife as you pull out toothpicks. Place candies in paper candy cups, then in tightly sealed box to store for a month at room temperature. Yield: 48 Fancies.

At right, starting from top: Super Fruit Cakes and Fondant-dipped Peach Halves. Dried Pears and Apricots dipped in Fondant. Peanut Clusters and Apricot Coconut Balls. Florenettes surround a Candied Rose

WILTON CARAMEL APPLES

Crisp apples covered with a soft, delectably rich caramel! That's the favorite treat-on-a-stick of all Americans. These caramel apples will never get too hard or chewy—the covering remains soft and toothsome.

    1 finished recipe Wilton Caramel for
      Dipping, page 61
    6 medium-size apples
    6 lollipop sticks, 4½'' (11.4cm) long

Before you begin, wash and dry the apples, remove stems and insert sticks. Set out six foil baking cups.

1. Make Wilton Caramel for Dipping as directed on page 61. Allow to cool for ten minutes, then dip apples, tilting pan to cover well. Lift apple by its stick and twirl, then hold upside down over pan for a minute to distribute caramel. Should caramel become too thick, stir in a tablespoon of cream, then continue dipping. Set dipped apples in foil baking cups.

2. Allow apples to firm about an hour. To store for several days, place firmed apples in small plastic bags, close with a twist tie and refrigerate. Yield: six apples.

CARAMEL APPLES IN VARIETY

For nutty apples, crisp one cup (240ml) of finely chopped nuts and place in shallow pan. As apples are dipped, set in pan of nuts for a moment, then in baking cup.

For varied flavors, use any of the caramel recipes starting on page 59 for dipping the apples. Instead of cooking to the temperature recommended in the recipe, cook to 242°F (117°C), or until a little of the carmel dropped in ice water forms a soft, firm ball.

CINNAMON CANDY APPLES

These are the prettiest candied apples! Glistening red hard candy covers the fruit and makes the apples sparkle like rubies!

    2 cups (480ml or 400g) granulated sugar

    1 cup (240ml) light corn syrup

    ½ cup (120ml) water

    6 drops cinnamon hard candy flavoring

    15 drops red liquid food coloring

    8 medium-size red apples

    8 lollipop sticks, 4½" (11.4cm) long

Before you begin, wash and dry the apples. Remove stems and insert lollipop sticks. Line a cookie sheet with foil and lightly butter the foil.

1. Combine sugar, corn syrup and water in a two-quart (two-liter) heavy saucepan. Set over high heat and stir constantly with a wooden spoon until all sugar crystals are dissolved. Wash down sides of pan with a pastry brush dipped in hot water and clip on thermometer. Now cook, without stirring, to 285°F (141°C). Remove from heat and quickly stir in flavoring and food color.

2. Tilt pan and quickly dip apples. When apple is covered, twirl to coat evenly. Set on prepared pan to harden. If syrup begins to harden, warm over low heat. Any leftover syrup may be poured on a small buttered pan, hardened and broken into bite-size treats. Serve apples within a few hours. If storing for two or three days, wrap in a square of plastic wrap, securing edges around stick with a twist tie or ribbon. The coating on these apples will attract moisture from the air and become sticky if not wrapped. Yield: eight candy apples.

FONDANT-DIPPED DRIED FRUITS

Turn dried fruits into decorative and elegant sweets by dipping in fondant. The creamy fondant softens and sweetens the intense flavors of the fruits. Try dried pears dipped in Chocolate Cream Fondant.

1. *Prepare fruit.* You will need about 15 dried apricots or seven or eight dried peach or pear halves. If fruit seems dry and hard, steam over simmering water for fifteen minutes to soften and plump. Cut peach or pear halves in half. Lay fruit on baking rack.

2. *Prepare Fondant.* You will need one cup (240ml or 400g) of finished fondant, either Wilton Corn Syrup (page 92), Cream of Tartar (page 94) or Chocolate Cream (page 95).

Melt the fondant in a small double boiler over simmering water. Break it up with a wooden spoon and stir constantly until temperature registers 105°F (40°C) and fondant is liquid. While stirring, add ½ teaspoon (2.5ml) of almond or vanilla extract, and, if you wish, one or two drops of liquid food color to the white fondant. Replace water in pan of double boiler with water at 105°F (40°C). Set top pan over lower pan.

3. *Dip fruit.* Holding fruit by one side, dip in fondant, covering only half of fruit. Lay dipped fruit on wax paper for fondant to set, only about ten minutes. Store leftover fondant in a tightly sealed container in the refrigerator to be used for dipping again.

TANGY APRICOT BALLS

Make this recipe for those who are watching their weight and prefer their candies not too sweet. It's deliciously wholesome.

    1 tablespoon (15ml or 15g) butter

    ¼ cup (60ml) light corn syrup

    2 teaspoons (10ml) water

    ¼ teaspoon (1.2ml) almond extract

    ⅓ cup (80ml) instant non-fat dry milk

    1 cup (240ml or 85g) flaked coconut

    1 cup (240ml or 227g) dried apricots, finely chopped

    ½ cup (120ml or 43g) flaked coconut for coating

Before you begin, chop and measure the apricots. It's easiest to do this with a scissors. Place ½ cup (120ml or 43g) coconut in a shallow pan. Line a cookie sheet with wax paper.

1. Stir butter and corn syrup together in a large mixing bowl. Add water and almond extract and stir until completely blended. Blend in dry milk.

2. Add one cup (240ml or 85g) of coconut and the apricots and knead mixture until it holds together. Take off portions with a teaspoon and roll firmly between your palms into balls. Roll balls in coconut to coat and set on prepared cookie sheet to dry, about 20 minutes. To store for several weeks, place balls in tightly sealed container and refrigerate. Yield: 30 candies.

FLORENETTES

The very best fruit-nut candy! This easy-to-make adaptation of an old European recipe has an intriguing flavor and a delicate crispness. Use metal tartlet circles (*without bottoms*) to form the candies. If you don't own them, you may substitute round metal cookie cutters, about 2½" (6.3cm) in diameter. Use your own homemade peel—the flavor is much better than purchased peel.

¼ cup (60ml or 56g) butter

15 large marshmallows, quartered

½ teaspoon (2.5ml) almond flavoring

½ cup (120ml or 100g) chopped candied orange peel

¼ cup (60ml or 56g) chopped candied cherries

1 cup (240ml or 100g) slivered almonds, crisped

½ pound (8 ounces or 227g) tempered milk or dark chocolate (page 107)

Before you begin, chop and measure the orange peel and cherries. Chopping is easiest done with a scissors dipped in cold water. Cut marshmallows in quarters. Toast the almonds. Line two cookie sheets with foil and brush with vegetable oil. Thoroughly brush inner surfaces of the tartlet rings with oil. Arrange them on the cookie sheets. Preheat oven to 350°F (177°C).

1. Melt butter in a two-quart (two-liter) saucepan over lowest heat. Add marshmallows and stir constantly with a wooden spoon until marshmallows are completely melted. Remove from heat and stir in almond flavoring.

2. Add orange peel, cherries and almonds and stir until well blended. Drop by teaspoon into prepared tartlet rings. Bake in 350°F (177°C) oven for ten minutes. As soon as candy is taken from oven lift rings from cookie sheet. Cool candy on cookie sheet, about 20 minutes, then remove from cookie sheet with a spatula. Cool completely on baking rack.

3. This final step may be done as soon as candy is completely cool or the next day. Cover flat cookie sheet smoothly with foil, shiny side up. Melt and temper the chocolate as directed in Chapter 11. Spread the bottom of a candy with chocolate, using a small spatula. Turn it over, and press it firmly, chocolate side down, on the cookie sheet. Repeat for all candies. Place cookie sheet in refrigerator for about ten minutes to harden the chocolate. Remove from sheet. Bottoms of candies will be smooth and shiny from being pressed against the foil. Store for up to two weeks in a tightly sealed container in a cool dry place (not the refrigerator). Yield: about 22 Florenettes.

DATE-NUT BALLS

Crunchy walnuts, tropic-sweet dates and creamy peanut butter are accented by the tang of fresh lemon. A favorite with youngsters and all peanut butter lovers.

1 tablespoon (15ml or 15g) butter, room temperature

2 tablespoons (30ml) sifted confectioners' sugar

1 tablespoon (15ml) fresh lemon juice

1 teaspoon (5ml) finely grated lemon rind

½ teaspoon (2.5ml) vanilla

¼ teaspoon (1.2ml) cinnamon

½ cup (120ml) creamy style peanut butter

¾ cup (180ml or 85g) chopped walnuts,

½ cup (120ml or 112g) finely chopped, pitted dates

1 pound (454g) milk chocolate tempered for dipping, page 107

Before you begin, line a cookie sheet with wax paper. Crisp the walnuts and chop and measure dates. Grate lemon rind.

1. Combine butter, sugar, lemon juice and rind, vanilla and cinnamon in a medium mixing bowl. Blend in peanut butter. Add walnuts and dates and stir with a wooden spoon until thoroughly mixed. Place bowl in refrigerator for one hour.

2. Take off portions of the mixture with a dessert spoon and form into balls by rolling between your palms. Place balls on prepared cookie sheet. Refrigerate about two hours.

3. Remove balls from refrigerator and allow to come to room temperature for about 30 minutes. Cover a second cookie sheet with wax paper. Dip balls into tempered chocolate, following directions on page 107. As balls are dipped, place on prepared cookie sheet. Set cookie sheet in refrigerator for five minutes only, then allow chocolate to harden completely at room temperature. Place candies in paper candy cups, then in sealed box. Store for up to a month in a cool place. Yield: 36 candies.

GLAZED FRESH FRUIT

The most beautiful and elegant dessert for a special dinner party! Glaze the fruits the day you plan to serve them—and make this recipe only in dry weather, unless your house is air-conditioned.

    1 medium grapefruit (to use as server)
    40 pieces of perfect fresh fruit (grapes, strawberries or cherries)
    fresh mint leaves
    40 lollipop sticks, 4½'' (11.4cm) long
    1 recipe Wilton Caramel Glaze (below)

1. Wash and carefully dry the fruit. Insert lollipop sticks. Place on paper toweling. Puncture the skin of the grapefruit to receive the lollipop sticks.

2. Make Wilton Caramel Glaze. Working quickly, dip each fruit into hot glaze, then insert in grapefruit. If glaze starts to harden, place over low heat to soften. To garnish the fruits, dip mint leaves into glaze and touch to sticks. *Caution:* do not let glaze dribble on your hands. It is very hot!

WILTON CARAMEL GLAZE

    2 cups (480ml or 400g) granulated sugar
    ⅔ cup (160ml) hot water
    ¼ teaspoon (1.2ml) cream of tartar
    3 drops oil of lemon

1. Combine sugar, water and cream of tartar in a two-quart (two-liter) heavy saucepan. Place over high heat and stir constantly with a wooden spoon until all sugar crystals are dissolved. Wash down sides of pan with a pastry brush dipped in hot water.

2. Continue cooking, without stirring, to 305°F (152°C). Remove from heat. Wash down sides of pan twice more as mixture cooks. Stir in the oil of lemon and dip fruits.

Note: leftover glaze may be poured onto buttered marble slab or cookie sheet, scored with a knife into squares and broken into candies when hardened.

CHOCOLATE-DIPPED STRAWBERRIES

There's absolutely nothing so luscious and luxurious as a fresh strawberry dipped in chocolate! Dip the berries the day you plan to serve them—this is a delicate treat.

>   40 perfect strawberries
>   1 pound (454g) milk chocolate, tempered for dipping (page 107)

Before you begin, set up your work area as diagram on page 107 shows. Strawberries will be on your left.

1. Carefully wash and dry the berries, then place on cookie sheet covered with paper toweling. Holding berry by stem, dip into tempered chocolate, leaving top of berry uncoated. Place on cookie sheet covered with wax paper.

2. Set cookie sheet in refrigerator for *five minutes only*, then complete hardening the chocolate at room temperature. Set each berry in a paper candy cup to serve. Store for a few hours at room temperature.

HOLIDAY BRANDIED CHERRIES

This is the easiest and most enjoyable way of making brandied cherries. Ask your friends to help—they'll feel more than repaid when they sample the delicious result of their labor! This candy rated four stars from our panel of tasters.

>   16-ounce jar (454g) maraschino cherries without stems
>   1 cup (240ml) brandy (approximate)
>   1 pound (454g) dry fondant (approximate)
>   1½ pounds (681g) dark chocolate, tempered for dipping, page 107

Days before you begin, drain the juice from the cherries. Let them remain in the sieve five minutes or more to drain as thoroughly as possible. Replace drained cherries in the empty jar and fill it with brandy. Cover the jar. Allow cherries to soak for at least a day or two—a week is even better.

Above: Chocolate-dipped Strawberries in a Sugar Candy Dish. Page 144 tells how to make the dish.

1. Drain the brandy-soaked cherries, letting them remain in the sieve at least five minutes. Reserve the brandy. Place about half of the cherries in a bowl with a rounded bottom. A two-quart (two-liter) metal mixing bowl is ideal. Rotate the bowl rapidly so the cherries roll briskly around the sides. Toss a handful of the dry fondant into the bowl as you continue rotating it. As soon as the cherries have picked up all the fondant, add a little more. When the cherries appear dry, add a spoonful of the reserved brandy, then more fondant. Never stop rotating the bowl.

2. Repeat the process three or four times until the cherries have built up a coating of brandy, and fondant and resemble round pink balls. Coat the other half of the cherries the same way.

3. As soon as all the cherries are coated, dip them in the tempered chocolate (see page 107). If you delay, the coating will break down. Make sure they are *well coated* with chocolate. If you see a spot not covered on a candy, touch it up with a little chocolate. Candies will "leak" unless the center has an air-tight chocolate coating. Store in a cool place for a day or two before serving. The fondant will have changed into a delightful cordial, with a flavorsome cherry swimming inside the chocolate shell. Store in a covered box in a cool place for up to three weeks. Yield: about 70 candies.

Note: Brandied cherries are best made by a congenial group. As one person tempers the chocolate, a second rotates the bowl and a third adds fondant and brandy. Any number may supervise. Have a second party in a few days to sample the finished candies.

VIENNA COMPOTES

A delightful and elegant European confection! The sunny flavors of fruit and nuts are enhanced with brandy, sweetened with honey, enriched with chocolate.

1 ounce (28g) pitted prunes
1 ounce (28g) pitted dates
1 ounce (28g) figs
1 ounce (28g) dried apples
1 ounce (28g) dried pears
1 ounce (28g) dried apricots
1 ounce (28g) dried peaches
1 ounce (28g) slivered almonds
1 ounce (28g) chopped pistachios
2 ounces (60ml) honey
3 ounces (90ml) brandy, approximate
½ cup (120ml) light corn syrup
2 pounds (908g) dark chocolate, tempered for dipping (page 107)
½ pound (227g) dark chocolate, prepared for piping (page 113)

Before you begin, crisp the almonds. Coarsely chop all the fruits on a cutting board with a long sharp knife. Line two cookie sheets with wax paper.

1. In a mixing bowl, combine fruits and almonds. Add honey, then just enough brandy to hold mixture together. Set aside to mellow for one hour or more at room temperature.

2. Take off portions of the mixture and form into ovals about 1¼" (3.2cm) long. Place on prepared cookie sheets. Heat corn syrup to boiling in a small saucepan and brush on ovals while hot. Allow to cool to room temperature, about 20 minutes.

3. Set up an area for dipping as shown on page 107. Dip the ovals into the tempered chocolate, using a loop-shaped dipping fork. Do not completely submerge the candies — leave an opening on top for a glimpse of fruit and nuts. Slide the dipped candy onto a cookie sheet covered with wax paper. Place cookie sheet in refrigerator for *five minutes only,* then complete hardening the chocolate at room temperature.

4. Prepare the half-pound (227g) of chocolate for piping. Drop tube 17 in a paper cone (page 26), half-fill with chocolate, and pipe a zigzag trim on each candy. Top with a piece of pistachio. Yield: about 90 candies.

Chapter 14

SPARKLING HARD CANDIES
TAFFY, TOFFEE, BRITTLES, TOO

In this chapter you'll find a treasure trove of old-fashioned sweets that are even more popular today. There's taffy, the satiny candy that's best made by a group so everyone can share in the fun of pulling it to long shining ropes. Toffee, the superlative buttery, crunchy confection crowned with chocolate and crisp nuts. And until you've tasted homemade brittle, you won't know how delicious brittle can be! All have one thing in common—they're cooked to high temperatures. Your thermometer is your most important tool.

Clear hard candy is the star of this group, and the simplest to make. By cooking a syrup mixture to the right temperature, you can turn out sparkling lollipops, brilliant confetti candy, old-fashioned butterscotch and anise drops, even shimmering serving trays to display your homemade candies. Just follow these guidelines to bring your hard candies to jewel-like perfection.

Use cane sugar. Beet sugar has the same degree of sweetness as cane sugar, but when brought to a high temperature, foams up too much for good results.

Use highest heat. The quicker hard candies are cooked, the better the results. Lower heat leads to longer cooking time and gives the candies a brownish color. When adding water, make sure it is hot.

Use a heavy pan of the right size. If you own pans with non-stick surfaces, they're ideal for cooking candies.

Stir hard candies with a wooden spoon after they've been put on the heat *only until all sugar crystals are dissolved.* Then wash down the sides of the pan with a pastry brush dipped in hot water. Remove spoon and clip on thermometer. After this, *do not stir*—stirring may cause crystallization, with the result of a sugary, dull candy. Don't scrape the pan when pouring out the cooked candy to cool.

Always oil the slab or pan on which the candy cools. Oil molds, too, for lollipops or molded "toys". Use a clear vegetable oil applied with a pastry brush. Be sure to use molds especially made for high-temperature candies.

Use only oil-based flavorings in hard candies. The flavors of extracts will waft away with the steam when they're added to the hot syrup.

Humidity is an enemy of hard candies. Make hard candies in a room free of steam. To compensate for some humidity, cook to a higher temperature. While 290°F-300°F (144°C-149°C) is sufficient for a dry atmosphere, cook to 310°F-320°F (155°C-160°C) on a more humid day. Don't attempt to make hard candy in damp weather.

Always wrap hard candies in clear plastic wrap as soon as they are cool. These candies absorb moisture from the air, and become sticky if not wrapped.

At left: glittering hard candy lollipops make a pretty party centerpiece. To learn the easy way to make them, please turn the page.

CREATE A SPARKLING CANDY DISH

Imagine your guests' surprise when they learn that the sparkling server that holds your homemade candies is made of candy itself! Put your creativity and this easy recipe together—you'll make this candy dish that glitters like cut glass in just half an hour or less. See it on page 140.

    3 cups (720ml or 600g) granulated sugar

    ¾ cup (180ml) hot water

    ¼ teaspoon (1.2ml) cream of tartar

    3 or 4 drops of food coloring
        (approximate)

    3 drops oil of peppermint

Before you begin, brush a marble slab or two cookie sheets with vegetable oil. Arrange, upside down, three metal or glass bowls about 4½" (11.4cm) in diameter to use as molds. Have ready a long sharp knife.

1. Combine sugar, hot water and cream of tartar in a heavy two-quart (two-liter) sauce-pan. Set over high heat. Stir with a wooden spoon to dissolve all sugar crystals. Wash down sides of pan with a pastry brush dipped in hot water and clip on thermometer. Cook, without stirring, until thermometer registers 310°F (154°C). Wash down sides of pan twice more while cooking—entire process takes about 10 minutes. Remove from heat and stir in food coloring and flavoring.

2. Now work quickly. Immediately pour cooked syrup into several circles on pre-pared slab or cookie sheets, making circles as well formed as possible and each about 6½" (16.5cm) in diameter. Do not scrape pan. Let set just a minute and form criss-cross designs by pressing with the knife. While circles are still hot, but can be touched, slide a spatula under each and place over bowls, *design sides next to bowls.* Press lightly with your hands to shape, and form casual flutes.

If a circle should harden before you have formed the shape, don't be concerned. Set bowl with circle over it in a 200°F (93°C) oven with the door open. In just a few minutes the candy will be soft enough to form.

3. Allow the candy dishes to harden on the bowls at room temperature about 15 minutes. When completely cooled, remove from bowls. Keep in a cool dry place for up to three weeks. Yield: three candy dishes.

SERVE DESSERT IN STYLE

Use these sparkling servers as dessert dishes. Place one on a doily on each plate. Just before serving, fill with a ball of ice cream and garnish with a fluff of whipped cream, a strawberry or cherry and a few fresh mint leaves.

LITTLE LOLLIPOPS

If you've never worked with hard candy before—start here! In just a few minutes you'll turn out ten perfect little lollipops— bright and shiny as jewels! Make sure the pan used for cooking is of no more than one- to two-quart (one- to two-liter) capacity— this is a small recipe.

- 1 cup (240ml or 200g) granulated *cane* sugar
- 1/3 cup (80ml) hot water
- 1/3 cup (80ml) light corn syrup
- 1/2 teaspoon (2.5ml) liquid food color
- 1/2 teaspoon (2.5ml) oil-based flavoring
- 10 small lollipop molds
- 10 paper lollipop sticks

Before you begin, line cookie sheet smoothly with foil and brush lightly with vegetable oil. Or you may oil a marble slab. Oil the molds and assemble with sticks on the cookie sheet or slab.

1. Combine sugar, hot water and corn syrup in a heavy one- or two-quart (one- or two-liter) saucepan. Place on high heat and stir with a wooden spoon until all sugar crystals are dissolved. Wash down sides of pan with a pastry brush dipped in hot water. Clip on thermometer. Continue cooking, without stirring, until thermometer registers 300°F (149°C), then remove from heat. Entire cooking process takes about nine minutes.

2. Let stand for two minutes until bubbles disappear. Add flavoring and food color and stir to blend. Pour into prepared molds. Let harden at room temperature about ten

minutes. Unmold and lay on a paper towel to absorb oil. Wrap each lollipop in clear plastic wrap and secure with a twist tie or ribbon around stick. These will keep at room temperature for up to six weeks. Yield: ten lollipops, about 2" (5.1cm) in diameter.

BIG LOLLIPOPS

It's just as quick and easy to make big all-day lollipops as little ones! This recipe uses cream of tartar instead of corn syrup to help keep the candy from turning grainy.

- 2 cups (480ml or 400g) granulated cane sugar
- 2/3 cup (160ml) hot water
- 1/4 teaspoon (1.2ml) cream of tartar
- 1 teaspoon (5ml) liquid food color
- 1 teaspoon (5ml) oil-based flavoring
- 6 large lollipop molds
- 6 paper lollipop sticks

Before you begin, oil your marble slab. Or line a cookie sheet smoothly with foil and oil the foil. Oil molds and assemble with sticks on slab. If your stove is electric, turn one unit to high.

1. Combine sugar, water and cream of tartar in a three-quart (three-liter) heavy saucepan. Place over high heat and stir constantly with a wooden spoon until all sugar crystals are dissolved. Wash down sides of pan with a pastry brush dipped in hot water, then clip on thermometer. Continue cooking, without stirring, washing down sides of pan twice more. When temperature reaches 300°F (149°C), remove from heat. Cooking time is about twelve minutes.

2. Let stand a minute or two until bubbles disappear. Stir in food color and flavoring, then immediately pour into prepared molds. Do not scrape pan. Let harden at room temperature for about 15 minutes. Unmold and wrap each lollipop in a square of plastic wrap. Secure with a twist tie or ribbon. Store at room temperature for up to six weeks. Yield: six lollipops, about 3 1/2" (8.9cm) in diameter.

Decorate lollipops with Wilton Royal Icing, (page 126), cut about 1/4" (.6cm) off the point and drop in tube 1. Fill with icing and pipe names, scallops or flowery designs. Perfect for birthday party favors or little gifts.

HARD CANDY HINTS

Never double a recipe for hard candy (except the recipe for Little Lollipops, page 145). Instead, repeat it. Larger batches will take too long to cook, and may discolor. The hot cooked syrup will be too heavy to control as you pour it into molds, and may solidify before you have time to pour all of it.

Hard candy "toys". Use molds for cartoon characters, bells, hearts, flowers or novelty shapes. Just be sure the molds are made of synthetic material for high temperatures, or of metal. These candies are favorites with children, look pretty in a gift box and make sparkling cake decorations. A recipe containing two cups of sugar will make about 50 small shapes.

Never stir hard candy after sugar crystals are dissolved. This could cause a grainy, dull appearance. (An exception: a recipe containing butter should be stirred occasionally to prevent scorching.) And do not scrape the pan as you pour out the candy to firm and cool.

Have everything you need at hand before you start cooking. Hard candy sets up fast!

When thermometer reaches 270°F (132°C), watch carefully. The temperature will rise very quickly from this point on.

The hard candy recipes on pages 144-146 may be used for patties, lollipops, "toys" or "pillows". For pillows, firm the candy in a shallow pan, or within metal candy bars. Score deeply with a sharp knife before the candy hardens—about four to five minutes. When cool, break into pieces.

The cooked syrup is very hot—so take care to avoid a painful burn.

BUTTERSCOTCH PILLOWS

Rich, smooth little amber pillows! Pack in a canister for a special gift!

- $^1/_2$ cup (120ml or 112g) butter
- 2 cups (480ml or 400g) granulated cane sugar
- $^1/_2$ cup (120ml) light corn syrup
- $^3/_4$ cup (180ml) hot water
- 1 teaspoon (5ml) lemon juice

Before you begin, oil a marble slab, arrange metal candy bars to form an 8" (20.3cm) square and oil inner sides of bars. Or line an 8" (20.3cm) square pan with foil and oil the foil.

1. Cut butter in small pieces and melt over medium heat in a heavy three-quart (three-liter) saucepan. Add sugar, corn syrup and water and stir constantly until all sugar crystals are dissolved. Clip on thermometer. Continue cooking, stirring occasionally, to 278°F (137°C). Remove from heat. Cooking takes about 55 minutes.

2. Add lemon juice, stirring until bubbles subside. Pour onto prepared slab or pan. Do not scrape pan. When candy has just set, only about four or five minutes, remove metal bars and score deeply with a sharp knife, almost through to base of candy. First score in $^1/_2$" (1.2cm) strips, then score in opposite direction every 1" (2.5cm). Allow to cool completely at room temperature, about an hour. Break into little "pillows". Wrap each candy in a square of clear plastic wrap, twisting ends to seal. Store at room temperature for up to six weeks. Yield: 128 candies.

BUTTERSCOTCH PATTIES

Three simple ingredients go together like magic to make shining patties with a rich buttery taste. Because butter is one of the ingredients, cook this candy at medium heat, rather than high heat.

- $^1/_2$ cup (120ml) dark corn syrup
- $^1/_4$ cup (60ml or 56g) butter
- $^3/_4$ cup (180ml or 150g) granulated cane sugar

Before you begin, oil your marble slab or a cookie sheet. Place mint patty funnel and stick in a pan of simmering water to heat. Keep water at simmer as you cook candy.

1. Combine all ingredients in a heavy one-quart (one-liter) saucepan. Place over medium heat and stir constantly with a wooden spoon until all sugar crystals are dissolved. Wash down sides of pan with a pastry brush dipped in hot water, then clip on thermometer.

2. Continue cooking, stirring occasionally, and washing down sides of pan twice more. When temperature reaches 270°F (132°C), remove from heat. Cooking time is about 20 minutes.

3. Insert stick in preheated funnel. Have a helper hold funnel and stick as you pour in

hot syrup. Drop patties on the prepared slab just as you would mint patties (page 98). Work quickly and rhythmically as you lift stick and then push down to form a patty about 2" (5.1cm) in diameter.

If you prefer, you may form the patties by dropping syrup from a spoon, but the funnel method is quicker, and produces more uniform patties.

4. Cool to room temperature, about 15 minutes. Wrap each pattie in a square of clear plastic to store for up to six weeks. Yield: about 30 patties.

AMBER LACE CANDY TRAYS

Here's a dazzling quick technique that displays the ability of a highly heated sugar mixture to form glistening, lace-like threads. With it, you can easily make a beautiful tray to display your confections that appears to be made of spun amber—and the whole process will take only about 20 minutes. You may make these beautiful serving pieces as much as a week ahead, but do not attempt them in hot humid weather.

   1 1/3 cups (320ml or 267g) granulated cane sugar
   1/2 cup (120ml) light corn syrup
   2/3 cup (160ml) water

Before you begin, select two trays to shape your creations. Any plate or tray up to 13"

(33cm) in diameter may be used.

Cover the *backs* of the trays smoothly with foil. Thoroughly but lightly grease the foil with solid white vegetable shortening.

1. Blend all ingredients in a three-quart (three-liter) heavy saucepan. Place on high heat and cook without stirring until syrup becomes a delicate amber. Wash down the sides of the pan several times with a pastry brush dipped in hot water as the syrup cooks. The amber color is the best way to judge if the syrup is cooked. but the temperature will reach 320°F to 330°F (160°C to 165°C). This will take about ten minutes.

2. Remove pan from heat and let stand until bubbles disappear. Grease a teaspoon lightly with solid white vegetable shortening. Dip it in the syrup and move your hand rapidly back and forth over the back of the prepared tray. Continue until tray is covered with a lace-like design. Build up the level surface a little more heavily for strength.

3. When tray is just warm, but not cooled completely, lift foil off form and peel foil away from lace design. Candy will still be flexible and you may shape it slightly with your hands. Cool thoroughly. Line the center of the tray with a grease-proof doily, then arrange your homemade candies for an exquisite display. Doily will keep the candies from sticking. Yield: two 12" (30.5cm) oval trays.

CONFETTI CANDY

For charming gifts, mix a variety of these candies together, then fill pretty glass jars or brandy snifters and dress up with ribbons. The method for making them is simple and fun to do. Make four or five batches of the Little Lollipop recipe (page 145), flavoring and coloring each differently. Tint yellow for lemon, green for peppermint, pink for raspberry, red for anise, or dream up your own combinations. Use oil-based flavorings only.

1. Sift confectioners' sugar liberally over a marble slab—or use the back of a large, heavy cookie sheet. (Sugar is used instead of oil.) Have a long sharp knife at hand.

2. Make Little Lollipop recipe through Step 1. Pour out on prepared slab or cookie sheet. Watch carefully as candy begins to set up—just a few minutes. Score with the knife into 1/2" (1.2cm) strips, then score again in opposite direction to form 1/2" (1.2cm) pieces.

3. Allow to harden, just a few minutes, then loosen candy from slab with spatula and break into pieces over edge of slab. Place pieces in a large strainer and shake to distribute sugar. Pack a variety of the candies in glass container and cover, or stretch clear plastic wrap over container and tie with a ribbon. Yield: about 90 candies from each batch.

OLD-FASHIONED ANISE DROPS

Just like the ones you remember!

1. Follow the recipe for Big Lollipops, page 145, through Step 1. Use 1 3/4 teaspoons (8ml) of oil of anise and 1 teaspoon (5ml) of red liquid food coloring.

2. Drop into patties 2" (5.1cm) in diameter with a teaspoon on oiled cookie sheets or marble slab. Or use the funnel-and-stick method, page 146, for more uniform patties. When cool, wrap each in a square of clear plastic to store for up to 6 weeks. Yield: about 85 candies.

To thin brittle the professional candymaker's way, use clean heavy work gloves, the palms soaked liberally with vegetable oil. After candy has cooled just a few minutes, loosen it from slab or cookie sheet with a spatula. Pick it up with gloved hands and pull and stretch to thin. Return to slab for scoring and final cooling.

FAVORITE PEANUT BRITTLE

This is the familiar "blonde" peanut brittle, loaded with crunchy nuts.

> 2 cups (480ml or 400g) granulated sugar
> 1 cup (240ml) light corn syrup
> 1/2 cup (120ml) hot water
> 1 tablespoon (15ml) butter
> 1 teaspoon (5ml) baking soda
> 2 cups (480ml or 288g) dry roasted salted peanuts

Before you begin, butter a marble slab or 12" x 18" (30.5cm x 45.7cm) cookie sheet.

1. Combine sugar, syrup and hot water in a three-quart (three-liter) heavy saucepan. Place on high heat. Stir constantly with a wooden spoon until all sugar crystals are dissolved. Wash down sides of pan with a pastry brush dipped in hot water, then clip on thermometer. Continue cooking, washing down sides of pan twice more, to 300°F (149°C). Remove from heat. Entire cooking time is about ten minutes.

2. Immediately stir in butter, baking soda and nuts. Mix well. Mixture will be foamy. Pour out on slab and flatten with spoon.

3. Allow to cool about five minutes, then loosen candy from slab with a spatula. Put on heavy gloves and grasp candy by edges to stretch and thin it. Return to slab and score into 1 1/4" (3.2cm) squares with a sharp knife. Allow to cool completely, about 30 minutes, then break into pieces. Store in a tightly sealed container, or plastic bag for up to a month. Yield: about 50 pieces.

TO VARY THIS RECIPE

Make Coconut Brittle by substituting 1 1/2 cups (127g) of toasted flaked coconut and 1/4 teaspoon (1.2ml) salt for the peanuts.

PUFFED RICE BRITTLE

If you like brittle, you'll love this candy! It has a glossy dark russet color, a deep caramel-like flavor and a crunchy crisp texture. The cereal is added when the candy has already cooked to a high temperature, so it has a roasted flavor like crisp nuts. This is an economy candy—but it doesn't taste like one! *Be sure to use a four-quart (four-liter) heavy pan to cook this candy. It foams up as it heats.*

   1 cup (240ml) water
   1 cup (240ml or 200g) granulated sugar
   1 cup (240ml or 170g) light brown sugar, lightly packed
   1½ cups (360ml) dark corn syrup
   1 cup (240ml or 150g) roasted Spanish peanuts
   2 cups (480ml or 56g) puffed rice
   1 teaspoon (5ml) butter
   1 teaspoon (5ml) salt
   1 teaspoon (5ml) baking soda

Before you begin, put nuts and cereal in a sheet cake pan and place in oven set at lowest temperature to warm. Butter a marble slab or butter a 12" x 18" (30.5cm x 45.7cm) cookie sheet.

1. Combine water, granulated and brown sugars and corn syrup in a four-quart (four-liter) heavy pan. Place over low heat and stir constantly with a wooden spoon until all sugar crystals are dissolved. Wash down sides of pan with a pastry brush dipped in hot water. Clip on thermometer.

2. Continue cooking, washing down sides of pan with a wet pastry brush three or four more times. Do not stir. When temperature reaches 270°F (132°C) reduce heat to low—it will rise quickly from this point. At 290°F (143°C) add butter, puffed rice and peanuts. Cook two minutes longer at low heat.

3. Remove from heat and stir in baking soda and salt. Pour onto prepared marble slab or cookie sheets. Do not scrape pan. While candy is still warm, score into 1¼" (3.2cm) squares with a sharp knife. Cool completely, about 30 minutes, then break into pieces. Store at room temperature in a tightly closed plastic bag for weeks. This candy keeps very well—it's ideal to send as a gift. Yield: about 60 pieces.

MOLASSES WALNUT BRITTLE

Lots of crunchy walnuts make this brittle a treat. The nuts are crisped by adding them before the brittle has completed cooking.

   ½ cup (120ml) hot water
   ¼ cup (60ml) molasses
   ¼ cup (60ml) light corn syrup
   1½ cups (360ml or 300g) granulated sugar
   1½ cups (360ml or 150g) walnuts, coarsely chopped
   1 tablespoon (15ml) butter
   ¼ teaspoon (1.2ml) salt
   ½ teaspoon (2.5ml) baking soda
   1 teaspoon (5ml) vanilla extract

Before you begin, butter a marble slab or a heavy 12" x 18" (30.5cm x 45.7cm) cookie sheet. Chop and measure the nuts.

1. Combine water, molasses, corn syrup and sugar in a heavy four-quart (four-liter) saucepan. Set over medium heat and stir constantly with a wooden spoon until all sugar crystals are dissolved. Wash down sides of pan with pastry brush dipped in hot water. Clip on thermometer. Continue cooking, without stirring, to 268°F (130°C), about 20 minutes. Wash down sides of pan again during this period. Gradually stir in walnuts, then butter and salt. Continue cooking, stirring constantly to 300°F (149°C), about eight minutes. Remove from heat and stir in soda and vanilla until thoroughly mixed. Candy will foam.

2. Pour onto prepared slab or cookie sheet and press with spoon to flatten. When candy has slightly cooled, about five minutes, loosen from slab with a spatula. Put on heavy gloves and grasp candy by edges to stretch and thin. Score with a sharp knife into 1¼" (3.2cm) squares. Allow to cool completely, about 30 minutes, then break into pieces. Store in a tightly sealed plastic bag for up to a month. Yield: about 60 pieces.

ALMOND TOFFEE

Surprisingly easy to make—rich, crisp and utterly delicious!

  1 pound (454g) butter

  2 tablespoons (30ml) water

  2 cups (480ml or 400g) granulated
    cane sugar

  $\frac{1}{2}$ teaspoon (2.5ml) salt

  2 cups (480ml or 320g) finely chopped
    almonds, crisped

  10 ounces (284g) milk chocolate,
    chopped

Before you begin, butter a 12" x 18" (30.5cm x 45.7cm) cookie sheet. Crisp the nuts and chop the chocolate.

1. Put butter (cut in thin slices) and water in a heavy 12" (30.5cm) skillet over medium-high heat. Stir with a wooden spoon until melted, then add sugar and salt as you continue stirring. When mixture loses its yellow color and becomes whitish, add one cup of the nuts. Continue cooking, stirring constantly, to 300°F (149°C). Mixture will be a caramel color. Remove from heat. Cooking takes about 20 minutes.

2. Turn into prepared pan and cool just until set, but not completely hardened. Score into $1\frac{1}{2}$" (3.8cm) squares with a sharp knife. Cool completely, about 30 minutes.

3. Melt chocolate in top pan of double boiler over hot water, stirring constantly. Spread over toffee with a spatula and sprinkle with the second cup of nuts, covering surface completely. Refrigerate until chocolate hardens, about 20 minutes. Break into squares. Store in a tightly sealed container at room temperature for up to three weeks. Yield: about 90 pieces.

WILTON TOFFEE

Make this superlative candy with just four ingredients—and at about one-third the cost of the purchased variety!

  1 pound (454g) butter

  3 cups (720ml or 600g) granulated sugar

  2 cups (480ml or 227g) finely chopped
    walnuts, crisped

  1 pound (454g) dark chocolate, chopped

Before you begin, crisp the nuts. Butter a heavy 12" x 18" (30.5cm x 45.7cm) cookie sheet.

1. Cut butter in thin slices and melt in a heavy, three-quart (three-liter) saucepan over medium heat. Add sugar and continue cooking, stirring constantly with a wooden spoon to 290°F (144°C). Remove from heat. Cooking takes about 40 minutes.

2. Spread on prepared cookie sheet and cool at room temperature until firm, about 25 minutes. Score with a sharp knife into $1\frac{1}{2}$" (3.8cm) strips before candy is completely set up. While candy cools, melt chocolate. Bring water in lower pan of double boiler to a simmer, remove from heat and place top pan in position. Pour in chopped chocolate, a third at a time, and stir until smooth and melted. Spread half the chocolate over the surface of the candy with a spatula, then sprinkle with half the nuts, covering chocolate completely. Refrigerate until chocolate hardens, about 30 minutes.

3. Loosen candy from cookie sheet with a spatula, cover cookie sheet with a second cookie sheet and invert to turn candy upside down. Re-melt remaining chocolate, if necessary. Spread over surface of candy and cover with remaining nuts. Refrigerate until chocolate hardens.

4. Break candy into scored strips, then into irregular pieces about $1\frac{1}{2}$" (3.8cm) square. Store in a tightly sealed container at room temperature for about three weeks. Yield: 90 pieces.

Pulling taffy is one of the pleasures of making candy at home! Pour out the candy on an oiled marble slab or cookie sheet, with a light dusting of sifted flour. Cool a few minutes, then use a spatula to fold the edges of the candy into the center to evenly distribute heat. When candy is cool enough to touch, oil your hands and pull and stretch the candy into long ropes. It's easier for two to do this. Continue pulling, folding ropes and stretching for about ten minutes. Cut into 1" (2.5cm) pieces with a scissors. Wrap each in a square of plastic wrap, twisting ends to seal.

SALT WATER TAFFY

This is the old-fashioned, best-loved favorite. Glycerine gives it a nice chewiness, and eliminates a too-sweet taste.

    2 cups (480ml or 400g) granulated cane sugar

    1½ cups (360ml) hot water

    1½ cups (360ml) light corn syrup

    2 tablespoons (30ml) glycerine

    1½ teaspoons (7.5ml) salt

    1 teaspoon (5ml) vanilla

    2 or 3 drops liquid food color

Before you begin, oil your marble slab and dust lightly with sifted flour. Or oil and dust a heavy cookie sheet.

1. Combine sugar, water, corn syrup, glycerine and salt in a four-quart (four-liter) heavy saucepan. Place over medium-high heat and stir constantly until all sugar crystals are dissolved. Wash down sides of pan with a pastry brush dipped in hot water, then clip on thermometer. Cook, without stirring, to 265°F (129°C), washing down sides of pan twice more. Remove from heat. Cooking takes about 25 minutes.

2. Stir in vanilla and food coloring, then pour out onto prepared slab or cookie sheet. Cool, pull, cut and wrap candy as described above. Store wrapped candy in a tightly sealed container for up to a month at room temperature. Yield: about 85 pieces.

SPICY MOLASSES TAFFY

A smooth, rich taffy with a full-bodied molasses flavor. Use a six-quart (six-liter) heavy saucepan or dutch oven for cooking — this candy foams up.

    1½ cups (360ml) light molasses

    1½ cups (360ml or 300g) granulated cane sugar

    1½ teaspoons (7.5ml) white vinegar

    ½ cup (120ml) hot water

    ¼ teaspoon (1.2ml) salt

    3 tablespoons (45ml or 43g) butter

Before you begin, oil a marble slab and lightly dust with sifted flour. Or oil and dust a 12" x 18" (30.5cm x 45.7cm) cookie sheet.

1. Combine molasses, sugar, vinegar, water and salt in a six-quart (six-liter) heavy saucepan or dutch oven. Place over medium heat and stir constantly with a wooden spoon until all sugar crystals are dissolved. Wash down sides of pan with a pastry brush dipped in hot water, then clip on thermometer. Cook to 250°F (121°C), washing down sides of pan twice more.

2. Add butter, cut in thin slices. Continue cooking, stirring occasionally, to 265°F (129°C). Remove from heat.

3. Pour out onto prepared slab or cookie sheet. Cool, pull, cut and wrap the candy as described at left. Store for up to a month in a tightly sealed container at room temperature. Yield: about 125 pieces.

Chapter 15

CONTINENTAL CHOCOLATES
CANDIES FOR CONNOISSEURS

Have you had the fun of working fondant, molding and dipping in chocolate and making marzipan? This chapter is for you! The recipes are all for classic European delicacies, refined, rich and elegant. What is needed to make them? The very finest ingredients, lots of love and care and just basic techniques taught in previous chapters of this book. Time is needed, too. These are not recipes that can be rushed through!

Almost all of these candies are composed, just as an artist would combine many elements to produce a masterpiece. This blending of several different mixtures in one candy gives them their subtle, refined flavor. You will notice that many of the recipes call for liqueur. The liqueur adds delicate flavor, and in addition, keeps the candies fresh for a relatively long period. These candies actually improve and mellow with age!

So make some candy masterpieces yourself. Select the recipe that appeals to you most, then delight your friends with a truly magnificent sweet—one that cannot be purchased in any store. And don't forget to study the picture of the finished candy. It will show you just how your candy will look with its final touch of decoration.

EGGNOG CUPS

Rich, mellow, with an exquisite subtle flavor —chocolates to crown a grand celebration!

2 pounds (908g) dark chocolate, tempered for molding (page 106)

3½ ounces (100g) almond paste

1 ounce (30ml) light corn syrup

2 ounces (60ml) sweetened condensed milk

3 ounces (90ml) eggnog liqueur

½ pound (227g) tempered milk chocolate, prepared for piping (page 113)

Before you begin, make dark chocolate shells to hold filling. Use the two pounds (908g) dark chocolate, flute candy molds and follow directions on page 111.

1. Crumble almond paste in a mixing bowl. Gradually add the syrup, kneading to form a smooth paste. Gradually stir in the condensed milk and liqueur. Mix well until smooth and fluffy. Put the mixture in a paper decorating cone (page 26), fold to seal and cut the point. With light pressure, pipe into the chocolate shells, filling just ¾ full. Set aside for ten minutes.

2. Fill a paper decorating cone with the leftover tempered dark chocolate, seal and cut point. Apply pressure to pipe the chocolate over the filled shells to seal. Refrigerate five minutes only. Unmold candies.

3. Fill a paper decorating cone with the half pound (227g) milk chocolate prepared for piping, fold to seal, cut tip and pipe a zigzag on top of each candy. Yield: about 100 Eggnog Cups.

To store continental chocolates, place each candy in a paper candy cup. Pack snugly in a box and cover with clear plastic wrap. Cover the box. Keep in a cool place, about 65°F to 72°F (18°C to 22°C). They will keep perfectly for up to six weeks.

At left: a luxurious assortment of Continental Chocolates. Starting at far left, outer edge of tray, Chocolate Mountains, Eggnog Cups, Orange Marzipan Wedges and Hazelnut Peaks, garnished with candied violet petals. On inner circle, Citron Bonbons, more Orange Marzipan Wedges, Pecan Delights and Royal Chocolate Prunes. In center, Mocha Crescents.

CHOCOLATE MOUNTAINS

These "chocolate mountains" resemble Mount Rigi, which towers above Lucerne in Switzerland. Make the marzipan bases first.

MARZIPAN FOR BASES

- 4 ounces (112g) almond paste
- 1 ounce (28g) sifted confectioners' sugar
- 1 ounce (30ml) light corn syrup (approximate)

Crumble almond paste in mixing bowl. Mix thoroughly with sugar. Knead by hand, adding just enough syrup to form a soft pliable mass. Roll out on surface dusted with confectioners' sugar to $1/8$" (.3cm) thick. Dust rolling pin with confectioners' sugar. Cut into 1" (2.5cm) circles and allow to dry, about one hour.

FILLING AND COATING

- 3 ounces (85g) unsalted butter, room temperature
- 3 ounces (150g) fondant, either Wilton Corn Syrup or Cream of Tartar (pages 92 and 94)
- 6 ounces (170g) dark chocolate, tempered for dipping (page 107)
- $2^{1}/_{2}$ ounces (75ml) cherry brandy
- $1^{1}/_{2}$ pounds (681g) dark chocolate, tempered for dipping (page 107)
- $1/2$ pound (227g) milk chocolate, tempered for dipping (page 107)

1. A hand-held mixer is best for mixing the filling. At medium speed, whip butter, then add fondant, broken in pieces. Gradually add the 6 ounces (170g) dark chocolate and brandy. Whip until fluffy and well mixed. Make a paper decorating cone (page 26), cut point and drop in tube 19. Fill $2/3$ full of mixture and fold to seal. Hold cone straight up and press gently to pipe a high mound on each marzipan base. Refrigerate one hour.

2. Dip candies in the $1^{1}/_{2}$ pounds (681g) tempered dark chocolate, using a loop dipping fork. Slide candies, *right side up*, off fork onto wax paper-lined tray. Place tray in refrigerator for *five minutes only*, then complete hardening at room temperature. Wear thin cotton gloves to hold candies upside down to dip the tips in the milk chocolate. Let harden. Yield: about 65 candies.

MOCHA CRESCENTS

Little chocolate half-moons with luscious almond-coffee filling and the garnish of milk chocolate hearts.

- about 60 molded milk chocolate hearts
- 4 ounces (112g) almond paste
- $3/4$ ounce (21g) sifted confectioners' sugar
- $1/2$ ounce (15ml) coffee liqueur (approximate)
- $1/2$ teaspoon (2.5ml) dry instant coffee
- $1^{3}/_{4}$ pounds (794g) dark chocolate, tempered for dipping (page 107)

Before you begin, follow the directions on page 106 to mold the hearts in milk chocolate, using a plastic mold.

1. Crumble almond paste in a mixing bowl and mix with sugar and instant coffee. Knead well, adding enough liqueur to form a pliable paste. Take off teaspoon-sized portions of the mixture and model into crescent shapes. Set on cookie sheet, lightly dusted with flour.

2. Dip the crescents in the tempered dark chocolate, according to directions on page 107. Place in refrigerator for *five minutes only,* then complete hardening at room temperature. Attach a molded heart to each crescent with a dot of soft chocolate. Yield: about 60 crescents.

PECAN DELIGHTS

Crisp fluted chocolate shells are filled with a melt-in-the-mouth truffle mixture. Inside, there's a surprise of a crisp nutmeat.

- 2 pounds (908g) dark chocolate, tempered for molding (page 106)
- 3 egg yolks
- 6 ounces (168g) granulated sugar
- 16 ounces (480ml) whipping cream
- 2 pounds (908g) dark chocolate, finely chopped
- 3 ounces (90ml) hazelnut liqueur*
- 4 ounces (112g) broken pecans, crisped
- $1/2$ pound (227g) milk chocolate, prepared for piping (page 113)

Before you begin, mold about 90 hollow chocolate shells in tempered dark chocolate (first item in list above), using fluted bonbon molds. Follow directions on page 111. Unmold shells carefully and line up on tray. Crisp the nuts.

154

1. Make filling. Whisk egg yolks and sugar together until fluffy. Bring cream to a boil in a small saucepan, stirring constantly. Remove from heat and add chopped chocolate. Stir until chocolate is melted and mixture is smooth. Blend a little of the chocolate mixture into the egg yolk mixture, then stir egg yolk mixture gradually into chocolate mixture. Stir in liqueur. Refrigerate about an hour.

2. Drop a pecan piece into each chocolate shell. Remove filling from refrigerator and beat just a moment or two with a hand-held electric mixer at high speed until fluffy. Fill a paper decorating cone (page 26) with mixture, cut point and pipe into chocolate shells, not quite to the top.** Seal shells with tempered dark chocolate, applied with a small spatula. Allow to harden at room temperature.

3. Make a paper decorating cone, cut point and drop in tube 17. Fill with the milk chocolate prepared for piping, seal, and pipe a decorative swirl on top of each chocolate. Yield: about 120 candies.

ORANGE MARZIPAN WEDGES

Smooth milk chocolate enrobes a marzipan filling with an intense but delicate orange flavor. Use your own homemade candied orange peel for best flavor.

    2 pounds (908g) almond paste

    3 ounces (85g) sifted confectioners' sugar

    1/2 cup (120ml) orange liqueur

    2 ounces (56g) orange-flavored powdered drink mix

    5 ounces (140g) finely chopped candied orange peel

    2 pounds (908g) milk chocolate, tempered for dipping (page 107)

    1/2 pound (227g) milk chocolate, prepared for piping (page 113)

    candied orange peel squares for garnish

Before you begin, cut the 5 ounces (140g) candied orange peel into tiny pieces with a scissors.

1. Make centers. Dust work surface with confectioners' sugar. Knead almond paste and sugar together, gradually adding liqueur. Add drink mix and chopped orange peel and knead to a smooth pliable mass.

Roll out on surface dusted with confectioners' sugar to 1/2" (1.2cm) thickness. Use confectioners' sugar to dust rolling pin. Cut into 1" (2.5cm) squares, then cut each square in half, diagonally, to form wedges.

2. Dip wedges in the two pounds of tempered milk chocolate with a two-tined dipping fork, (see page 107). Deposit, upside down, on cookie sheet covered with wax paper. Lightly press fork on surface of candy to form ridges. Place cookie sheet in refrigerator for *five minutes only.*

3. Make a paper cone (page 26), cut point and drop in tube 17. Fill with the 1/2 pound (227g) milk chocolate for piping, and pipe an "S" shape at wider edge of each wedge. While chocolate is still soft, press a square of candied orange peel on each "S". Yield: about 90 Orange Marzipan Wedges.

CITRON BONBONS

The tang of lemon, the sweetness of raisins and the richness of marzipan are combined, then enrobed in a creamy coating. Superb!

    1 recipe Continental Marzipan (page 126)

    1 ounce (28g) lemon-flavored powdered drink mix

    4 ounces (120ml) lemon liqueur

    2 1/2 ounces (70g) golden raisins, chopped

    2 pounds (908g) white confectionery coating prepared for dipping (page 22)

    golden raisins for garnish

Before you begin, chop the 2 1/2 ounces (70g) of raisins. Place in glass jar, pour liqueur over them and cover jar. Let stand at room temperature for one hour or more.

1. Make centers. Drain raisins, reserving liqueur. Crumble marzipan in mixing bowl, add powdered drink mix and chopped raisins. Blend. Knead well, adding enough reserved liqueur to form a pliable paste. Form into centers as directed on page 97. Set on lightly floured cookie sheet to crust, about 30 minutes.

2. Dip centers following directions on page 22. Garnish each candy with a whole raisin. Yield: about 90 bonbons.

*You may substitute cognac.
**Leftover filling may be piped into paper candy cups for serving.

HAZELNUT PEAKS

Whimsically shaped chocolates concealing a ganache (truffle) mixture and a toasted hazelnut, all mounded on krokant bases. Each is crowned with a candied violet petal. If these are not obtainable in your area, substitute tiny violets piped with royal icing (page 103) and tube 225.

    1 recipe Krokant (below) for bases
    1 recipe Hazelnut Ganache (at right) for
      filling
    about 60 hazelnuts, roasted
    2 pounds (908g) milk chocolate, tem-
      pered for dipping (page 107)
    Candied violet petals for garnish

Before you begin, cut out bases for candies from Krokant. Make Hazelnut Ganache.

1. Set Krokant bases on tray. Make a paper decorating cone (page 26), cut point and drop in tube 10. Fill cone with Ganache, fold to seal, and pipe a spot of Ganache on each base. Top with a hazelnut. Now pipe three peaks around each nut, pointing outward. Refrigerate about 30 minutes to firm.

2. Bring candies to room temperature. Dip in the tempered milk chocolate as described on page 107. Slide dipped candies off fork, right side up onto cookie sheet covered with wax paper. Refrigerate five minutes only, then complete hardening the chocolate at room temperature. Dip end of a candied violet petal in soft chocolate and lightly press to centers of candies. Yield: about 60 Hazelnut Peaks.

HAZELNUT KROKANT, shown at right

    10 ounces (284g) granulated sugar
    3½ ounces (105ml) honey
    4 ounces (112g) unsalted butter
    ½ pound (227g) sliced hazelnuts

Before you begin, butter a heavy flat cookie sheet. Crisp the nuts.

1. Melt sugar in a heavy frying pan over medium heat. Put about one-third of the sugar in the pan and stir constantly with a wooden spoon until liquid and a very light brown. Add another third of the sugar, stir until melted, then repeat until all the sugar is liquid and bubbly.

2. Gradually add the honey and butter (cut in small pieces) to the sugar, stirring constantly. Be sure to add honey and butter in small amounts, so butter will be well incorporated. Blend in nuts.

3. Pour out onto prepared cookie sheet. Allow to cool slightly, about ten minutes. Butter a rolling pin and roll to ¼" (.6cm) thickness. Cut into 1" (2.5cm) circles with a buttered cookie cutter. If krokant is difficult to cut, place in oven set at 200°F (93°C), with door open, for a few minutes until it softens. Leftover scraps of krokant may be crushed and stirred into tempered chocolate, then dropped in mounds on wax paper to firm. Yield: 60 bases for candy.

HAZELNUT GANACHE

    1 cup (240ml) whipping cream
    1 pound (454g) milk chocolate, chopped
    2½ ounces (70g) ground hazelnuts
    1½ ounces (45ml) rum

1. Bring cream to a boil in a small saucepan over low heat, stirring constantly. Remove from heat and add chocolate. Stir constantly until mixture is smooth and chocolate is melted. Stir in ground nuts, then rum. Set pan in refrigerator about one hour, or until mixture is firm.

2. Beat mixture with hand-held electric mixer until fluffy. Pipe as directed in Step 1, at left. Leftover ganache may be piped into paper candy cups and served.

COGNAC CHERRIES

Make these irresistable candies as a treat for Christmas, or the most special occasion! The whole family will share in the excitement of their preparation.

- 16 ounces (454g) canned pitted sour cherries
- 1 cup (240ml) cognac (approximate)
- 1½ pounds (681g) dark chocolate, tempered for molding (page 106)
- 1 cup (240ml or 400g) Wilton Fondant, either Corn Syrup or Cream of Tartar (pages 92 and 94)
- ½ pound (227g) milk chocolate prepared for piping (page 113)

A month before you make the candies, marinate the cherries. Drain them well, then place in a glass jar and pour enough cognac over them to cover well. Seal the jar and refrigerate.

1. Make the hollow chocolate shells for the cherries as directed on page 111. Set about 75 foil candy cups on a cookie sheet. Make a paper decorating cone (page 26), half-fill it with tempered dark chocolate and cut a tiny opening from the point. Fold the top of the cone to seal and fill each foil cup to the top, using light pressure on the cone. Place filled foil cups in the freezer for just a moment, then empty excess chocolate from cups and allow to harden completely at room temperature.

2. Drain cherries well, reserving liquid, then dry on paper towels. Place a cherry in each chocolate cup.

3. Bring fondant to room temperature, place in top pan of small double boiler and break up with a wooden spoon. Place over simmering water in lower pan and stir constantly to melt. Add a little of reserved cognac, by teaspoon (5ml) to soften the fondant. Remove from heat, take off top pan, and continue stirring until fondant is at room temperature and consistency of ketchup. Fill a paper decorating cone with the fondant, cut a tiny opening from point, fold to seal, and fill the chocolate cups, not quite to the rim.

4. With a small spatula, seal the tops of the candies with tempered dark chocolate. Allow to stand about 30 minutes at room temperature to harden. Fill a paper decorating cone with prepared milk chocolate, fold

top and cut a tiny opening from point. Pipe a decorative swirl on each candy.

5. Store the candies in a covered box at about 68°F (20°C) for two weeks—then serve. The fondant will have been transformed into a delightful liqueur-flavored syrup with a cherry swimming inside the chocolate shell! Yield: about 75 cognac cherries.

VIENNESE WHIRLS

A delicious and decorative confection with a rich chocolate filling subtly flavored with cherry brandy. Hazelnuts add crunch.

FOR BASES:

> 1 recipe Continental Marzipan (page 126)

FOR FILLING

> 6 ounces (180ml or 168g) unsalted butter
>
> 1½ ounces (42g) sifted confectioners' sugar
>
> 3 ounces (90ml) cherry brandy
>
> ½ pound (227g) dark chocolate, tempered for dipping (page 107)
>
> 3 ounces (90ml or 85g) ground hazelnuts
>
> 90 whole roasted hazelnuts

FOR DIPPING AND GARNISH

> 2 pounds (908g) dark chocolate, tempered for dipping (page 107)
>
> ½ pound (227g) milk chocolate, prepared for piping (page 113)

Before you begin, make bases for filling. Roll out marzipan about ⅛" (.3cm) thick on surface dusted with confectioners' sugar. Cut out circles with a 1" (2.5cm) cutter.

1. Make filling. Beat butter and sugar with an electric mixer at medium speed until fluffy. Gradually beat in brandy. Fold in chocolate, then ground nuts. Refrigerate, if necessary, until stiff enough to pipe with. Make a paper decorating cone (page 26), cut point and drop in tube 12. Fill with filling and fold to seal. Pipe mounds of filling on prepared marzipan bases. Top each candy with a hazelnut.

2. Dip candies in tempered dark chocolate. Slide off fork, *right side up,* onto wax paper. Refrigerate *five minutes only.*

3. Make a paper cone (page 26) and fill with the milk chocolate. Cut a tiny opening in point and pipe a spiral on each candy. Make a second cone, cut point and drop in tube 17. Fill with remaining milk chocolate. Hold cone straight up and pipe a star on top of each candy. Yield: about 90 candies.

VODKA CHERRIES

Plan well ahead to make these sweets. The delightful results are well worth the wait.

> 100 maraschino cherries, stems on
>
> 2 cups (480ml) vodka (approximate)
>
> ½ recipe either Wilton Corn Syrup or Cream of Tartar Fondant, pages 92 and 94
>
> 4 pounds (1.8kg) milk chocolate, tempered for dipping (page 107)
>
> ½ pound (227g) milk chocolate, prepared for piping (page 113)

Eight weeks, or more, before you begin, marinate the cherries. Drain well, place in glass jar, then cover with vodka. Refrigerate for eight or more weeks.

1. Drain cherries well and dry on paper towels about 30 minutes. Prepare fondant for dipping (page 100), omitting food coloring and flavoring. Dip cherries, holding by stems. Dry on wax paper ten minutes.

2. The cherries are dipped twice in chocolate to make sure there are no leaks in the finished candies. Holding by stems, dip cherries into tempered chocolate to just one-third of their height. Place in refrigerator for *five minutes only.* Dip again in chocolate, covering about ¼" (.6cm) of stem to provide a firm seal. Refrigerate five minutes, then complete hardening chocolate at room temperature.

3. Make a paper decorating cone (page 26), cut point and drop in tube 65. Fill with the piping chocolate and pipe two leaves on each candy. Yield: about 100 Vodka Cherries.

CHOCOLATE DRUMS

Simply delightful, superbly rich and easy to put together.

> 8 ounces (227g) Wilton Basic Marzipan (page 117), about ⅓ of recipe
>
> 1 recipe Classic Chocolate Truffles (page 8)
>
> 3 pounds (1.4kg) dark chocolate, tempered for dipping (page 107)
>
> ½ pound (227g) milk chocolate prepared for piping (page 113)

Before you begin, make truffle recipe through Step 3. Dust work surface and rolling pin with sifted confectioners' sugar.

1. Roll out marzipan on prepared surface to a thickness of about $\frac{1}{8}$" (.3cm). Try to roll to a rectangular shape. Stir truffle well, then spread evenly over marzipan with a spatula.

2. Roll up like a jelly roll into a cylinder. When cylinder is about 1" (2.5cm) in diameter, cut it off with a sharp knife. Roll marzipan again for a second 1" (2.5cm) cylinder. Repeat for several of these cylinders. Wrap each lightly in wax paper and refrigerate one hour.

3. Cut cylinders in 1" (2.5cm) pieces, bring to room temperature, then dip in tempered dark chocolate. Refrigerate for *five minutes only*, then complete hardening chocolate at room temperature. Make a paper decorating cone (page 26), fill with milk chocolate, seal and cut tiny opening in point. Pipe two lines on each candy. Yield: about 100 Chocolate Drums.

KROKANT STICKS

Crunchy, crisp little sticks are dipped in chocolate, then garnished.

> 1 recipe Almond Krokant (see Step 1, below)
> $1\frac{1}{2}$ pounds (681g) milk chocolate, tempered for dipping (page 107)
> $\frac{1}{2}$ pound (227g) dark chocolate, prepared for piping (page 113)

1. Make Krokant just as on page 156, substituting $\frac{1}{2}$ pound (227g) slivered almonds for the hazelnuts. Use a buttered rolling pin to roll out about $\frac{1}{2}$" (1.2cm) thick. While still warm, cut into sticks about $\frac{1}{2}$" x 1" (1.2cm x 2.5cm) with a sharp knife. Cool to room temperature.

2. Dip in milk chocolate (page 107). Place in refrigerator for *five minutes only*, then complete hardening at room temperature. Make a paper decorating cone (page 26), cut point and drop in tube 17. Fill with dark piping chocolate. Holding cone straight up, pipe two stars on each candy. Yield: about 50 Krokant Sticks.

TO VARY THIS RECIPE

Make Krokant Squares, cut krokant into $\frac{3}{4}$" (1.9cm) squares, then dip in tempered dark chocolate. Make a crisscross on each candy with tempered milk chocolate prepared for piping, using tube 46.

PRUNE KISSES

Prunes are mellowed in bourbon, filled with perfumed almond paste, then covered with rich chocolate. A delightful blend of flavors!

> 80 small pitted prunes
> 2 cups (480ml) bourbon whisky (approximate)
> 8 ounces (227g) almond paste
> 3 ounces (90ml) apricot brandy (approximate)
> 2 pounds (908g) dark chocolate, tempered for dipping (page 107)
> $\frac{1}{2}$ pound (227g) milk chocolate prepared for piping (page 113)

A week before you make the candy, place prunes in a glass jar. Pour in enough whisky to cover the prunes, seal the jar and allow the prunes to marinate at room temperature for a week. Rotate the jar daily to make sure prunes are evenly soaked with the whisky.

1. Drain prunes, then set on a cake rack covered with a paper towel to air-dry while you make the filling.

2. Crumble almond paste in a mixing bowl. Add brandy, one tablespoon (15ml) at a time, kneading to form a smooth, soft paste.

3. Cut a slit in side of each prune. Fill the prunes with the almond paste mixture using a small spoon. Close the prunes over the filling. Set prunes on cookie sheet and refrigerate for an hour.

4. Remove prunes from refrigerator and allow to come to room temperature. Set up your work area for dipping as shown on page 107. Dip prunes in the tempered dark chocolate and place on cookie sheet covered with wax paper. Place dipped candies in refrigerator for *five minutes only*. Complete hardening at room temperature. When chocolate has hardened, use a paper cone (page 26), tube 65, and the milk chocolate to pipe a leaf on each candy. Go back and pipe a tube 17 rosette at base of each leaf. Place candies in paper candy cups, then in a covered box to store for up to six weeks. Yield: 80 Prune Kisses.

Above, starting at top: Viennese Whirls, Prune Kisses, Chocolate Drums, Krokant Squares flanked by Krokant Sticks, Vodka Cherries and Walnut Truffles.

WALNUT TRUFFLES

The richest truffle is piped onto marzipan bases, garnished with walnuts, then dipped in chocolate.

FOR BASES:

> ½ recipe Continental Marzipan (page 126)

FOR TRUFFLE FILLING:

> 9 ounces (252g) unsalted butter
>
> 2½ ounces (70g) confectioners' sugar
>
> 4½ ounces (135ml) rum
>
> 1 pound, 5 ounces (594g) milk chocolate, tempered for dipping (page 107)
>
> 70 walnut halves, roasted (approximate)

FOR DIPPING AND GARNISH

> 2 pounds (908g) milk chocolate, tempered for dipping (page 107)
>
> ½ pound (227g) milk chocolate, prepared for piping (page 113)

Before you begin, make marzipan bases. Roll out marzipan on surface dusted with confectioners' sugar to a thickness of ⅛" (.3cm) or less. Cut out circles with a 1" (2.5cm) round cutter. Allow to air-dry on wax paper.

1. Make filling. With electric mixer set on medium speed, beat butter until fluffy. Gradually beat in sugar, then rum. Fold in the 1 pound, 5 ounces (594g) tempered chocolate and stir until smooth. Refrigerate 30 minutes, or until thickened.

2. Make a paper decorating cone (page 26), cut point and drop in tube 12. Fill with the prepared filling and pipe mounds onto the marzipan bases. Top each with a walnut half.

3. Dip in the two pounds (908g) tempered milk chocolate just up to the walnut halves. Slide dipped candies off fork, walnut on top, onto wax paper. Refrigerate just *five minutes*. Make another paper decorating cone, cut point and drop in tube 17. Fill with the chocolate prepared for piping and pipe a zigzag in center of each walnut. Yield: about 70 Walnut Truffles.

ROYAL CHOCOLATE PRUNES

The flavors of almond, brandy and chocolate combine for a delectable fruit candy.

> 50 small pitted prunes
>
> ½ cup (120ml) brandy (approximate)
>
> ½ recipe Continental Marzipan (page 126)

> 1½ pounds (681g) dark chocolate, tempered for dipping (page 107)
>
> ½ pound (227g) dark chocolate, prepared for piping (page 113)

Before you begin, place prunes in a glass jar, pour in the brandy, cover jar and allow to marinate at room temperature for an hour. Drain prunes, reserving brandy, and dry on paper towels.

1. Put marzipan in a mixing bowl and knead in enough of the reserved brandy to form a soft paste. Take off portions and roll between your palms into ovals. Stuff prunes with ovals and place on wax paper-covered cookie sheet.

2. Dip prunes into the tempered dipping chocolate and place on second cookie sheet covered with wax paper. Place in refrigerator for *five minutes only*.

3. Make a paper decorating cone, half-fill with the piping chocolate and cut a tiny opening in point of cone. Pipe a "shoe-lace" design on top of each candy. Yield: 50 Royal Chocolate Prunes.

BUTTER ALMONDS

> 3 cups (720ml or 340g) slivered almonds
>
> 3 tablespoons (45ml or 42g) unsalted butter
>
> 1 tablespoon (15ml or 15g) vanilla sugar
>
> 3 pounds (1.4kg) milk chocolate, chopped

Before you begin, make vanilla sugar. Bury a vanilla bean in one cup of sifted confectioners' sugar, cover container and leave for a week or longer. This sugar may be used over fresh fruit or in a recipe. Line two cookie sheets with wax paper.

1. Melt butter in a heavy frying pan over low heat. Stir in almonds and sprinkle with the vanilla sugar. Stir constantly with a wooden spoon until almonds are golden. Cool to room temperature, about 30 minutes.

2. Melt the chocolate in top pan of a double boiler over hot water. Stir in almond mixture. Drop from dessert spoon in oval shapes on prepared cookie sheets. Let harden at room temperature, about 25 minutes. To store, place candies in paper candy cups, then in tightly sealed box. They will keep for several weeks at a cool temperature. Yield: about 100 candies.

CHOCOLATE KIRSCH HEARTS

Are you ready for an adventure? Make this candy to amaze and delight everyone who samples it. The original version was created in the 19th century for royalty by a German *patissier*. These "Kirschwassertropfen" are still being made in Europe today, and enjoyed by all who can afford their very high price.

Study the pictures as you read the recipe, then make your own rare and deluxe candies.

- 5 pounds (2.3kg) cornstarch (approximate)
- 13½ ounces (378g) cubed sugar
- 4½ ounces (135ml) hot water
- 1½ ounces (45ml) kirsch (you may substitute rum, brandy or other 80 to 90 proof liqueur)
- 2 pounds (908g) dark chocolate, tempered for dipping (page 107)

Before you begin, have at hand a plastic mold for heart-shaped candies, sheet cake pans, a soft, clean pastry brush and a clean ruler or strip of stiff cardboard.

1. Sift cornstarch into sheet cake pans to fill to overflowing. Draw the ruler across the pans to level. Carefully press the mold into the cornstarch to make clear, heart-shaped depressions. This recipe makes about 150 candies, so you will need that many depressions. Set pans in a warm place, about 100°F (37°C). The top of your stove over an oven set at lowest temperature will provide this warmth.

2. Combine sugar cubes and hot water in a two-quart (two-liter) saucepan and set over medium heat. Stir with a wooden spoon to break up cubes and dissolve sugar. Wash down sides of pan with a pastry brush dipped in hot water and clip on thermo-

meter. Cook, without stirring, to 224°F (107°C), just a few minutes. Remove pan from heat.

3. Blend in kirsch, then cover pan with a damp cloth. (This prevents kirsch from evaporating). Let stand five minutes, then pour into a pitcher with a small spout. Syrup will still be hot.

4. Carefully fill the depressions in the cornstarch with the syrup. Gently sift more cornstarch over the syrup to completely cover. Allow to stand at a temperature of 100°F to 110°F (37°C to 43°C) for about four hours. The syrup will have formed a thin crisp crust. Use a fork to gently turn the candies over, and allow to remain in cornstarch four more hours, at 100°F to 110°F (37°C to 43°C).

5. Lift the candies out of the pans and

TEA CHOCOLATES

The center of these candies is a meltingly rich truffle mixture surprisingly flavored with tea! Use your favorite best-quality tea —most people prefer a black tea for its decided flavor.

    8 ounces (240ml) whipping cream

    ½ ounce (15ml) tea

    7 ounces (198g) dark chocolate,
        finely chopped

    13 ounces (369g) milk chocolate,
        finely chopped

    1½ pounds (681g) milk chocolate,
        tempered for dipping (page 107)

    ½ pound (227g) milk chocolate,
        prepared for piping (page 113)

1. Combine cream and tea in a small saucepan over low heat. Stir constantly until mixture comes to a boil. Remove from heat and strain.

2. Add finely chopped dark and milk chocolate to cream mixture and stir until chocolate is melted and mixture is smooth. Refrigerate about fifteen minutes, or until stiff. Beat with a whisk or hand-held electric mixer for just a minute or two until fluffy.

3. Make a paper decorating cone (page 26), cut point and drop in tube 10. Fill with truffle mixture and pipe into long ovals on wax paper. Refrigerate about one hour. Dip in the tempered milk chocolate as directed on page 107. Refrigerate dipped candies *for five minutes only.* Decorate with the milk chocolate prepared for piping. Pipe a band across each candy with tube 46, then pipe a tube 17 star in the center of each band. Yield: about 45 Tea Chocolates.

gently brush off excess cornstarch. Dip in the tempered chocolate and place on wax paper-covered surface to harden. Dip the candies very gently. Do not shake the fork or tap it on the side of the pan. This might break the delicate crust. Place tray of dipped candies in the refrigerator for *five minutes only.* Store in a cool place for up to six weeks.

Warn everyone to put the whole candy into his mouth at once—where it will explode in a burst of delicious syrup. Yield: about 150 Kirsch Hearts.

APPENDIX

HOW TO GIFT-WRAP
YOUR HOMEMADE CANDIES

Half the fun of making candy is sharing it with someone else! Wrap the candies in a pretty, imaginative way that reflects the love and care you put into making it.

Choose a container that's a gift, too. Use a pretty gelatin mold, a serving tray or a soufflé dish. Other good containers for candies: baskets, brandy snifters, bake-and-serve casseroles or the shiny new pan the candy was firmed in.

For a plant lover, line a new clay flower pot with plastic wrap, fill with candy and plant an artificial daisy in the center. Or pack a ceramic pot with candy and add a green ribbon.

For a lavish presentation, fill a jewel box with candy for a lady, a leather dresser box for a man.

Children take special joy in brightly wrapped gifts. For a double treat, fill a pan shaped like a child's favorite character or toy with candy. Mom can bake the cake later.

Two-piece clear plastic molds make fine candy containers to save for future use. Fill an egg mold with pastel confectionery coating eggs, or a ball mold with glittering hard candy. A bright ribbon covers the seam.

Dress up a plain-jane box. You can "slip-cover" any neat clean box to give it a perky personality. Carefully measure the length of the box, and add twice its height. Do the same with the width. Add 1" (2.5cm) to both of these measurements and draw an accurate rectangle on the back of pretty gift paper or colored foil and cut out. Spray with artist's adhesive.

Lay the cover of the box, top down, in the center of the sprayed paper and bring edges of long sides smoothly around the cover. The extra inch will turn down on the inside edges of the box. Do the same on two short sides, folding smoothly at corners.

Add your own decorative touches to the "slip-covered" box. Lavish ribbon bows, sprays of artificial flowers or cut-out hearts may all be taped or cemented on. Try a small paper doily, a plastic cupid figure, a small toy, or a group of lacy plastic bells tied with ribbons. You'll dream up lots of ways to suit the décor to the gift occasion.

On the inside of the box cement the cut-off lacy edges of square or rectangular paper doilies to frame the candies. Or use purchased paper lace strips. And make sure each piece of candy is set in its own paper candy cup. When the box is opened, the contents will look dainty and appealing.

Paper cornucopias are easy to make. Paper doily cornucopias are dainty. Just fold a 10" or 12" (25.4cm or 30.5cm) round doily in half, then twirl into a cone as shown on page 26. Tape or staple to secure, then add a ribbon loop, stapling ends of ribbon on opposite sides of the cone. Dress up with bows or artificial flowers, fill with candy. These look showy hanging on the Christmas tree, or from a chandelier. Make tiny cornucopias from 6" or 8" (15.2cm or 20.3cm) round doilies and fill with spiced nuts as place-markers for a shower, or a party for a little girl.

As variations, make cornucopias from a folded circle of gift-wrap, or a half-circle of construction paper in a bright color. Line with a doily cornucopia.

Save metal containers to hold your candy gifts. Boxes or one- or two-pound (454g or 908g) coffee cans can be covered with self-adhesive paper. These containers are strong and have well-fitting covers, so they're ideal for mailing.

THE DO-IT-YOURSELF
CANDY BAR

Bring back the good old days when a candy bar was a substantial treat, eagerly looked forward to. Your candy bars will be much better—because you make them yourself.

You can be very creative when you make candy bars. Almost any type of candy tastes even better when it's formed into a bar. Read the suggestions below, then dream up your own delectable versions.

Dipped candy bars. Cut firmed candy in 3" x 1" (7.6cm x 2.5cm) pieces, about ³/₄" to 1" (1.9cm x 2.5cm) high. Or form into logs, about 3" x 1" (7.6cm x 2.5cm). Dip in confectionary coating or chocolate. Embellish to your own taste with crisp nuts, candied fruits, chocolate or confectionery coating cut-outs (pages 112 and 30)—even piped decorations or buttercream flowers (pages 113, 30 and 31).

Cereal bars. Chocolate Cereal Bars. Peanut Crunch Squares or Peanut Supremes are all good dipped in confectionery coating or chocolate.

Fudge bars. Use any of the fudge recipes in Chapter 1 or Chapter 5 (starting on page 6 or page 44). Fold nuts, fruit or coconut into the candy.

Caramel bars. Cut any caramel in Chapter 6 (except Wilton Caramel for Dipping) into bars, then dip. While chocolate or coating is still soft, roll in chopped, crisped nuts.

Divinities and nougats are naturals for candy bars. For real luxury, top the candy with a slice of Wilton Caramel for Dipping (page 61). Firm caramel to a thickness of ¹/₄" (.6cm), cut in 1" x 3" (2.5cm x 7.6cm) strips, brush tops of divinity or nougat bars with corn syrup and top with strips of caramel. Dip in butterscotch confectionery coating or in chocolate.

Marshmallows (pages 76 to 78) make light fluffy bars, especially attractive when dipped in pastel confectionery coating. Add trims. (See page 79.)

Truffle bars are the ultimate! Try Cherry Kirsch Truffles (page 84) or the centers of Chocolate Almond Balls (page 87). Set on a strip of marzipan (pages 117 or 126) brushed with corn syrup. Dip in chocolate only.

Brittle or toffee bars are favorites. Score candy into 1¹/₂" x 2¹/₂" (3.8cm x 6.3cm) bars before candy sets up, dip bars in chocolate, then cover with crisped chopped nuts.

Molded bars are quick to make. Flavor melted confectionery coating or tempered chocolate with *oil based* flavorings. Pour into candy bar molds, chill and unmold. For more interest, fill just bottom of mold, add a ¹/₄" (.6cm) thick strip of caramel or rolled marzipan or fondant, then complete filling mold. Or fill bottom of mold, then add roasted nuts, snipped marshmallow or dried or candied fruit. Fill mold, chill and unmold.

Below: Cherry Divinity and Grasshopper Divinity (page 68) dipped in chocolate, trimmed with candied cherries and confectionery coating cut-outs. Lemon Coconut Nougat (page 69) dipped in confectionery coating, trimmed with candied peel.

HOW TO STORE YOUR HOMEMADE CANDIES

It's important to store your homemade candies properly, so their delicious flavors and freshness will be maintained. The brief notes at the end of each recipe concerning storage should be observed. The times they give for safe duration of storage are conservative — the candies will probably remain in top condition for even longer than stated. The following notes will give you the reasons for storage procedures, and help you to store your candies for longer periods.

Air is the enemy of candies' freshness. The texture and eating quality of all candies deteriorate when exposed to air.

These candies dry out, lose moisture and may become hard or sugary when exposed to air for more than one or two hours:

Candied peel	Half-dipped dried fruit
Caramels	Jellies
Cereal candies	Marshmallows
Divinities	Marzipan*
Fondant candies	Mixed fruit candies
Fudges	Nougats

These candies pick up moisture and become sticky when exposed to air. This is true of all high-temperature candies:

Brittles	Clear hard candies
Candied fruits	Taffies

All candies pick up foreign odors. Never pack a strongly flavored candy in the same container as one with a delicate flavor. Dipped or molded chocolate or confectionery coating candies are especially susceptible to foreign odors.

Always wrap candies to protect them from drying out, becoming sticky, or developing off-flavors. Even if you are only keeping the candies for a day or two, make sure they are well wrapped.

Clear plastic wrap is the most convenient material for protecting your candies from the effect of air. Double-fold the edges and tape securely. For additional protection, slip wrapped package into a plastic bag, press to exclude air and seal with a twist tie. Any candy that is firmed in a square or a rectangle should be wrapped uncut, as a block. Candies may be scored into squares with a sharp knife before they firm.

Wrap pralines, bars of cereal candy and popcorn or cereal balls in squares of plastic wrap. Tape to seal or seal with a twist tie, then put in plastic bag and seal again.

Most candies can be refrigerated for several weeks to keep them at peak flavor. Make sure they are securely wrapped as described above, so that the candies are not exposed to moisture. Bring the candies to room temperature *before unwrapping.*

These candies should not be refrigerated: any clear hard candy, cereal or popcorn candies, marshmallows, taffies, toffees or brittles. Never refrigerate dipped or molded chocolates, or candies based on chocolate, such as Rocky Road.

Many candies can be frozen to keep well for up to six months. Nougat seems to improve with freezing! Logs covered with caramel freeze well. (Do not cut in slices, freeze whole logs.) Take care that candies do not pick up moisture by double-wrapping in plastic. Freeze candies firmed in a square or rectangle uncut. Divinities with gelatin as an ingredient freeze well.

Do not freeze: jellies, clear hard candies, cereal or popcorn candies, marshmallows, candies dipped or molded in chocolate or confectionery coating. Do not freeze divinities unless they contain gelatin. They become grainy.

To defrost candies successfully, it is necessary to raise the temperature gradually. First place the frozen candies, still in plastic wraps, in a brown paper bag, or wrapping of unglazed paper. This will absorb the condensed moisture that will collect during the defrosting period.

Place candies in refrigerator until defrosted. Bring to room temperature before unwrapping. They will have a flavor as fresh as if just made.

Be sure to freeze fresh candies only. Candies that are frozen while fresh will last as long as if they were not frozen. Candies frozen when a week or more old will taste fine the day they are defrosted, but after that the flavor will deteriorate rapidly.

*Marzipan candies coated with Corn Syrup Glaze do not dry out rapidly.

STORING CANDIES DIPPED OR MOLDED IN CHOCOLATE OR CONFECTIONERY COATING

Special conditions must be observed to keep these candies looking and tasting their best. Freezing may not affect their flavor, but will cause them to become too brittle, and take away their glossy finish. Chocolates may lose their "snap".

Place chocolate or bonbons (dipped in confectionery coating) in paper candy cups, then pack snugly in a box. Cover with clear plastic wrap, tucking in at edges of box. This adds to the appetizing appearance of the candies and keeps air out. Put lid on box.

Wrap larger molded pieces in clear plastic wrap, or in thin foil. Candies based on chocolate or confectionery coating, such as barks or Rocky Road, should be wrapped uncut. You may score the candy into squares before it has completely hardened.

Store in a cool dry place. Temperature should be between 60°F and 72°F (16°C and 22°C) and humidity no higher than 50% to 60%. A cool dry basement, cupboard or hallway is ideal. Make sure the temperature is even and does not fluctuate greatly.

Most dipped candies, chocolates or confectionery coating bonbons, store very well. This is because the coating is airtight, and keeps the center fresh and moist. Times given in individual recipes are accurate.

Never allow chocolates to stand in the sun, even if the day is cool. This may cause white streaks or melting. Confectionery coating candies should not be exposed to sunlight, either. They may melt.

Protect pastel confectionery coating from strong light. It may fade the delicate colors. Pastel confectionery coating will fade especially rapidly under fluorescent light.

TIME-SAVERS, WORK-SAVERS

Non-stick pans are wonderful for cooking candies. Caramels and jellies roll right out, even traditional fudges leave the pan easily. Much less of the candy clings to the pan. Much less danger of scorching, too.

Use the right size pan as directed in the recipe. Too large and the candy may scorch, or you may get an incorrect reading on the thermometer. (The bulb may not be submerged.) Too small—there's a messy boil-over and a stove to clean.

One-pound coffee cans are perfect gift containers for caramel corn, spiced nuts or cereal candies. Dress them up with foil, gift wrap or felt.

Keep a metal ruler in the kitchen for accurately sized, uniform centers or squares of candy. Wash it with the dishes.

A large angled spatula makes it easy to loosen fudge, caramels or brittle from a marble slab.

Does your candy threaten to boil over? Lay a wooden spoon across the pan.

Always oil the molds or surface onto which you pour hard candy. Use vegetable oil and a pastry brush.

Keep a container of hot water on the stove when you're cooking candy. A two-cup, heat-proof glass measuring cup is ideal. Into it, place your thermometer, pastry brush and later, spoon. Tools are at hand and washing is half done.

Group small bottles of flavorings and food colors in a shallow open box. They won't tip over and are easy to find.

Use hot water if a recipe calls for a cooked syrup containing water and sugar. Fondants, nougats, divinities and hard candies will have a shorter cooking time, a clearer, whiter color. Use hot water from the tap.

Preheat a unit of your electric stove before cooking fondants, hard candies or any recipe using a cooked syrup. Cooking time will be shorter.

Use cane sugar, not beet sugar, for candies. Beet sugar foams too much.

Wrap your firmed candy in the foil used for lining the pan. When you line the pan, let the foil extend a few inches beyond the pan edges (page 18). Lift the candy out of the pan, fold the foil around it, then place in a plastic bag. Fold bag to fit snugly, then seal with a twist tie.

Screw a cup hook in the wall behind your counter to hang your thermometer on. This is much safer than storing it in a drawer where it may be jostled.

Continued on next page

Use only metal measuring cups with handles for measuring dry ingredients. These are convenient, too, for filling two-piece molds with tempered chocolate or confectionery coating. Good for taking out a small quantity of hot syrup as you do in making nougat.

When measuring two different liquids, such as corn syrup and water, use the same measuring cup. Less waste, less dishwashing.

To save space in your pan cupboards, invest in metal candy bars. You'll be able to form the exact area you need for firming candies with very little storage space.

For bargains in good quality heavy saucepans, other equipment, too, shop at a restaurant supply store. Look one up in the yellow pages of your directory.

Decorate your candies for the final, professional touch. Half a candied cherry, a square of candied peel or a nutmeat add a finished look. Make drop flowers in royal icing or cutouts from confectionery coating or chocolate to keep on hand.

Melting confectionery coating to use in a recipe? Bring water in lower pan of a double boiler to a simmer, then remove from heat. Place top pan in position and fill with chopped coating or wafers. Cover pan. Coating will be melted in about five minutes.

Get everything ready before you begin! This is the most important rule for success. Measure all your ingredients and line them up within reach. Have all needed equipment at hand. Then all you need do is follow the recipe, step by step.

COOKING TO CORRECT TEMPERATURE IS ESSENTIAL

In making fine candies, cooking temperatures are critical. Accordingly, a thoroughly reliable thermometer is an important tool of the serious candy maker. Practice true economy by getting a good quality thermometer, handling it with care and having the peace of mind of working with a good and dependable tool for years.

Since the recipes *in this book give temperatures at sea level,* it may be necessary for you to *compensate for a higher altitude in your community.* As the *altitude increases,* temperature *readings decrease.* You will note from the chart at right that for every 500 feet above sea level your location may be, the boiling point of water drops one degree Fahrenheit.

As a guide to determining your community's altitude above sea level, a representative number of United States cities are listed at right. The altitude of each city is indicated, together with the temperature at which water boils in this location. If you are unable to compare the altitude of your location with any of these, then we suggest you get *specific information* locally. Call your library, community newspaper or any weather service office, all of whom should be able to provide the "sea level" figure.

Compensating for altitudes above sea level
Here's how a resident of Boise, Idaho, would *compensate on temperature reading* when making Corn Syrup Fondant from the recipe on page 92. In Step 1, after the mixture has come to a boil, the pan is washed down and the thermometer is clipped on. Recipe indicates cooking should continue until temperature reaches 240°F (116°C). Since this is the temperature at *sea level* and the recipe is being followed in Boise, Idaho, compensation must be made for Boise's *2,704 altitude above sea level.* From the chart it is seen that water boils at 207°F (98°C) at 2500 feet above sea level — a figure 5° lower than the 212°F (100°C) reading at sea level. Compensating for this 5° difference, the Boise candymaker should bring the fondant mixture to 235°F (113°C), rather than 240°F (116°C).

Boiling points change as altitude rises

altitude in feet	Fahrenheit boiling point	centigrade boiling point
SEA LEVEL 0	212°	100°
500	211°	99°
1,000	210°	99°
1,500	209°	98°
2,000	208°	98°
2,500	207°	97°
3,000	206°	97°
3,500	205°	96°
4,000	204°	96°
4,500	203°	95°
5,000	202°	95°
5,500	201°	94°
6,000	200°	94°
6,500	199°	93°
7,000	198°	93°

ALTITUDES AND BOILING POINTS OF WATER IN U.S. CITIES

STATE	CITY	altitude in feet	boiling point	STATE	CITY	altitude in feet	boiling point
Alabama	Birmingham	600	211°F	Montana	Butte	5,765	200°F
Alaska	Anchorage	118	212°F	Nebraska	Lincoln	1,150	210°F
Arizona	Phoenix	1,090	210°F	Nevada	Las Vegas	2,030	208°F
Arkansas	Little Rock	286	212°F	N. Hampshire	Manchester	175	212°F
California	Sacramento	30	212°F	New Jersey	Trenton	599	211°F
Colorado	Denver	5,280	201°F	New Mexico	Santa Fe	6,950	198°F
Connecticut	Waterbury	260	212°F	New York	Syracuse	400	211°F
Delaware	Wilmington	135	212°F	North Carolina	Durham	405	211°F
Florida	Orlando	70	212°F	North Dakota	Bismarck	1,674	209°F
Georgia	Atlanta	1,050	210°F	Ohio	Cleveland	660	211°F
Hawaii	Honolulu	21	212°F	Oklahoma	Okla. City	1,195	210°F
Idaho	Boise	2,704	207°F	Oregon	Portland	77	212°F
Illinois	Chicago	595	211°F	Pennsylvania	Pittsburgh	745	211°F
Indiana	Indianapolis	510	211°F	Rhode Island	Providence	80	212°F
Iowa	Des Moines	805	210°F	South Carolina	Columbia	190	212°F
Kansas	Wichita	1,290	209°F	South Dakota	Sioux Falls	1,395	209°F
Kentucky	Louisville	450	211°F	Tennessee	Nashville	450	211°F
Louisiana	Baton Rouge	57	212°F	Texas	San Antonio	650	211°F
Maine	Bangor	20	212°F	Utah	Salt Lake City	4,390	203°F
Maryland	Baltimore	20	212°F	Vermont	Burlington	110	212°F
Massachusetts	Worcester	475	211°F	Virginia	Richmond	160	212°F
Michigan	Detroit	85	212°F	Washington	Spokane	1,890	208°F
Minnesota	Minneapolis	815	210°F	West Virginia	Charleston	601	211°F
Mississippi	Jackson	298	211°F	Wisconsin	Milwaukee	635	211°F
Missouri	Kansas City	750	211°F	Wyoming	Cheyenne	6,100	200°F

METRIC CONVERSIONS FOR OFTEN-USED CANDY INGREDIENTS

Weight Conversion to Metric: 1 ounce equals 28 grams (can be rounded to 30 grams)

INGREDIENT	AMER.	METRIC	INGREDIENT	AMER.	METRIC
Butter	1 tbl.	15ml or 15g	Nuts		
	2 tbls.	30ml or 28g	almonds, chopped	¼ cup	60ml or 38g
	¼ cup	60ml or 56g	ground	1 cup	240ml or 98g
	½ cup	120ml or 112g	cashews, dry roasted	½ cup	120ml or 56g
	1 cup	240ml or 227g	peanuts, dry roasted	1 cup	240ml or 112g
Candied cherries	½ cup	120ml or 112g	pecans, chopped	½ cup	120ml or 56g
pineapple	½ cup	120ml or 112g	walnuts, chopped	½ cup	120ml or 56g
Chocolate	1 pound	480ml or 454g	Peanut butter	½ cup	120ml or 112g
	2 pounds	960ml or 908g	Popcorn, unpopped	½ cup	120ml or 112g
Coconut, flaked	1 cup	240ml or 85g	popped	1 cup	240ml or 28g
Confectionery coating	1 pound	480ml or 454g	Marshmallows, min.	1 cup	240ml or 56g
	2 pounds	960ml or 908g	Sugar		
Dried apricots	½ cup	120ml or 112g	brown	1 cup	240ml or 200g
dates, pitted	½ cup	120ml or 112g	confectioners' sifted	1 cup	240ml or 100g
pears	½ cup	120ml or 112g	granulated	1 cup	240ml or 200g
raisins	1 cup	240ml or 130g	superfine	1 cup	240ml or 200g

INDEX

MAKE EVERY DAY A PARTY WITH HOMEMADE CANDY

WHERE TO BUY IT

For most equipment, tools and materials needed for fine candy-making, write:

Wilton Enterprises
Department C-10
2240 West 75th Street
Woodridge, Illinois 60517

For oil-based flavorings, such as oil of peppermint or oil of lemon, or for rosewater, check with your pharmacist.

For confectionery coating or chocolate in ten-pound blocks, consult a bakery supply firm. Find one in the yellow pages of your telephone directory.